The Commentary Of PappusOn Book X Of Euclids Elements – Primary Source Edition

Junge,Gustav., Thomson William.

*[English] introduction : p. 38

THE COMMENTARY OF PAPPUS
ON
BOOK X OF EUCLID'S ELEMENTS

LONDON HUMPHREY MILFORD
OXFORD UNIVERSITY PRESS

THE COMMENTARY OF PAPPUS
ON
BOOK X OF EUCLID'S ELEMENTS

ARABIC TEXT AND TRANSLATION

BY

WILLIAM THOMSON

WITH

INTRODUCTORY REMARKS, NOTES, AND
A GLOSSARY OF TECHNICAL TERMS

BY

GUSTAV JUNGE AND WILLIAM THOMSON

CAMBRIDGE
HARVARD UNIVERSITY PRESS
1930

Druck von J J Augustin in Glückstadt und Hamburg

Contents

I. BEMERKUNGEN ZU DEM VORLIEGENDEN KOMMENTAR
GUSTAV JUNGE

II. INTRODUCTION

WILLIAM THOMSON

Bemerkungen
zu dem vorliegenden Kommentar.

Von Gustav Junge in Berlin-Lichterfelde.

LITERARISCHES — Im Jahre 1850 kam Dr Woepcke nach Paris. In der damaligen Bibliothèque impériale war ein Sammelband von 51 arabischen Handschriften, auf den Woepcke durch den Katalog aufmerksam wurde. Er muß sogleich mit dem Studium begonnen haben, jedenfalls erschienen schon 1851 mehrere Abhandlungen von ihm uber einige dieser Handschriften. Bald beschaftigte er sich auch mit unserem Kommentar, der die Nummern 5 und 6 des Bandes bildet.

Dieser Kommentar bringt einige Andeutungen uber ein verlorenes Werk des Apollonius (I §§ 1, 21, 22, 23; II § 1), die Woepcke besonders interessierten. Er legte der Académie des Sciences einen Bericht uber den Kommentar vor, unter dem Titel. „Essai d'une restitution de travaux perdus d'Apollonius sur les quantités irrationelles". — Dieser Bericht enthalt unter anderem ein Verzeichnis der samtlichen Handschriften des Bandes, bringt einige Stucke des Kommentars, etwa den 15. Teil des ganzen, arabisch und in französischer Übersetzung, und den Schluß der Abhandlung bildet eine Inhaltsangabe des ganzen Kommentars. Das arabische Manuskript zerfallt in zwei Teile, diese sind aber im Original in keiner Weise weiter gegliedert.

Woepcke's Essai hat offenbar lange auf den Druck warten mussen, er erschien erst 1856[1]. Schon 1853 gab Chasles, der Mathematiker und Historiker der Mathematik, einen Vorbericht uber Woepcke's Abhandlungen, der kurz und klar sowohl den Gegenstand des Kommentars, namlich das 10. Buch Euklid's, wie auch die Abhandlung Woepcke's charakterisiert[2]. Vortrefflich ist die Bemerkung von Chasles, der Inhalt des ganzen Buches 10 von Euklid lasse sich wiedergegen durch die eine Formel

$$\sqrt{A+B} = \sqrt{\frac{A+\sqrt{A^2-B^2}}{2}} + \sqrt{\frac{A-\sqrt{A^2-B^2}}{2}}$$

Chasles macht auch auf mehrere Schwierigkeiten aufmerksam, die Woepcke nicht gelost hat. Es sind folgende Warum hat

EUKLID sowohl die Linien von der Länge 2, 3 wie auch die von der Länge $\sqrt{2}$, $\sqrt{3}$ als rational, als rheta, bezeichnet? — Welchen Sinn hat die Bezeichnung „ungeordnet" für die Irrationalen des Apollonius? — Und endlich· Wie sind die Andeutungen über die durch Subtraktion entstehenden Irrationalen des Apollonius zu verstehen? — Wir werden auf diese Fragen nachher (S 21, 27 und 29) eingehen —

Merkwürdigerweise erwähnt WOEPCKE in seinem Essai, der 1856 erschien, mit keinem Worte, daß er inzwischen den vollständigen arabischen Text des Kommentars herausgegeben hatte Dieser war 1855 in Paris bei Firmin-Didot erschienen, aber ohne Angabe des Jahres, Ortes und ohne Nennung von WOEPCKE's Namen. Es ist ein kleines Buch von 68 Seiten, das außer dem arabischen Text nur einige lateinische Anmerkungen enthält. Es scheint, daß von dieser Text-Ausgabe nur wenige Exemplare existieren Eins ist in der Bibliothek der Akademie der Wissenschaften in Berlin, ein zweites war im Besitz von Herrn Professor Heiberg in Kopenhagen, ein drittes, das Suter in Händen hatte, ist nicht mehr nachzuweisen. Wegen der angegebenen Eigenschaften ist diese Ausgabe natürlich in den Katalogen schwer zu finden

WOEPCKE hatte eine vollständige Übersetzung des Kommentars ins Französische geplant Die Berliner Akademie hatte 1854 für die Veröffentlichung des Textes einen beträchtlichen Zuschuß, 300 Taler, gezahlt, und 1856 wurde sogar eine zweite Rate von 400 Talern bewilligt. Aber die Akademie hatte schon 1854 den Wunsch geäußert, Übersetzung und Anmerkungen möchten in lateinischer Sprache abgefaßt werden. WOEPCKE ist ja diesem Wunsche in bezug auf die Anmerkungen nachgekommen Er machte aber die Akademie in einem Schreiben auf die Schwierigkeit aufmerksam, die vielen Fachausdrucke des Kommentars in lateinischer Sprache wiederzugeben

Vielleicht ist an dieser Uneinigkeit die Herausgabe einer Übersetzung gescheitert Übrigens starb WOEPCKE schon 1864, mit 38 Jahren

Wahrscheinlich haben bei den Publikationen von 1855 und 1856 noch andere Umstände mitgespielt, die sich heute nicht mehr sicher feststellen lassen[3]. Vielleicht ist die arabische Ausgabe von 1855 überhaupt nur in wenigen Exemplaren hergestellt worden, jedenfalls war sie schon wegen der Sprache immer nur wenigen zugänglich, und sie wird fast nie in der Literatur erwähnt. Auch die gegenwärtigen Herausgeber hatten von ihr keine Kenntnis, als sie ihr Unternehmen begannen.

Dagegen ist WOEPCKE's Abhandlung von 1856 viel beachtet worden, und sie war geeignet, übertriebene Erwartungen über den Wert des ganzen Kommentars zu erwecken. Die von WOEPCKE mitgeteilten Stücke bringen nicht nur die schon erwähnten Andeutungen über Apollonius, sondern der Anfang gibt auch einige neue Aufschlüsse über die Leistungen Theätets. So konnte man wohl hoffen, daß auch die Stücke, von denen im Essai nur kurz der Inhalt skizziert war, dem Mathematiker oder Historiker etwas bringen würden. Namentlich schienen WOEPCKE's Nummern 6 und 10 (bei uns § 10 und § 17) des ersten Teiles Berichte über die Mathematik Theätets und Platos zu versprechen.

Die richtige Einschätzung des ganzen Kommentars hat Professor HEIBERG schon im Jahre 1882 und nochmals 1888—89 dadurch angedeutet, daß er den Kommentar neben die Euklid-Scholien stellte, insbesondere die soeben erwähnte Nummer 6 neben das ziemlich nichtssagende Scholion 62 (Band V S. 450) der HEIBERG'schen Euklid-Ausgabe[4]. — In der Tat hat unser Kommentar viele Stellen, die wörtlich mit den von HEIBERG gesammelten Scholien übereinstimmen. Wir haben diese Koinzidenzen S. 57 angegeben.

Das genaue Studium des Kommentars bestätigt auch sonst, was HEIBERG schon vor Jahrzehnten vorausgeahnt hat: unser Kommentar steht kaum höher als die besseren Euklid-Scholien, er bringt nicht viel mehr historische und sachliche Aufschlüsse als diese. Man kann auch hier von Goldkörnern sprechen, wie HEIBERG es tut, und die größeren Goldkörner sind schon von WOEPCKE gefunden worden.

Indes die Hoffnung auf reichere Ausbeute, die ja nach WOEPCKE's Auszug wohl zu verstehen war, hatte zunächst die Folge, daß H. SUTER in den letzten Jahren seines Lebens die Textausgabe von WOEPCKE ins Deutsche übersetzte, und sie hat auch die jetzigen Bearbeiter des Gegenstandes zu ihrem Unternehmen ermutigt.

SUTERS Übersetzung erschien 1922 unter dem Titel „Der Kommentar des Pappus zum X. Buche des Euklides" in den „Beiträgen zur Geschichte der Mathematik", Heft IV der „Abhandlungen zur Geschichte der Naturwissenschaften und der Medizin", Erlangen 1922.

SUTER hat wahrscheinlich die arabische Handschrift nicht benutzt, sondern nur WOEPCKE's Textausgabe von 1855. WOEPCKE hat öfter Stellen der Handschrift nicht lesen können oder Worte vom Rande in den Text aufgenommen, und in allen Fällen richtet sich SUTER nach ihm.

Suter's deutsche Übersetzung gibt natürlich, da sie von einem guten Kenner der arabischen Mathematik stammt, den Sinn des Kommentars genügend wieder, und es kann einem deutschen Leser, der sich schnell über den Kommentar unterrichten will, nur empfohlen werden, zunächst Suter's Übersetzung durchzusehen. Immerhin war Suter zuerst Mathematiker und in zweiter Linie Arabist, wir hoffen, daß in der vorliegenden englischen Übersetzung ein Arabist vom Fach doch manche Feinheiten jener so einfachen, aber gerade wegen ihrer Kargheit schwierigen Sprache richtiger wiedergegeben hat als Suter. Hinzu kommt, daß Suter nur selten die Übereinstimmung mit den Scholien bemerkt hat: die Kenntnis des Scholions und damit des griechischen Urtextes erleichtert natürlich das Verständnis des Arabischen außerordentlich. Endlich hat Mr. Thomson nach dem arabischen Original übersetzt, während Suter, wie soeben bemerkt, nach allem Anschein nur die Textausgabe Woepcke's vor sich hatte.

Hiermit ist schon zum Teil die Rechtfertigung gegeben dafür, daß die jetzigen Herausgeber ihr Unternehmen nicht nur begonnen haben, sondern auch fortgesetzt, nachdem sie erfahren hatten, daß der arabische Text schon gedruckt vorlag und daß auch eine deutsche Übersetzung existierte. Wir gestehen nämlich, daß wir bei Beginn unserer Arbeit oder doch unserer Vorbereitungen im Jahre 1924 auch von Suter's Übersetzung keine Kenntnis hatten. Zwar waren schon Besprechungen erschienen, von H. Wieleitner in „Mitteilungen zur Geschichte der Medizin", Bd. XXI, S. 171, 1922 und von Sarton in „Isis", Bd. V, S. 492, 1923. Aber zur Entschuldigung mag doch angeführt werden, daß das „Jahrbuch über die Fortschritte der Mathematik" erst 1925 einen Bericht über Suter's Übersetzung gebracht hat —

Wir haben uns zu einer Neuausgabe des arabischen Textes entschlossen schon deswegen, weil von der Ausgabe Woepcke's nur wenige Exemplare bekannt und zugänglich sind. Auch eine eingehende Bearbeitung des Kommentars einschließlich der Übersetzung ins Englische schien uns die Mühe zu lohnen. Mag auch unser Kommentar einer Verfallsperiode der Mathematik angehören, so hat er doch seinen kulturgeschichtlichen Wert. Gerade der erste, mathematisch schwächere Teil zeigt, wie religiös und philosophisch interessierte Gelehrte von den begrifflichen Schwierigkeiten der Mathematik, insbesondere der Lehre vom Irrationalen, einen Weg zu den ewigen Geheimnissen des Lebens gesucht haben.

Wir hoffen auch, daß die recht beträchtliche philologische

Arbeit nicht umsonst gewesen ist. Das beigefügte Verzeichnis arabischer mathematischer Fachausdrücke wird das erste seiner Art sein. —

Unser Kommentar handelt vom 10. Buche Euklids, dessen Gegenstand die irrationalen Größen sind. Wir werden zunächst versuchen, einen Überblick über die Geschichte des Irrationalen zu geben, von den Anfängen, die bei Plato nachweisbar sind, bis zu der systematischen Behandlung bei Euklid und den Zusätzen, die APOLLONIUS gemacht hat. Hierbei wird schon vieles aus dem Inhalt unseres Kommentars zur Sprache kommen. Was sonst noch daran für den Mathematiker erwähnenswert ist, soll im Schlußkapitel angeführt werden.

PLATO UND THEÄTET — Die ersten Spuren des Irrationalen finden sich in den Platonischen Dialogen. „Menon", „Der Staat", „Parmenides", „Theätet" und „Die Gesetze": alle bringen Andeutungen über die neue Lehre, meist freilich in kurzer und für uns kaum verständlicher Form.

Im „*Menon*" heißt es: Wenn die Seite des Quadrats = 2 ist, so ist die Fläche = 4; wie lang ist nun die Seite des 8-füßigen Quadrats? — Der Sklave meint erst, sie sei = 3. Es stellt sich heraus, daß dieser Wert falsch ist, und Sokrates spricht: „Aber wie groß muß sie denn sein? Versuche es uns genau anzugeben. *Und wenn du es nicht ausrechnen (arithmein) willst*, so zeige uns in der Figur die Linie" In der Tat wird nicht weiter gerechnet, sondern gezeichnet.

Auf die Worte, die wir hier hervorheben (Menon 83—84) scheint bisher noch niemand aufmerksam gemacht zu haben. Sie lassen durchblicken, daß die Rechnung nicht einfach ist, und PLATO wird gewußt haben, daß sie sich überhaupt nicht genau ausführen läßt. die Linie ist irrational.

Der „*Staat*" (546 c) bringt die berühmte Platonische Zahl, aus der für die Geschichte des Irrationalen zu entnehmen ist, daß der Näherungswert 5 7 für das Verhältnis von Seite zur Diagonale damals bekannt war

Im „*Parmenides*" (140 b, c) heißt es von dem „Einen": „Ist es größer oder kleiner, so wird es, wenn es sich um kommensurable Größen handelt, mehr Maßeinheiten haben als das Kleinere und weniger als das Größere; handelt es sich aber um inkommensurable Größen, so wird es im Vergleich zu dem einen aus kleineren, im Vergleich zu dem anderen aus größeren Maßeinheiten bestehen."

Bei kommensurablen Größen ist die Sache klar. Sei die eine = 10, die andere = 15 Fuß, so ist 5 Fuß das Maß, und dies ist in dem kleineren Stück 2mal, in dem größeren 3mal enthalten.

Wie aber im Falle inkommensurabler Größen? Es ist wahrscheinlich dieselbe Vorstellung von den zwei Maßen, die auch ARISTOTELES dunkel andeutet: „Die Diagonale wird von zwei Maßen gemessen, die Seite und alle Großen⁵" Verständlicher sind die Ausführungen in unserem Kommentar (§ 16 Ende und § 17 Ende) Soll die Seite des Quadrats meßbar sein, dann ist die Maßeinheit entweder die Seite selbst oder deren Hälfte oder Drittel usw. Die Diagonale muß dann als inkommensurabel gelten. Die Diagonale ist zu *anderen* Längen kommensurabel, und für die Gesamtheit dieser Längen läßt sich auch ein Maß aufstellen, das aber ein anderes ist als das erste, es ist etwa die Diagonale selbst oder irgend ein Bruchteil, vielleicht auch ein Vielfaches von ihr Es sind also zweierlei Maße zu unterscheiden· das Maß für die Seite und die mit ihr kommensurablen Längen, und das Maß für die Diagonale und alles was zu ihr kommensurabel ist, *diese beiden Maße sind immer von einander verschieden.* — Der heutige Mathematiker wird eine gewisse Verwandtschaft mit dem Begriff des *Körpers der rationalen Zahlen* erkennen Die Griechen betrachteten die Gesamtheit der Längen, die entstehen, wenn die Seite (oder Diagonale) mit allen Zahlen dieses Körpers multipliziert wird

Schon viel erörtert ist die „*Theätet*"-Stelle (147—148) THEODOR zeichnet die Quadrate von 3,5 bis zu 17 Quadratfuß und beweist von jedem, daß die Seite inkommensurabel ist zur Seite des Einheitsquadrates, also zu 1 Fuß THEATET faßt diese vielen Sätze und Beweise in einen zusammen, indem er alle ganzen Zahlen einteilt in Quadrat- und Nicht-Quadrat-Zahlen. Zu den ersten gehören Quadrate, deren Seiten kommensurabel zur Einheit sind, nämlich = 2, 3, 4 usw Fuß, dagegen zu den Nicht-Quadrat-Zahlen gehören Quadrate, deren Seiten nicht einfach als Längen anzugeben sind; diese Seiten werden vielmehr als „dynameis" definiert, d h durch ihr Vermögen, ein Quadrat von bekannter Fläche zu erzeugen, oder, wie die Mathematiker noch heute sagen, durch ihre *Potenzen*⁶.

Endlich die „*Gesetze*" (819—820) bringen allgemeinere Betrachtungen· nicht alle Längen sind untereinander meßbar, und niemals Längen gegen Flächen. eine dankbare Aufgabe ist es, zu untersuchen, wie sich die meßbaren und die nichtmeßbaren Großen zueinander verhalten.⁷ —

In unserem Kommentar wird die „Theatet"-Stelle ausführlich besprochen (§§ 10, 11, 17), aus den „Gesetzen" wird eine Stelle angeführt (§ 12), „Parmenides" immerhin erwähnt (§ 13). Doch zur Aufklärung der mathematischen Schwierigkeiten trägt unser Kommentar in der Regel wenig bei. —

Über den historischen Theatet erfahren wir einiges durch den schon länger bekannten Anfang des Kommentars (§ 1). THEÄTET hat die Medial-Linie dem geometrischen Mittel zugeteilt, das Binomium dem arithmetischen und die Apotome dem harmonischen Mittel. Begnügen wir uns vorerst mit einem Zahlenbeispiel, so ist zwischen 1 und $\sqrt{2}$ das geometrische Mittel $= \sqrt{2}$, eine Mediale, das arithmetische Mittel $= \dfrac{1 + \sqrt{2}}{2}$ ist ein Binomium, endlich das harmonische Mittel zwischen x und y ist $= \dfrac{2xy}{x+y}$; in unserem Falle kommt

$$\frac{2\sqrt{2}}{1 + \sqrt{2}} = 2\sqrt{2}\,(\sqrt{2} - 1) \ \text{oder}\ 2\,(2 - \sqrt{2}),$$

und dies ist eine Apotome. — Hierin liegt die Erkenntnis, daß $(\sqrt{2} + 1)$ und $(\sqrt{2} - 1)$ multipliziert einen rationalen Wert, nämlich 1 ergeben, oder in der Ausdrucksweise der Griechen: ein Rechteck aus einem Binomium und einer gleichnamigen Apotome ist rational.

Diese Aussage findet sich in verschiedenen Fassungen in den Sätzen 112 bis 114 im 10. Buche Euklids. HEIBERG hält die Sätze 112 bis 115 für interpoliert[8]. Wir wollen hieran nicht zweifeln, wenn uns auch der Satz 115, der höhere geometrische Mittel wie $\sqrt[3]{2}$, $\sqrt[4]{2}$ betrachtet, weiter vom sonstigen Inhalt der Elemente abzuführen scheint als die Sätze 112 bis 114.

Jedenfalls ist die Einfügung der Sätze 112 bis 114 vor der Zeit des Pappus (etwa 300 n. Chr.) erfolgt, denn unser Kommentar schreibt den Satz dem Euklid zu (§ 22 Anfang). Hierauf macht schon SUTER aufmerksam (S. 54 Anm. 201). Wir können noch hinzufügen: der Grund der Einschaltung der Sätze 112 bis 114 war wohl, daß sie altes mathematisches Gut darstellen, nämlich *auf Theatet zurückgehen*.

Ähnlich steht es ja mit dem Satze über die Inkommensurabilität der Quadrat-Diagonale zur Seite, der früher als der letzte des 10. Buches geführt wurde (Euklid ed. Heiberg, III 408—412). Er ist wahrscheinlich noch älter und wohl auch eben wegen seines Alters interpoliert worden.

EUKLIDS ZEHNTES BUCH. — Unter den 13 Büchern der Elemente Euklids ist das 10. bei weitem das umfangreichste. Während die übrigen Bücher untereinander einigermaßen gleichen Raum einnehmen, erfüllt das 10. Buch in den Textausgaben so viele Seiten wie drei oder vier andere Bücher zusammen. Es bildet für sich allein den vierten Teil des ganzen Werkes.

Diese ungefuge Ausdehnung ist nur eine Folge der Schwierigkeit des Gegenstandes. Hierüber klagte Petrus RAMUS (gest 1572), er habe nie etwas so Verworrenes und Verwickeltes gelesen wie das 10 Buch Euklids. nie in menschlichen Schriften und Kunsten eine solche Dunkelheit gefunden. — RAMUS war mehr Logiker als Mathematiker. Doch auch STEVIN, der vlamische Mathematiker, schrieb 1585, fur manche sei das 10. Buch Euklids ein Schrecken, so daß sie es „das Kreuz der Mathematiker nennen. einen gar zu schwer verstandlichen Gegenstand, an dem man außerdem keinerlei Nutzen bemerken konne." — Endlich CASTELLI, ein hervorragender Schuler GALILEIS, schrieb 1607 in einem Brief an diesen, er sei bei dem 40. Satze des 10. Buches stecken geblieben, „erstickt von der Menge der Vokabeln, der Tiefe der Gegenstande und der Schwierigkeit der Beweise "9

Ein Mathematiker liest nicht wie andere Menschen, er ist schon immer auf einige Schwierigkeit gefaßt. Was uns Neuere beim Studium des 10. Buches abschreckt, das ist, wie schon RAMUS hervorhebt, nicht so sehr die schwere Verstandlichkeit der einzelnen Satze Manche Exhaustions-Beweise im 12. Buche mit ihren Vorbereitungen sind kaum eine angenehmere Lekture als die Satze des 10. Buches. Man versuche es einmal mit Satz 17 des 12. Buches uber die Einbeschreibung eines Polyeders zwischen zwei konzentrischen Kugeln! —

Eher konnte schon die „Menge der Vokabeln" angefuhrt werden, die vielen Bezeichnungen fur die einzelnen Irrationalitaten. Diese sind in der Tat fur unsere Begriffe ein primitives, langst uberholtes Hilfsmittel; die Zeichensprache, die auch um 1600 schon einigermaßen entwickelt war, gibt eine viel bessere Übersicht.

Das Entscheidende ist aber doch wohl, daß zu der sachlichen Schwierigkeit und der umstandlichen Nomenklatur des 10. Buches noch ein drittes Moment hinzutritt, welches vor allem das Studium erschwert· uns fehlt der Faden. der uns durch das Gewirr der uber 100 Satze hindurchleitet.

Es gab eine Zeit, die das Studium der irrationalen Größen und die Muhseligkeiten von Euklids 10 Buch geduldig auf sich nahm, weil man darin einen Weg zur Philosophie zu finden meinte Aus solcher Stimmung heraus ist, wie wir schon andeuteten, unser Kommentar geschrieben worden, jedenfalls große Stucke des ersten Teiles, und ahnlich urteilte auch KEPLER, als er Euklid gegen RAMUS verteidigte: „Du magst tadeln, was du nicht verstehst, mir aber, der ich die Ursachen der Dinge erforsche, hat sich nur im 10. Buche Euklids der Weg zu diesen eröffnet. — Durch einen rohen Richterspruch wurde dies 10 Buch ver-

dammt, nicht gelesen zu werden, welches gelesen und verstanden
die Geheimnisse der Philosophie aufschließen kann[10]."

Aber unsere Zeit ist hiermit nicht zufrieden, auch nicht mit
der unbestimmten Erklärung des Proklus, der KEPLER sich
anschließt das Ziel der Elemente sei die Konstruktion und Berechnung der regularen Korper[11].

Doch es ist nicht schwer, von hier aus den genaueren Sinn des
10. Buches nachzuweisen' *Das Buch ist in der Tat eine Theorie
derjenigen einfachen und doppelten quadratischen Irrationalitaten,
die bei der Berechnung der regularen Korper auftreten.*

Im letzten, 13. Buche Euklids finden sich Berechnungen, die
wir in der heutigen Zeichensprache wiedergeben wollen.

Wird die Strecke 1 nach dem goldenen Schnitt geteilt und das
größere Stück x genannt, so ist $(x + \frac{1}{2})^2 = 1$, woraus folgt
$x = \frac{1}{2}(\sqrt{5} - 1)$ — (Satz 1 von Buch 13; — der 6. Satz, der
aber als interpoliert gilt, geht hierauf noch genauer ein).

Im Kreise vom Radius 1 ist die Seite des regelmäßigen Funf-
ecks $= \frac{1}{2}\sqrt{2(5 - \sqrt{5})}$ — (Satz 11)

In der Kugel vom Radius 1 ist die Seite des Ikosaeders
$= \frac{1}{4}\sqrt{10(5 - \sqrt{5})}$ — (Satz 16);

endlich ist die Seite des Dokekaeders $= \dfrac{\sqrt{5} - 1}{\sqrt{3}}$ oder
$= \frac{1}{3}(\sqrt{15} - \sqrt{3})$. (Satz 17.)

Da Euklid unsere Zeichensprache nicht hat, so muß er die ver-
wickelten algebraischen Vorgange alle durch Worte wiedergeben
und seine Darstellung ist darum fur uns schwer lesbar. In einem
Punkte geht aber Euklid viel weiter als die gewöhnlichen Dar-
stellungen in den Schulbuchern   Er stellt nicht nur die genann-
ten Ausdrucke auf, sondern er beweist auch von allen in
seinen Rechnungen vorkommenden Größen, von den Formen
$\sqrt{a},\ a \pm \sqrt{b},\ \sqrt{a} \pm \sqrt{b}$, *daß sie sich durch keine anderen gleich-
artigen und erst recht nicht durch einfachere Ausdrucke ersetzen
lassen.*

Wir werden den gordischen Knoten des 10. Buches am
schnellsten lösen, wenn wir mit der schwierigsten Frage anfangen.

Ist $\sqrt{5 - \sqrt{5}}$ durch eine einfachere Formel ersetzbar? Es
ist doch z. B.

$$\sqrt{6 - 2\sqrt{5}} = \sqrt{5} - 1 \text{ und}$$

$$\sqrt{3 - \sqrt{5}} = \frac{\sqrt{5} - 1}{\sqrt{2}}.$$

Ist es sicher, daß sich aus $5 - \sqrt{5}$ nicht auch auf ähnliche Weise die Wurzel ziehen läßt?

Wir wollen die Frage in moderner Form behandeln und $\sqrt{a - \sqrt{b}} = x - y$ setzen. a und b mögen ganze Zahlen sein, doch b keine Quadratzahl. Es folgt

$$a - \sqrt{b} = x^2 - 2 x y + y^2$$

Nehmen wir nun an, x oder y oder auch beide sind einfache Irrationalitäten von der Form $\sqrt{m}$, dann ist $x^2 + y^2$ rational (im modernen Sinne), dagegen $2 x y$ irrational. Es folgt

$$x^2 + y^2 = a$$
$$2 x y = \sqrt{b} \quad \text{und hieraus weiter}$$
$$x^2 - y^2 = \sqrt{a^2 - b}.$$

Es kommt also darauf an, ob der letzte Ausdruck rational ist oder nicht, und diese Bedingung ist auch von Euklid klar erkannt worden. Ist $\sqrt{a^2 - b}$ gleich dem rationalen Werte c, so folgt

$$x = \sqrt{\tfrac{1}{2} (a + c)}, \quad y = \sqrt{\tfrac{1}{2} (a - c)},$$
$$\sqrt{a - \sqrt{b}} = \sqrt{\tfrac{1}{2} (a + c)} - \sqrt{\tfrac{1}{2} (a - c)}.$$

In diesem Falle läßt sich also die gegebene doppelte Irrationalität durch zwei einfache ersetzen. Nehmen wir z. B. $a = 3$, $b = 5$, so wird $c = 2$ und es folgt

$$\sqrt{3 - \sqrt{5}} = \sqrt{\tfrac{5}{2}} - \sqrt{\tfrac{1}{2}},$$

wie wir schon erwähnten.

Ist dagegen $a = 5$, $b = 5$, so ist $c = \sqrt{20} = 2\sqrt{5}$, also nicht rational. Die Umformung ist auch jetzt möglich, bringt aber keine Vereinfachung. Es wird

$$\sqrt{5 - \sqrt{5}} = \sqrt{\tfrac{5}{2} + \sqrt{5}} - \sqrt{\tfrac{5}{2} - \sqrt{5}}. \tag{1}$$

Diese Unterscheidung, ob $\sqrt{a^2 - b}$ rational ist oder nicht, ist unseres Erachtens der Kern des ganzen 10. Buches. Eine Andeutung hiervon hat schon CHASLES gegeben in seinem oben (S. 11) angeführten Ausspruch. —

In seinem 10. Buche betrachtet EUKLID nicht nur die „Apotome" $a - \sqrt{b}$ und die zugehörige Wurzel $\sqrt{a - \sqrt{b}}$, sondern auch das „Binomium" $a + \sqrt{b}$ und dazu $\sqrt{a + \sqrt{b}}$. Als guter Alexandriner, der die Vollständigkeit liebte, hat er auch noch die Formen $\sqrt{\sqrt{a} \pm b}$ und $\sqrt{\sqrt{a} \pm \sqrt{b}}$ dazugenommen.

Seine Überlegung für die beiden letzten Formen wird am einfachsten an Zahlenbeispielen erklärt. Es war doch

$$\sqrt{6 - 2\sqrt{5}} \qquad = \sqrt{5} - 1. \text{ Hieraus folgt}$$
$$\sqrt{6\sqrt{5} - 10} \qquad = \sqrt[4]{5}\,(\sqrt{5} - 1) \text{ und} \qquad\qquad (2)$$
$$\sqrt{6\sqrt{2} - 2\sqrt{10}} \quad = \sqrt[4]{2}\,(\sqrt{5} - 1).$$

Dies sind die Fälle, die eine Vereinfachung zulassen; die vierte Wurzel, die rechts auftritt, wird von EUKLID als *Mediale* bezeichnet.

Um die anderen Fälle zu erhalten, die sich nicht vereinfachen lassen, beginnen wir mit $\sqrt{5 - \sqrt{5}}$ und gehen über zu $\sqrt{5\sqrt{5} - 5}$ oder auch zu $\sqrt{\sqrt{5} - 1}$ und endlich zu $\sqrt{5\sqrt{2} - \sqrt{10}}$. Es ist klar, daß für die Zerlegung die Formel (1) die Grundlage bildet, es ist nur $\sqrt[4]{5}$ als Faktor oder Divisor und im letzten Falle $\sqrt[4]{2}$ als Faktor zuzufügen. —

Hiermit wäre für den modernen Leser über das Buch 10 genug gesagt, wenn es sich nicht darum handelte, in das Verständnis unseres Kommentars einzuführen. Dazu ist es aber unerläßlich, über die Terminologie EUKLIDS genauere Aufklärung zu geben.

Zunächst wollen wir den besonderen Gebrauch des Wortes „rational" bei EUKLID besprechen, auf den schon anfangs (S. 11—12) hingewiesen wurde.

DIE RATIONALE LINIE — Wie auch unser Kommentar hervorhebt (I, § 19 Schluß), sind medialen und rationalen Flächen ebensolche Quadratseiten zugeordnet. Also z. B. das Quadrat von der Fläche $\sqrt{2}$ Quadratfuß hat eine mediale Fläche, und die Seite, $= \sqrt[4]{2}$ Fuß, ist eine mediale Länge. Das Quadrat von der Fläche 4 Quadratfuß hat eine rationale Fläche, die Seite ist $= 2$ Fuß, sie ist rational, und hier stimmen antiker und moderner Sprachgebrauch überein. Aber auch bei dem Quadrat von der Fläche 3 Quadratfuß ist für EUKLID nicht nur die Fläche, sondern auch die Seite rational, und diese ist doch $= \sqrt{3}$ Fuß.

Diese eigentümliche Ausdehnung des Begriffs *rational* hängt also damit zusammen, daß die Griechen die Strecke und das zugehörige Quadrat gleichsam als untrennbare Einheit auffaßten. Die Linie von der Länge 3 Fuß ist mit der Einheit „in Länge kommensurabel", die Linie $\sqrt{3}$ Fuß ist „in Potenz kommensurabel", wobei, wie schon erwähnt, das Wort „Potenz" nicht nur im Sinne von „Quadrat" aufzufassen ist, sondern auch in dem von ARISTOTELES her bekannten Sinne von „Vermögen".

Die genauere Erklärung läßt sich nach unserem Kommentar geben, und zwar besonders nach I § 5 Anfang und § 6 Anfang. Beide Stellen sind auch als Scholien in griechischer Sprache

erhalten (EUKLID ed HEIBERG, V, Scholion Nr. 2, S. 418 Z. 7—9
und Z. 14—23)

Es wird gefragt· „Wie kann es *irrationale* Größen, aloga,
geben, da doch für alle begrenzten Großen, wenn sie vervielfältigt einander übertreffen, ein Verhältnis, *ratio*, logos existiert?"
— Die Antwort lautet· „Die irrationalen sind die, die kein
*Zahlen*verhaltnis haben; es gibt nämlich drei Arten des Ver-
hältnisses. eins für alle begrenzten und homogenen Größen, eins
für die kommensurablen und eins für die (sonstigen) rationalen."

Das Verhältnis der endlichen und homogenen Großen, so
heißt es weiter, wird nach „großer und kleiner" behandelt, — das
heißt, die eine kann vervielfacht die andere übertreffen, vielleicht
ist auch gemeint, daß ein Vielfaches der einen ein Vielfaches der
anderen übertreffen kann, womit auf die 5 Definition des
5. Buches EUKLIDS über die Gleichheit beliebiger Verhältnisse
angespielt wäre.

In den beiden anderen Fällen ist das Verhältnis „rational"
(im griechischen Sinne), es ist durch Zahlen festgelegt, und zwar
bei den „in Länge kommensurablen" Strecken unmittelbar,
sagen wir „actu"; dagegen bei den übrigen rationalen namlich
nur „in Potenz kommensurablen", besteht das Verhältnis
„potentiā", nämlich für die über den Strecken gezeichneten
Quadrate — *Hierin scheint uns die Erklärung zu liegen.* —
Das Verhältnis des (im griechischen Sinne) Rationalen zur Einheit ist aussprechbar, rheton, das des Irrationalen nicht· diese
Auffassung zeigt sich auch in der Art, wie EUKLID im 13 Buch
die Satze über die Kantenlängen der regulären Körper angibt.
Fur Tetraeder, Oktaeder und Wurfel ist das Verhältnis zum
Durchmesser der umschriebenen Kugel „in Potenz kommensurabel", die Seite ist also nach griechischem Sprachgebrauch
rational In diesem Falle wird das Zahlenverhältnis einfach
angegeben, z. B. lautet Satz 15· der Durchmesser der Kugel ist
in Potenz das Dreifache von der Seite des Wurfels

Dagegen für Ikosaeder und Dodekaeder (Satz 16 und 17) sagt
der Satz nur: die Seite ist die „kleinere Irrationale" und die
„Apotome". Mit diesen Worten ist nur die Natur der Beziehung,
sozusagen der algebraische Charakter, angegeben dagegen die
zahlenmäßige Abhängigkeit, die wir oben S. 19 durch moderne
Quadratwurzeln wiedergegeben haben, wird nur im Beweise
entwickelt. —

Man mag einwenden, daß hier von „Größer und Kleiner" oder
von den Euklidischen Definitionen 4 und 5 des Buches 5 nicht
die Rede ist. *Immerhin werden diese Definitionen aber vorausgesetzt.* Kugeldurchmesser und Ikosaeder-Seite haben *deswegen*

ein Verhältnis zueinander, weil sie doch vervielfältigt einander
übertreffen können. Und der Anfang des 6 Buches beschäftigt
sich damit, zu zeigen, daß gewisse geometrische Konstruktionen,
etwa das Zeichnen einer Parallelen zu einer Dreiecksseite inner-
halb des Dreiecks, zu proportionierten Stücken im Sinne der
Definition 5 führen; diese Erkenntnis wird weiterhin stillschwei-
gend angewendet.

Besonders glücklich ist die EUKLIDische Fassung des Begriffs
rational sicher nicht. Auch unserem Kommentator gefällt sie
nicht Er meint, sie sei nicht recht durchdacht und habe Ver-
wirrung angerichtet (I § 17). Sie hat sich ja auch nicht lange
gehalten, schon HERON und DIOPHANT haben sie nicht mehr.[12]

DIE IRRATIONALEN LINIEN EUKLIDS. — $\sqrt{5}$ oder
$\sqrt[3]{5}$ bedeutet für uns eine irrationale *Zahl*. Dergleichen gab es
für die Griechen nicht, EUKLID handelt nur von rationalen und
irrationalen *Strecken und Flächen*[13] Eine Einheitsstrecke r von
bestimmter Länge etwa $= 1$ Fuß wird als Maß angenommen
Dann ist also für EUKLID $(5 - \sqrt{5})\, r$ eine Apotome, $(5 + \sqrt{5})$
r ein Binomium. Auch $(\sqrt{5} - 1)\, r$ und $(\sqrt{5} - \sqrt{2})\, r$ sind
Apotomen, allgemein $(\sqrt{a} - \sqrt{b})\, r$; dabei bedeuten a und b
Brüche, es ist $a > b$, und a und b sollen sich nicht wie Quadrat-
zahlen verhalten. — Entsprechendes gilt für das Binomium.

Auch unser Ausdruck $\sqrt{5 - \sqrt{5}}$ existiert für EUKLID nicht
in dieser Form Er betrachtet vielmehr das Rechteck, dessen
Seiten $= r$ und $(5 - \sqrt{5})\, r$ sind. Dies Rechteck wird in ein
Quadrat verwandelt, und die Seite des Quadrats ist dann in
unserer Schreibweise $= \sqrt{5 - \sqrt{5}}\; r$.

Um mit EUKLID die verschiedenen Fälle von $\sqrt{\sqrt{a} - \sqrt{b}}$ zu
unterscheiden, wollen wir noch einmal die Quintessenz des
Buches 10 in der Form von CHASLES anführen:

$$\sqrt{A \pm B} = \sqrt{\frac{A + \sqrt{A^2 - B^2}}{2}} \pm \sqrt{\frac{A - \sqrt{A^2 - B^2}}{2}}. \quad (3)$$

Wir lassen das Vorzeichen unbestimmt, um zugleich Binomium
und Apotome sowie die aus beiden abgeleiteten irrationalen
Linien zu umfassen. A und B sind Quadratwurzeln aus
rationalen Zahlen, $= \sqrt{a}$ und $\sqrt{b}$ mit der soeben angegebenen
Beschränkung, daß nicht beide zu einander kommensurabel
sein dürfen. — Wir kommen der Vorstellung EUKLIDS näher,
wenn wir in (3) überall den Faktor r hinzugefügt denken.

Wann ist die rechte Seite von (3) einfacher als die linke? Dann und nur dann, wenn $\sqrt{A^2 - B^2} = C$ kommensurabel zu A ist. Dann stehen rechts im allgemeinen zwei vierte Wurzeln. EUKLID drückt die Bedingung für das Binomium so aus. „Der größere Name (A) potenziert um das Quadrat einer ihm in Länge kommensurablen Größe (nämlich C) über den kleineren (B)" (Definitionen II, vor Satz 48 des 10. Buches)[14]. Die Bedingung ergibt sich jetzt also in etwas umständlicherer Form als in unserer vorläufigen Betrachtung oben S 20, wo wir A als ganze Zahl vorausgesetzt hatten. —

Nehmen wir als Beispiel $\sqrt{\sqrt{18} \pm \sqrt{10}}$, also $A = \sqrt{18}$, $B = \sqrt{10}$, dann ist $\sqrt{A^2 - B^2} = \sqrt{8}$, kommensurabel zu $\sqrt{18}$. Die Bedingung ist erfüllt, die rechte Seite von (3) wird einfach, nämlich

$$= \sqrt[4]{2} \left(\sqrt{\tfrac{3}{2}} \pm \sqrt{\tfrac{1}{2}} \right) —$$

EUKLID unterscheidet 6 Formen des Binomiums. $A + B$ ist ein 1., 2. oder 3. Binomium, wenn C zu A kommensurabel ist. wenn nicht, so haben wir das 4., 5. oder 6. Binomium — Beim 1. und 4. Binomium ist, wie schon oben angedeutet, A „in Länge kommensurabel mit der Einheit", beim 2. und 5. gilt das gleiche von B, beim 3. und 6. von keinem von beiden

Bezeichnen wir die 6 Binomien mit $bn_1, bn_2, \ldots bn_6$, so können wir, teilweise in Anlehnung an S 20 oben, die folgenden Beispiele aufstellen

$$bn_1 = (3 + \sqrt{5})\, r \ \text{oder auch} = (2 + \sqrt{3})\, r,$$
$$bn_2 = (3\sqrt{5} + 5)\, r \ \text{oder} \ (2\sqrt{3} + 3)\, r,$$
$$bn_3 = (3\sqrt{2} + \sqrt{10})\, r \ \text{oder} \ (2\sqrt{2} + \sqrt{6})\, r,$$
$$bn_4 = (5 + \sqrt{5})\, r,$$
$$bn_5 = (\sqrt{5} + 1)\, r,$$
$$bn_6 = (5\sqrt{2} + \sqrt{10})\, r \ \text{oder auch} \ (\sqrt{5} + \sqrt{2})\, r.$$

Werden diese Ausdrücke der Reihe nach in (3) für $A + B$ eingesetzt, so ergeben sich rechts die „6 Linien durch Addition"[15]. Wir wollen diese mit $la_1, la_2, \ldots la_6$ bezeichnen. Dann ist also

$$\sqrt{r \cdot bn_1} = la_1$$
$$\sqrt{r \cdot bn_2} = la_2$$
$$\cdot \quad \cdot \quad \cdot$$
$$\sqrt{r \cdot bn_6} = la_6.$$

Die Linien durch Addition haben alle besondere Namen. Die erste ist, wie leicht zu sehen, ein Binomium. Die zweite heißt „erste Bimediale", die dritte „zweite Bimediale". Nehmen wir als Beispiel

$$la_3 = r \cdot \sqrt{2\sqrt{2} + \sqrt{6}} = r\sqrt{2} \left(\sqrt{\tfrac{1}{2}} + \sqrt{\tfrac{3}{2}} \right) = r \left(\sqrt[4]{\tfrac{1}{2}} + \sqrt[4]{\tfrac{9}{2}} \right).$$

Rechts steht die Summe zweier vierten Wurzeln oder nach EUKLID die Summe zweier *medialen* Linien, daher „Bimediale". — Vergleiche auch die Beispiele S 21 unter (2) und die zahlreichen Beispiele bei SUTER, „Beiträge" S 67.—70

la_4 heißt „größere Irrationale" diese kurze Bezeichnung für den Typus $r \sqrt{5 + \sqrt{5}}$ neben der entsprechenden „kleineren Irrationale" für den Typus $r \cdot \sqrt{5 - \sqrt{5}}$ läßt vermuten, daß anfangs, etwa von Theätet, überhaupt nur diese beide Formen untersucht worden sind[16].

Endlich la_5 und la_6 heißen „die ein Rationales und Mediales Potenzierende" und „die zwei mediale Potenzierende" Wir brauchen nur eine dieser Bezeichnungen zu erklären und setzen

$$la_5^2 = (\sqrt{5} + 1) r^2.$$

Das Quadrat oder die „Potenz" von la_5 ist die *mediale* Fläche $\sqrt{5} \cdot r^2$ vermehrt um die *rationale* Fläche r^2. —

Es sei uns erlaubt, die 6 Apotomen $ap_1, \ldots ap_6$ und die entsprechenden Linien durch Subtraktion, nämlich $ls_1, \ldots ls_6$ jetzt sehr kurz abzumachen

Es ist natürlich $\sqrt{r \cdot ap_1} = ls_1$, $\sqrt{r \cdot ap_2} = ls_2$ usw. Wir wollen noch die Bezeichnungen angeben.

ls_1 = Apotome,
ls_2 = erste Medial-Apotome,
ls_3 = zweite Medial-Apotome,
ls_4 = kleinere Irrationale,
ls_5 = die mit einem Rationalen ein Mediales ergebende,
ls_6 = die mit einem Medialen ein Mediales ergebende.

Die beiden letzten Ausdrücke bedürfen vielleicht der Erklärung Wir begnügen uns mit dem letzten. Es sei $ls_6^2 = (\sqrt{5} - \sqrt{2}) \cdot r^2$, durch Hinzufügung einer medialen Fläche, nämlich $\sqrt{2} \cdot r^2$, wird ls_6^2 ergänzt zu einer anderen medialen Fläche, nämlich $\sqrt{5} \cdot r^2$.

Konsequenterweise könnte man die „kleinere Irrationale" auch nennen „die mit einem Medialen ein Rationales ergebende". — Entsprechend könnte die „größere Irrationale" la_4 auch den umständlichen Namen tragen, den EUKLID an la_5 gegeben hat. Der Unterschied ist der, daß bei la_4 wie bei ls_4 die größere Fläche rational ist, bei la_5 wie bei ls_5 die kleinere

Ein hübsches Beispiel zu ap_1 findet sich in dem — allerdings wohl interpolierten — Satz 6 des 13. Buches Wird die Seite 1 nach dem goldenen Schnitt geteilt und das größere Stück x genannt, so ist $x^2 = 1 - x$. Da nun x und $1 - x$ Apotomen sind, so kann man wegen $x = \sqrt{1-x}$ sofort schließen, daß $1 - x$ eine erste Apotome ist

Die Ausrechnung gibt $x = \dfrac{\sqrt{5}}{2} - \dfrac{1}{2}$, übrigens eine 5. Apotome,

und $1 - x = \dfrac{3}{2} - \dfrac{\sqrt{5}}{2}$, dies ist in der Tat eine erste Apotome, wie wir auch aus früheren Beispielen schon wissen.

APOLLONIUS EUKLIDS Buch 10 ist schon einigermaßen verschnörkelt, aber ein klares Ziel immerhin vorhanden, nämlich, wie wir hoffen gezeigt zu haben, die Untersuchung von $\sqrt{5 - \sqrt{5}}$. Die Arbeit des Apollonius, soweit sich aus den Andeutungen unseres Kommentars schließen läßt, stellt dagegen lediglich einen tastenden Versuch dar, durch Verallgemeinerungen über EUKLID hinaus zu kommen, ohne daß ein Ziel oder ein befriedigender Erfolg zu erkennen wäre

Das euklidische Binomium mag in der Form $a + \sqrt{b}$ dargestellt werden. APOLLONIUS bildet nun das Trinomium $a + \sqrt{b} + \sqrt{c}$, das Quadrinomium $a + \sqrt{b} + \sqrt{c} + \sqrt{d}$ usw. Hierüber besteht kein Zweifel. (Siehe unten die Übersetzung des Textes, I § 21, S. 85.)

Die euklidische Apotome ist entsprechend $= a - \sqrt{b}$. Es liegt nahe, wenn ein dreigliedriger Ausdruck dieser Art entstehen soll, etwa an $a - \sqrt{b} + \sqrt{c}$ zu denken, und wir werden zeigen, daß diese Vermutung mit dem Wortlaut des Textes sehr wohl verträglich ist (s S. 29).

Die euklidische Mediale ist in modernen Zeichen $= \sqrt{\sqrt{a}} = \sqrt[4]{a}$ Mit den Hilfsmitteln der euklidischen Geometrie lassen sich ebenso gut wie 4 Wurzeln auch 8., 16. usw. Wurzeln konstruieren Der Text ist zwar an dieser Stelle nicht ganz in Ordnung, wir werden es aber wahrscheinlich machen, daß APOLLONIUS in der Tat an 8 , 16 usw Wurzeln, oder, was dasselbe ist, an immer wiederholte Quadratwurzeln gedacht hat

Diese drei angeführten Erweiterungen stellen nun gerade keine sonderlichen mathematischen Fortschritte dar. Es wird APOLLONIUS gereizt haben, zu den übrigen „Linien durch Addition und Subtraktion" EUKLIDS ebenfalls allgemeinere Formen zu finden, und dies scheint ihm nicht gelungen zu sein.

Man könnte denken, APOLLONIUS wollte Ausdrücke von der Form $\sqrt{a + \sqrt{b} + \sqrt{c}}$ untersuchen Solche lassen aber nie eine Vereinfachung zu, wie eine leichte Rechnung ergeben wird.

Naturlich nehmen wir an, daß $\sqrt{b}$ und $\sqrt{c}$ nicht etwa kommensurabel zu einander sind. Ist dies der Fall, z. B vorgelegt $1 + \sqrt{2} + \sqrt{8}$, so läßt sich der Ausdruck durch ein Euklidisches Binomium ersetzen, in unserem Fall durch $1 + \sqrt{18}$. —

Wir wollen für einen Augenblick setzen, ähnlich wie oben S. 20.

$$\sqrt{a} + \sqrt{b} + \sqrt{c} = x + y + z$$

x, y und z seien einfache Irrationalitaten von der Form $\sqrt{m}$ oder, aber höchstens in einem Falle, $= m$. Ohne Schaden für die Allgemeinheit der Untersuchung dürfen wir m als ganze Zahl annehmen Auch von den Großen x, y und z sollen nicht etwa zwei miteinander kommensurabel sein

Es wird

$$(x + y + z)^2 = x^2 + y^2 + z^2 + 2xy + 2xz + 2yz$$

Die drei ersten Glieder rechts sind ganze Zahlen, die drei letzten samtlich Quadratwurzeln aus solchen, und untereinander nicht kommensurabel, wenn x, y, z es nicht sind. Ware ferner etwa $2xy$ gleich einer ganzen Zahl, so mußten x und y sich wie ganze Zahlen zueinander verhalten, was doch ausgeschlossen war. — Rechts steht also erst eine ganze Zahl, namlich $x^2 + y^2 + z^2$, und dann folgen drei einfache Quadratwurzeln, die sich nicht etwa auf zwei reduzieren lassen.

Wir haben hiermit nachgewiesen, daß wohl ein viergliedriger Ausdruck von der Form $a + \sqrt{b} + \sqrt{c} + \sqrt{d}$ das Quadrat eines ähnlichen dreigliedrigen sein kann, aber niemals ein dreigliedriger selbst.

Gleichwohl untersucht APOLLONIUS Ausdrucke von der Form $x + y + z$, indem er etwa die Bedingungen stellt es sei $x^2 + y^2$ rational, also $= m$, ebenso $x^2 + z^2 = m'$, dagegen $2yz$ sei medial. $= \sqrt{n}$ (§ 22). Wir vermogen in diesen Dingen nur ein „leeres Spiel des Kalkuls" zu erkennen und werden uns nicht weiter damit befassen, zumal wir zu den Analysen von WOEPCKE und CHASLES kaum etwas hinzuzufugen haben

Nur auf drei Fragen wollen wir eingehen· auf die erweiterte Mediale und Apotome, von denen schon S 26 die Rede war, und auf den Namen der „ungeordneten" Irrational-Linien.

Zur *Medial-Linie* heißt es (§ 22 Anfang). Wir konnen zwischen zwei rationalen, in Potenz kommensurablen Linien — wie 1 und $\sqrt{2}$ — nicht nur eine mittlere Proportionale nehmen, sondern auch 3, 4 und mehr

Eine mittlere Proportionale fuhrt auf $\sqrt[4]{2}$, die Medial-Linie EUKLIDS Wenn namlich

$$1 : x = x : \sqrt{2}, \text{ so ist } x = \sqrt[4]{2}$$

Wir wollen auch den Fall von zwei Zwischengliedern nehmen, der allerdings im Texte fehlt. Es wird

$$1 \quad z = x \quad y = y \quad \sqrt{2} \text{ und hieraus}$$

$$x = \sqrt[3]{2}, \quad y = \sqrt[3]{2}.$$

Bei drei „mittleren Proportionalen" entsteht die Reihe:
$1, \sqrt[8]{2}, \sqrt[4]{2}, \sqrt[8]{8}, \sqrt{2}$ oder $2^0, 2^{\frac{1}{4}}, 2^{\frac{1}{2}}, 2^{\frac{3}{4}}, 2^{\frac{4}{4}}$, bei vier Zwischen-gliedern.

$$1, \sqrt[10]{2}, \sqrt[5]{2}, \sqrt[10]{8}, \sqrt[5]{4}, \sqrt{2} \text{ oder}$$
$$2^0, 2^{0,1}, 2^{0,2}, 2^{0,3}, 2^{0,4}, 2^{0,5} \text{ —}$$

Es treten also nicht nur 4, 8, 16 Wurzeln auf, die sich elementar-geometrisch konstruieren lassen, sondern auch 5. Wur-zeln, und wenn man den Fall von zwei Zwischengliedern mit-nimmt, 3 Wurzeln usw —

Hiergegen sprechen nun mehrere Bedenken

Zunächst wenn man auf $\sqrt{2}$ und $\sqrt[3]{2}$ kommen will, so ist es nicht nötig, von 1 und $\sqrt{2}$ auszugehen, sondern es liegt doch näher, 1 und 2 als Endglieder zu nehmen Im Falle der 3. Wurzel oder des Delischen Problems waren allgemein zwei mittlere Proportionalen einzuschalten zwischen zwei Linien, die sich wie Zahlen, aber nicht gerade wie Kubikzahlen verhalten.

Ferner muß es auffallen, daß unser Text gar nicht von *zwei* mittleren Proportionalen redet, sondern daß es heißt 3, 4 und mehr Unsere Vermutung ist diese *Es hat ursprünglich geheißen 3, 7 und mehr* Die weiteren zu ergänzenden Zahlen sind 15, 31, allgemein $2^n - 1$ Das arabische Zahlwort für 4 hat einige Ähnlichkeit mit dem Worte für 7, so daß ein Versehen wohl möglich ist. Schalten wir zwischen 1 und $\sqrt{2}$ drei mittlere Proportionalen ein, so kommen wir auf 8 Wurzeln, bei sieben auf 16 Wurzeln *Alle diese sind geometrisch konstruierbar,* während etwa die 5 Wurzel für die klassische griechische Geome-trie völlig abseits lag

Eine Korrektur des Textes ist auf jeden Fall nötig. WOEPCKE scheint allerdings am Text keinen Anstoß genommen zu haben, dagegen SUTER fügt als seine Vermutung *zwei* mittlere Propor-tionale hinzu, so daß es heißen wurde 2, 3, 4 und mehr. Die von uns vorgeschlagene Lösung der Schwierigkeit wurde gut passen zu der schon einmal (oben S 17) erwähnten Vermutung HEIBERGS, daß der Satz 115 im 10. Buch EUKLIDS von APOLLO-NIUS herrührt, also interpoliert ist. Dieser Satz sagt nämlich: aus einer Medial-Linie können unzählige Irrational-Linien ent-stehen; das Verfahren ist die immer wiederholte Einschaltung eines geometrischen Mittels, so daß 8., 16. usw. Wurzeln gebildet werden[17] —

Nun zur *Apotome*. EUKLID hat die zweigliedrige Apotome vom Typus $5 - \sqrt{5}$. Unser Kommentar sagt dazu, in § 23, von der subtrahierten Linie wird eine weitere „rationale" Linie weggenommen. WOEPCKE hat hierbei an $\sqrt{5} - \sqrt{3}$ gedacht, wodurch man allerdings nicht weiter kommt. Die richtige Auffassung ist wohl die, man soll *vorläufig* $\sqrt{5} - \sqrt{3}$ bilden und dann die so erhaltene Linie anstatt $\sqrt{5}$ vom ersten Gliede, namlich von 5, abziehen, auf diese Weise entsteht

$$5 - (\sqrt{5} - \sqrt{3}),$$

und dies ist in der Tat eine dreigliedrige Apotome.

Die viergliedrige Apotome wäre bei unserer Auffassung des Textes von dem Typus

$$5 - (\sqrt{5} - (\sqrt{3} - \sqrt{2})). \text{ —}[18]$$

Endlich die Frage der *ungeordneten Irrationalen*. Welchen Sinn hat der Name „geordnete Irrational-Linien" für die des EUKLID, im Gegensatz zu den „ungeordneten" des APOLLONIUS?

PROKLUS braucht in seinem Kommentar (S 220) dieselben Ausdrücke für *Probleme: geordnet* sind solche, die *eine Lösung* haben, *gemischt* die *mit einer endlichen Anzahl* von Lösungen, endlich *ungeordnet* solche Aufgaben, die *unendlich viele* Lösungen zulassen.

Man konnte sich nun denken, wenn die Linien von der Länge 1 und $\sqrt{2}$ gegeben sind, so ist durch sie *eine* Euklidische Mediale, *ein* Binomium und *eine* Apotome bestimmt, namlich $\sqrt[4]{2}$, $1 + \sqrt{2}$ und $\sqrt{2} - 1$. Aus diesen lassen sich aber unbestimmt viele Irrational-Linien des APOLLONIUS ableiten, namlich die Medialen $\sqrt[4]{2}$, $\sqrt[8]{2}$ usw., die Binomien $1 + \sqrt{2} + \sqrt{3}$, $1 + \sqrt{2} + \sqrt{5}$ usw., Apotomen etwa $\sqrt{2} - (1 - \sqrt[4]{\tfrac{1}{3}})$ usw. —

Man mag diese Deutung, wenigstens für die Binomien und Apotomen, etwas oberflächlich finden. In der Tat ist die richtige Auffassung doch die, daß das Euklidische Binomium durch zwei Stücke bestimmt ist, die angeführten Binomien des APOLLONIUS durch drei, von denen das dritte genau so wichtig ist wie die beiden ersten.

Aber wir müssen bedenken, daß die Arbeit des APOLLONIUS durchaus auf den Voraussetzungen der „Elemente" beruht. Eine selbständige Definition der dreigliedrigen Apotome würde z. B. lauten: zwei Linien werden addiert und eine dritte davon abgezogen. APOLLONIUS aber geht von der Euklidischen Festsetzung aus und ersetzt nur den Subtrahenden durch einen anderen

NOCH EINIGE MATHEMATISCHE ERKLÄRUNGEN.

Der erste Teil des Kommentars bringt die philosophischen Grund-
lagen der Theorie des Irrationalen: besprochen werden die
Auffassungen von PLATO und ARISTOTELES und die Begriffe
Maß, kommensurabel, rational; es folgen einige Bemerkungen
über die Irrationalitaten EUKLIDS und des APOLLONIUS, und
endlich wird eine Einteilung des 10. Buches gegeben.

Der zweite Teil geht genauer auf die irrationalen Linien durch
Addition und durch Subtraktion ein, die wir oben mit la und ls
bezeichnet haben   Einige mathematische Schwierigkeiten des
Textes, die nur kurzer Erklarung bedurfen, sind in den Anmerkungen erledigt.   Dagegen erfordern wohl die §§ 10, 19 und 26
eine etwas ausführlichere Wiedergabe in modernen Zeichen.

§ 10 handelt von den drei ersten la und ls Hier sind die
Stücke x und y, die addiert oder subtrahiert werden, zueinander
kommensurabel in Potenz, aber nicht in Lange.   Es wird nun die
Bemerkung gemacht: je nachdem $x^2 + y^2 = m$ oder $= \sqrt{m}$,
also rational oder medial ist, sind auch x und y selbst rational
oder medial, das heißt $= \sqrt{n}$ oder $= \sqrt[4]{n}$

Dies ist leicht einzusehen.   Da nämlich x^2 kommensurabel zu
y^2 sein soll, so ist auch jede dieser Größen kommensurabel zu
$x^2 + y^2$.   Die Gleichung $x^2 + y^2 = m$ hat also zur Folge
$x^2 = m'$ und $y^2 = m''$.   Ebenso folgt im anderen Falle aus
$x^2 + y^2 = \sqrt{m}$, daß $x^2 = m' \sqrt{m}$ und $y^2 = m'' \sqrt{m}$

Der erste Fall führt auf la_1 und ls_1, Binomium und Apotome,
der zweite auf la_2, la_3, ls_2 und ls_3, die ja samtlich durch Zu-
sammenfugung medialer Linien entstehen —

In § 19 wird entwickelt: wenn zwei Stücke x und y zusammen
eine Linie durch Addition la ergeben, so ist das harmonische
Mittel aus x und y die entsprechende ls

Wir erwähnten schon S 17, daß das harmonische Mittel
zwischen x und y dargestellt ist durch

$$\frac{2\,x\,y}{x + y} \quad \text{oder} \quad \frac{2\,x\,y\,(x - y)}{x^2 - y^2}.$$

Wenn nun $x + y = la$, so ist $x - y = ls$, und zwar von
derselben Ordnung, sogar von denselben „Namen", wie es bei
den Griechen heißt, d. h. von denselben Komponenten.   Wir

haben nur zu zeigen, daß der Faktor $\dfrac{2\,x\,y}{x^2 - y^2}$ von der Form

$\sqrt{m}$ ist und deswegen die Ordnung von ls nicht beeinflußt.
Wir benutzen wieder die Formel (3) von S. 23 und zwar zerlegt:

$$\left. \begin{array}{l} x + y = \sqrt{A + B}, \\ x - y = \sqrt{A - B} \end{array} \right\} (3\,a)$$

x und y seien der Einfachheit halber als Zahlen gedacht, der Faktor r mag wegbleiben. Es folgt

$$x^2 - y^2 = \sqrt{A^2 - B^2}.$$

Durch Addition bez. Subtraktion der Gleichungen (3a) ergibt sich

$$2x = \sqrt{A + B} + \sqrt{A - B}$$
$$2y = \sqrt{A + B} - \sqrt{A - B}$$
$$4xy = 2B$$
$$2xy = B$$

Da von A und B die Form $\sqrt{m}$ vorausgesetzt ist, so haben auch $2xy$ und $x^2 - y^2$ dieselbe Form, ebenso ihr Quotient, und dies war zu beweisen.

Als Beispiel sei eine 6. Linie durch Addition oder Subtraktion vorgelegt, nämlich

$$x \pm y = \sqrt{\sqrt{5} \pm \sqrt{3}} = \sqrt{\frac{\sqrt{5} + \sqrt{2}}{2}} \pm \sqrt{\frac{\sqrt{5} - \sqrt{2}}{2}}.$$

Es folgt

$$x^2 + y^2 = \sqrt{5} = A,$$
$$2xy = \sqrt{3} = B,$$
$$x^2 - y^2 = \sqrt{2}.$$

Das harmonische Mittel aus x und y ist

$$= \frac{\sqrt{3}}{\sqrt{2}} (x - y), \text{ und dieser Ausdruck ist für}$$

Euklid gleichartig mit $x - y$. —

Endlich § 26 besagt in unseren Zeichen.

$$la^2 \text{ entweder } = \sqrt{m} \cdot r \cdot la_2 \text{ oder } = \sqrt{m} \cdot r \cdot la_3,$$
$$ls^2 \text{ entweder } = \sqrt{m} \cdot r \cdot ls_2 \text{ oder } = \sqrt{m} \cdot r \cdot ls_3 \text{ —}$$

Wir hatten gesehen, daß nach Definition $la^2 = r \cdot bn$ ist (oben S. 24). Aus den dortigen Formeln und Beispielen wird der Leser auch ersehen, daß la_2 und la_3 sich durch den Faktor $\sqrt{m}$ unterscheiden von la_1 oder, was ja dasselbe ist, von bn, während der Faktor $\sqrt{m}$ auf die Art der Linie ohne Einfluß ist. Entsprechendes gilt von ls und ap. Hiermit ist unser Satz bewiesen.

Als Beispiel nehmen wir, ähnlich wie soeben und wieder ohne den Faktor r

$$la^2 = \sqrt{5} + \sqrt{3}$$

Für m sei 2 gesetzt und also gefragt: von welcher Art ist z, wenn die Gleichung gilt

$$\sqrt{5} + \sqrt{3} = \sqrt{2} \cdot z^2$$

Offenbar wird

$$z = \frac{1}{\sqrt{2}} \left(\sqrt{5} + \sqrt{3} \right) = \sqrt{2} \left(\sqrt{\frac{5}{2}} + \sqrt{\frac{3}{2}} \right).$$

Dies ist eine la_3

Eine la_2 entsteht. wenn wir $m = 15$ wahlen, namlich

$$la_2 = z = \frac{1}{\sqrt{15}} \left(\sqrt{5} + \sqrt{3} \right) = \sqrt{15} \left(\sqrt{\frac{1}{3}} + \sqrt{\frac{1}{5}} \right).$$

Das Quadrat ist $= \sqrt{15} \left(\frac{8}{15} + \frac{2}{\sqrt{15}} \right) = \frac{8}{\sqrt{15}} + 2$, und dies ist

ein bn_2, denn das erste Glied der rechten Seite enthalt eine Wurzel und ist großer als das zweite

Anmerkungen.

[1] Mémoires présentés par divers savants à l'Ac des Sc , 14, 1856, S. 658 bis 720.

[2] Comptes Rendus de l'Ac des Sc., 37, 1853, S. 553; -- noch einmal abgedruckt in Journal de math , 19, 1854, S. 413.

[3] Die Mitteilungen des Textes beruhen zum Teil auf den Akten der Berliner Akademie der Wissenschaften Außerdem sind drei bald nach WOEPCKE's Tode erschienene Nachrufe benutzt ein von WOEPCKE's Vater herruhrender, im Archiv der Math. und Physik (Grunerts Archiv) 42, 1864, Heft 1, Literar Bericht S 1, eine sehr schone Wurdigung des früh Verstorbenen durch MOHL im Journal Asiatique, 6 Ser , 4, 1864, S 20, — endlich NARDUCCI in Bulletino di bibl e di storia delle sc. mat e fis , 2, 1869, S 119 — NARDUCCI gibt an, W habe die 400 Taler zumeist zurückgezahlt Dies ist an sich glaubhaft, doch sagen die Akten der Akademie nichts davon.

Vielleicht lassen sich die Ratsel der Ausgabe von 1855 am ersten psychologisch erklaren *Woepcke wollte nicht, daß die Pariser Akademie von der Ausgabe etwas erfahre* Er hatte dieser doch 1853 oder noch früher sein Essai eingereicht Er war verwöhnt durch den schnellen Abdruck seiner ersten Pariser Aufsatze, außerdem von jugendlicher Ungeduld — er war 1826 geboren — und vielleicht war er über die Verzögerung des Druckes seines Essai so verstimmt, daß er sich an die Berliner Akademie wandte. Nachdem nun das Geld von dort bewilligt und der Druck des Textes vorbereitet war, da hatte er, ein wenig zaghaft wie er war, vielleicht wieder Besorgnis, diese Veröffentlichung möchte in Paris einen ungunstigen Eindruck machen, und so richtete er den Druck des Textes so ein, daß allerdings außer den Mitgliedern der Berliner Akademie wohl nicht viele Menschen davon erfahren haben werden.

[4] Studien über Euklid, Leipzig 1882, S 171. K. DANSKE Vid Selsk. Skr , 6 RAEKKE, Hist og philos. Afdel 2, 1888 89, S 238, Die Bemerkung über die Goldkorner S 229

[5] Metaphysik 10, 1, 1053a 17; s. dazu ROSS, Aristotle's Metaph II, Oxford 1924, S 283.

[6] s STENZEL, Zahl und Gestalt bei Platon und Aristoteles, Leipzig 1924, S 90 und 94

[7] s EVA SACHS, Die funf Platonischen Korper, Philolog Unters Heft 24, Berlin 1917, S 160—182

[8] Prolegomena critica, Band 5 der Euklid-Ausgabe (1888) S LXXXV; – über den nachher erwahnten Satz von der Diagonale ebendort S LXXXIV

[9] P RAMUS, Scholae mathematicae, Buch 21 (zum ersten Mal gedruckt 1567) STEVIN, Arithmétique, Def 30 — Der Brief von CASTELLI in A FAVARO, G GALILEI e lo studio di Padova, Firenze 1883, II, 267

[10] Harmonices mundi, Anfang

[11] Proclus in Euclidem, ed Friedlein, Leipzig 1873, S. 68 und 71

[12] Bei HERON gibt es eine bisher nicht beachtete Stelle, s. Bd 3, ed. SCHOENE, Lpzg. 1903, S 18, Z. 22, ἐπεὶ οὖν ψκ ῥητὴν τὴν πλευρὰν οὐκ ἔχουσι, da nun 720 eine rationale Wurzel nicht hat. Die Stelle fehlt im Register unter ῥητός. -- Für DIOPHANT s das Register der TEUBNER'schen Ausgabe (ed TANNERY, Lpzg. 1893—95).

[13] Die ersten Satze des 10. Buches bilden zwar den Anfang einer Theorie kommensurabler und inkommensurabler *Größen* Aber diese Theorie wird nicht durchgeführt Euklid verstrickt sich in eine Terminologie, die doch immer an Linien und Flächen haften bleibt Für den von uns angegebenen Zweck des 10. Buches, nämlich die Untersuchung der Kanten der regulären Körper, ist dies ja auch kein Schade.

[14] Unser Pappus-Kommentar geht auf dies sachgemäße, freilich etwas schwierige Euklidische Kriterium nur einmal kurz ein, nämlich in § 24 des zweiten Teiles Große Stücke des Kommentars (II §§ 6--16) scheinen geradezu in der Absicht geschrieben, das Euklidische Kriterium entbehrlich zu machen

[15] Dies ist die gewöhnliche Bezeichnung unseres Kommentars, und entsprechend gibt es die „Linien durch Subtraktion" Auch in den griechischen Scholien heißt es „Hai kata synthesin hex alogoi", z. B. Scholion Nr 189, 204, 309, 358, 359. — Siehe auch Euklid ed Heiberg III S. 107 Anm. 20 und S 224 Anm 5

In Euklids Text heißt es nur (Bd III S. 222, Z. 9) „das Binomium und die darauf (folgenden) Irrationalen"; S 224, 4 einfach „Die Irrationalen". Entsprechend für Apotome usw S. 352, 18 und 354, 14 ft

[16] Daß Theatet sich mit der Form $\sqrt{5} - \sqrt[4]{5}$ beschäftigt hat, ist zwar nicht unmittelbar bezeugt; es ist aber wahrscheinlich, denn 1 gewinnt die Apotome, die Theatet eingeführt haben soll, erst Interesse durch eine solche weitergehende Betrachtung, und 2. wird Theatet die Behandlung der regulären Körper zugeschrieben, sogar die Konstruktion von Oktaeder und Ikosaeder (s. EVA SACHS a a O. S. 29 und 76-87). Beim Ikosaeder tritt aber gerade die Form

$\sqrt{5} - \sqrt[4]{5}$ auf

[17] Der Verfasser hat schon einmal darauf hingewiesen, daß wahrscheinlich der Anfang der 3. Definition des 10 Buches (Euklid ed Heiberg Bd. V, S. 2, Z. 9—12) auch interpoliert ist. Hier werden die unendlich vielen Irrational-Linien erwähnt, womit wahrscheinlich auf die immer wieder eingeschalteten mittleren Proportionalen angespielt ist; siehe Jahresbericht der Deutschen Mathematiker Vereinigung Band 35, S 170.

[18] Die Auffassung SUTERS (Beiträge S. 67 Nr. 8) scheitert doch wohl an der klaren Bedeutung des Euklidischen Wortes prosarmozousa = Subtrahendus

Inhalt des Kommentars.

3*

Zweiter Teil

INTRODUCTION

by WILLIAM THOMSON.

1. DESCRIPTION OF THE M S

The commentary of Pappus on the tenth book of Euclid's Elements is preserved only in Arabic, and the Arabic text is to be found, so far as is yet known, only in MS. 2457 of the Bibliothèque Nationale in Paris[1]. This manuscript contains some fifty treatises, of which Nos. 5 and 6 constitute our commentary The whole manuscript has been described by F. WOEPCKE in his *Essai d'une restitution de travaux perdus d'Apollonius sur les quantités irrationnelles* (Paris 1856)[2], where WOEPCKE also gives a fairly accurate analysis of the content of our commentary and quotes four extracts from the manuscript with translations (pp. 57—63, 28—45). WOEPCKE also published, anonymously, and without date or place of publication, the full text of the commentary with the title, *The commentary on the tenth book of Euclid's Elements by Bls*, and his work cannot be praised too highly, especially if one considers the nature of the subject in the first part of the commentary and the state of the manuscript, which is written for the most part without the usual diacritical marks that ordinarily distinguish similarly formed letters in Arabic.

In 1922 a translation of WOEPCKE's text by HEINRICH SUTER was published posthumously in Abhandlungen zur Geschichte der Naturwissenschaften und der Medizin, Erlangen. Heft IV, pp. 9—78, under the title of *Der Kommentar des Pappus zum X. Buche des Euklides*. As Dr. JUNGE has observed, SUTER's translation is on the whole reliable, so far as the mathematical content of the commentary is concerned. Nevertheless it has its defects SUTER evidently did not consult the MS., as might be conjectured from statements which he has made, on pages 1 and 3 of his *Einleitung* His translation reproduces, therefore, for the most part, the errors of WOEPCKE's text[3], and occasionally misrepresents the text entirely, especially when philosophical ideas are introduced[4]. Sometimes indeed it is misleading even when it deals with mathematics For example, in his notes, 54, 65, and 85, SUTER supposes that Pappus had abandoned the Euclidian idea of rationality and had approached that of Diophantes. But in each case SUTER's notes are based on mistranslations of the Arabic text, for, as will be shown later, Pappus uses the terms, *rational* and *irrational*, in this commentary at least, in their Euclidian signification[5].

On page 17 of his *Essai* WOEPCKE assigns the commentary to Valens; in all probability, he says, the astronomer, Vettius Valens, of the time of Ptolemy. SUTER discusses this suggestion in the first two pages of his *Einleitung* and rightly assumes that Pappus was the author, pointing out that the Fihrist ascribes a commentary on Book X to Pappus but makes no reference to Valens in this connection. SUTER has omitted, however, an important point, namely, that the Fihrist states that the commentary of Pappus was in two books, like the present commentary.

The source of WOEPCKE's error was his reading of the consonantal skeleton of the author's name as *Bls*. SUTER quite correctly suggests that the *L* may be a *B* with a longer upward stroke than is usual. But as he did not, apparently, consult the MS., he was unable to state positively that WOEPCKE's reading was false. As a matter of fact, however, WOEPCKE was deceived by a trick of the Arab copyist, who almost invariably prolongs the second letter upward more than is usual, whenever three such letters as *B*, *T*, *Th*, *N*, or *Y*, follow one-another in succession in an Arabic word[6]: and two *B*'s followed by an *S* present the same general pattern and would be subject to the same treatment. Hence. probably, the unusual length upward of the second *B* of the name and WOEPCKE's conjecture concerning Valens.

Although SUTER ascribes the commentary in general to Pappus, he raises the question whether (in its present form) it represents the original work of the author of the famous *Collectiones*, so astonishingly prolix appears to him the discussion, so frequent the repetitions, so many the omissions, and so confusingly obscure oftentimes the expression[7]. He acknowledges, indeed, that prolixity and repetitiousness are rather common characteristics of Greek mathematics, but the omissions and the obscurity of expression he imputes to the Arab translator and copyist. SUTER's judgment is, however, unjust, as, it is hoped, the present translation will prove. Not only is the commentary, as SUTER himself says (p 73), well constructed, which opinion seems to contradict the charge of the many omissions, it is also for the most part lucid in statement, a good example of the best period of Arab translation.

SUTER again raises the question of authorship in the last paragraph of his *Anhang* (p. 78). Some of the ideas expressed in the commentary (cf especially Part I, para 9) are in his opinion Neoplatonic in character and impell him, therefore, to ask whether, in the last analysis. the authorship should not be ascribed to Proclus, whose commentary on Euclid may have covered the whole of the Elements and not merely Book I, as it now stands.

The answer to SUTER's query is simple Not one of the philosophical ideas in Part I of the commentary is peculiarly Neoplatonic[8]. The doctrine of the Threeness of things that appears in Part I, para. 9, is found in Aristotle[9] and goes back to the early Pythagoreans or to Homer even; paragraph 8 is mathematical in content rather than philosophical, SUTER notwithstanding, although there is an allusion in it to the Monad as the principle of finitudes, again a very early Pythagorean doctrine[10], and these two paragraphs are the source of SUTER's suggestion of the authorship of Proclus[11]. As a matter of fact, the philosophical notions in Part I have been borrowed for the most part directly from Plato, with two or three exceptions that are Aristotelian in origin. PLATO's Theaetetus, Parmenides, and the Laws, are specifically mentioned[12]. The Timaeus forms the background of much of the thought[13]. And the Platonism of a mathematician of the turn of the third century A. D. need not surprise us, if we but recall Aristotle's accusation that the Academy tended to turn philosophy into mathematics[14]

It is also problematical whether Proclus could have ever written such a clear, sober, and concise piece of work His predominant interest in any subject, even mathematics, is always the epistemological aspect of it He must ever inquire into the how and the why of the knowledge relevant to that subject, and its kind or kinds[15], and such speculation is apt with him to intrude into the discussion of even a definition or proposition[16].

Moreover Proclus can never forego theologizing in the Pythagorean vein. Mathematical forms are for him but veils concealing from the vulgar gaze divine things[17]. Thus right angles are symbols of virtue, or images of perfection and invariable energy, of limitation, intellectual finitude, and the like, and are ascribed to the Gods which proceed into the universe as the authors of the invariable providence of inferiors, whereas acute and obtuse angles are symbols of vice, or images of unceasing progression, division, partition, and infinity, and are ascribed to the Gods who give progression, motion, and a variety of powers[18].

This epistemological interest and this tendency to symbolism are entirely lacking in our commentary, and another trait peculiar to Proclus is also absent, namely, his inordinate pedantry, his fondness of quoting all kinds of opinions from all sorts of ancient thinkers and of citing these by name with pedagogical finicalness. Obviously the author of our commentary had a philosophical turn of mind. but he was a temperate thinker compared with Proclus His philosophy is the handmaid of his mathematics, serving to give his mathematical notions a more or less firm metaphysical basis and no more Philosophical ideas do not seem to have interested him for their own sake

The superscription of Part I and the postscript of Part II give the Arab translator as *Abū 'Uthmān Al-Dimishqī.* According to *Ibn Abī Useibia* (ed., A. MULLER, 1884), p. 234 (cf. p. 205), *Abū 'Uthmān Sa'īd Ibn Ya'qūb Al-Dimishqī* was a famous physician of Bagdad attached to the person of the vizier of that time, *'Alī Ibn 'Īsā*, who in the year 302 H. (i e., 914 A D) built and endowed a hospital in Bagdad and put Al-Dimishqī in charge not only of it but of all the hospitals in Bagdad, Mecca, and Medina Al-Dimishqī flourished, therefore, in the first quarter of the tenth century.

He was famous not only as a physician but also as an author and translator[19]. According to Al-Qiftī he wrote some books on medicine[20] and also a commentary on Ishāq's translation of the commentaries of Ammonius and Alexander of Aphrodisias on Aristotle's Topics[21]. He is most often cited, however, as a translator of philosophical, medical, and mathematical works.

Of his translations the following are recorded· (1) The fourth book of Aristotle's Physics (The Fihrist. p. 250). (2) Books 1, 2, and part of 3, of the commentary of Alexander of Aphrodisias on the fourth book of Aristotle's Physics (Al-Qiftī, p 38, l 18)[22], (3) Aristotle's De Generatione et Corruptione (The Fihrist, p 251, Al-Qiftī, p. 40, l 18), (4) Seven books of Aristotle's Topics (The Fihrist, p. 249, Al-Qiftī, p 36, l. 19), (5) Porphyry's Isagoge (The Fihrist, p. 253, Al-Qitti, p. 257, l. 6)[23], (6) An abstract of Galen's book on the qualities (i. e of character), the De Moribus, (Ibn Abī Useibia, p. 234), (7) An abstract of Galen's Little Book on the Pulse, the De Pulsibus ad Tirones or the Book on the Pulse to Teuthras and other beginners (Ibn Abī Useibia, p 234)[24], (8) Several books of Euclid, of which Al-Nadīm, the author of The Fihrist, saw the tenth in the library of 'Alī Ibn

Ahmad Al-'Imrānī (died 344 H., i. e. 955/56 A. D.) in Mosul (The Fihrist, p 265, Al-Qiftī, p. 64, l 5), (9) The commentary of Pappus on Book X of Euclid (MS. 2457 of the Bibliothèque Nationale in Paris) Al-Dimishqī is also said to have revised and improved many translations made by others (The Fihrist, p 244), but this statement could quite well refer to some of the works already mentioned, as, for instance, his translations of Euclid and Aristotle[25].

The postscript to Part II (Book II of the Treatise) states that this copy of the commentary was written by *Ahmad Ibn Muhammad Ibn 'Abd Al-Jalīl* in Shīrāz in the month of Jumādā 1. of the year 358 H (March 969 A D). According to WOEPCKE the whole MS. 2457 of the Bibliothèque Nationale is an autograph of this well-known Persian geometer. On page 14 of his *Essai* he says· — "Les cent quatre-vingt-douze premiers feuillets du volume présentent une seule et même écriture Ainsi que l'attestent les post-scriptum ci-dessus mentionnés, cette partie a été écrite à Chīrāz, principalement pendant les années 969 et 970 de notre ère, par le géomètre Ahmad Ben Mohammed Ben Abd-al-jalîl Alsidjzî, qui formait probablement ce recueil pour son propre usage Depuis le folio 192 v⁰ a 216 v⁰, on trouve une ou plutôt plusieurs écritures, différentes de celle de la première partie du volume, mais qui, cependant, en quelques endroits, ressemblent beaucoup à cette dernière écriture Les trois derniers feuillets, 217 à 219, sont d'une écriture complétement différente"

In his *Die Mathematiker und Astronomen der Araber und ihre Werke* SUTER accepted WOEPCKE's judgment of the MS. with the proviso that Al-Sijzī must have written it as a very young man of about twenty years of age, since he was a contempory of Al-Bīrūnī (972 3—1048 A D.). Later, in 1916, however, he revised his judgment, and in his *Uber die Ausmessung der Parabel von Thābit b. Kurra al-Harrānī*, p 65,[26] he questions whether Al-Sijzī wrote even those parts which have postscripts stating

that he did so. Postscripts, he remarks, were often copied by
later copyists, and there are so many omissions, repetitions,
and bad figures, for example, in the treatise on the paraboloids
(MS 2457, 24⁰, Fol 95 v⁰—122 r⁰) that it is impossible to believe
that such a good geometer as Al-Sijzī is known to have been,
ever wrote it In his *Der Kommentar des Pappus zum X. Buche
des Euklides* (1922) Suter does not mention Al-Sijzī at all

Suter's argument is not very convincing Postscripts were
occasionally copied by later copyists mechanically, but the later
copyist usually appended his own name to the MS also; and the
accusations which Suter levels against the MS of Thābit's
work on the paraboloids, are the same, with the exception of
that concerning bad figures, as those which he has brought
against the MS of the present commentary on Book X of Euclid,
which will be found, it is hoped, unjustified Al-Sijzī also, as
Suter has said, may have been quite young when he wrote
his copies, although this also is subject to doubt, since he seems
to have been already well known as a mathematician. He may,
of course, have developed his mathematical genius early
in life, but Suter's argument would not be improved by
this fact

The noteworthy points concerning MS 2457 are as follows It
contains five treatises which are described as the work of Al-
Sijzī himself, viz., 10⁰ (Fol 52 v⁰—53 v⁰), 27⁰ (Fol 136 v⁰,
l. 5—137 r⁰), 28⁰ (Fol. 137 v⁰—139 r⁰), 31⁰ (Fol. 151 r⁰—156 v⁰,
l 11), 46⁰ (Fol 195 v⁰—198 r⁰). Three of these 10⁰, 27⁰, and
28⁰, are letters of Al-Sijzī on mathematical subjects, the other
two are treatises by him 27⁰ is dated, Oct., 970, 28⁰, Feb , 972,
but the place of writing is in neither case given. 31⁰ is undated,
but was written in Shīrāz. Significant, perhaps, is the fact
that 46⁰ occurs in that part of the MS. where Woepcke found
"Une ou plutòt plusieurs écritures différentes de celle de la première
partie du volume, mais qui, cependant, *en quelques endroits,*
ressemblent beaucoup à cette dernière écriture.

Four treatises are stated to have been copied by Al-Sijzī, viz., 1^0 (Fol 1 r^0—18 v^0), 5^0—6^0 (Fol. 23 v^0—42 v^0), 15^0 (Fol. 60 r^0—75 v^0) These are said to have been written in Shīrāz, the first three in the year, 969 the last in the year, 970. They are all by the same hand, occuring in the first 192 leaves

Seven treatises, according to the postscripts, were written in Shīrāz, viz., 14^0 (Fol 59 r^0, l. 18—60 r^0, l. 8), 16^0 (Fol 76 r^0—78 r^0), 24^0 (Fol. 95 v^0—122 r^0), 26^0 (Fol 134 v^0, l 14—136 v^0, l. 4), 32^0 (Fol 156 v^0, l. 12—160 r^0, l 4), 38^0 (Fol 170 v^0, l 12—180 v^0, l. 7) 41^0 (Fol 181 v^0, l 16—187 r^0, l. 12), 24^0, 26^0, 38^0, and 41^0 in the year, 969, 14^0 and 32^0 in the year, 970 16^0 has no date, but was copied from a text of Nazīf Ibn Yomn, as was 15^0, which is dated 970 The name of the copyist is not given in any of these treatise, but they are all by the same hand as those already mentioned

The treatises in the MS deal predominantly with mathematical or astronomical subjects One or two, such as 3^0 and 4^0, have topics belonging to the field of physics one 22^0, treats of medicine It is also perhaps worthy of observation that eleven of the treatises are devoted to the consideration of irrationals, viz, 5^0, 6^0 (our commentary), 7^0, 16^0, 18^0 34^0, 39^0, 41^0, 42^0, 48^0, and 51^0

All of the works, therefore, attributed to Al Sijzī, or stated to have been copied by him or written in Shīrāz, fall within the first 192 leaves, which are the work of one hand, excepting only 46^0, a treatise of Al Sijzī on the measurement of spheres by means of spheres, which occurs in that part of the MS, where, as WOEPCKE says, we find "Une ou plutôt *plusieurs écritures* différentes de celle de la première partie du volume, mais qui, cependant, *en quelques endroits*, ressemblent beaucoup à cette dernière écriture" Even if, therefore, 46^0 were shown to be an autograph of Al-Sijzī, that would not prove that the whole MS., with the exception of the last three leaves, is, as WOEPCKE claims, the work of Al-Sijzī In the second part of the MS., moreover, there is no date except at the end of a table of contents to the whole MS (Fol 215 v⁰—216 v⁰), and this date is the eleventh of Muharram of the year 657 H. (the eighth Jan , 1259 A.D.).

In view, therefore, of the facts that have just been set forth, the most reasonable assumption would appear to be that the first part of the MS (Fol. 1—192) constitutes a collection formed by Al-Sijzī and written in his own hand, but that the second part (Fol. 192—216)²⁷ is another collection of the same type added to the first at a later date. The later collection contains works by the same authors as the first, and it is not necessary to suppose that they were written much later than those in the first collection, if at all. It is quite possible that 46⁰, the treatise by Al-Sijzī, is in his own hand But it is to be presumed that the second collection was added to the first in the year 1259, when a table of contents was supplied for the whole MS. No 71⁰ (Fol. 217 r⁰—219 v⁰) would be added later. It deals with irrationals, the subject which bulks most in the whole collection

*Ahmad Ibn Muhammad Ibn 'Abd Al-Jalīl Abū Saʿīd Al-Sijzī*²⁸ was a contemporary of Al Bīrūnī (972/3—1048 A D.), but his exact dates are uncertain. In his *Chronologie Orientalischer Völker*²⁹, p. 42, Al-Bīrūnī states that he personally heard Al-Sijzī citing the names of the Persian months on the authority of the ancients of Sijistān. On the other hand, in his treatise on the trisection of an angle³⁰ Al-Sijzī quotes three propositions from Al-Bīrūnī, and the latter also wrote him concerning a proof of the theory of sines³¹. One of Al-Sijzī's works is dedicated to 'Adud Al-Daulah, who reigned from 949 to 982 A.D ³², another to an Abd emir, Al Malik Al-'Adil Abū Ja'far Ahmad Ibn Muhammad.

On the basis of his being a contemporary of Al Bīrūnī, SUTER gives as approximate dates for Al Sijzī's life, 951—1024 A D., which would make him a young man of about eighteen years of age in 969, when he was active in Shīrāz both as a copyist and as an original writer on mathematical subjects. But it seems certain from the facts that have been advanced, that he was already a mathematician of some note, and he might quite well have been born ten years earlier and still remain a contemporary of Al-Birūnī.

None of his works have yet been published[33], but one or two have been discussed by European scholars. These are. — (1) *On lines drawn through given points in given circles* (MS 2458, 1⁰, of the Bibl. Nat., Paris) by L. A. Sédillot in *Notices et Extraits des MSS. de la Bibliothèque Nationale*, 1838, t 13, pp. 126—150, (2) *On the determination of definite mathematical rules* (MS. 2458, 2⁰) by L. A Sédillot (ibid), (3) *On the solution of certain propositions from the Book of Lemmas of Archimedes* (MS. 2458, 3⁰) by L. A. Sédillot (ibid), (4) *Concerning conic sections* (Leyden, 995) by F. WOEPCKE in *Notices et Extraits*, 1874, t. 22, pp. 112—115, (5) *Concerning the division of an angle into three equal parts and the construction of a regular heptagon in a circle* (Leyden, 996) (Cairo, 203) by F WOEPCKE in *L'Algebre d'Omar Alkhayyami*, pp 117—127 and by C. SCHOY in *Graeco-arabische Studien*, Isis, 8, pp 21—35, 1926 (Translation), (6) *On the attainment of the twelve proportions in the plain transversal figure by means of one operation* (Leyden, 997) by H. BURGER and K. KOHL in *Abhandlungen zur Geschichte der Naturwissenschaften und der Medizin*, Heft 7, Erlangen, 1924, (*Thabits Werk uber den Transversalensatz*, A BJORNBO, pp 49—53 b).

The rest of Al-Sijzī's works lie buried in manuscript in the libraries of Europe or throughout the East In the libraries of Europe we find: —

(1) *A letter on the solution of a problem from the Book of Yūhanna b Yūsuf, namely, the division of a straight line into two equal parts, together with a demonstration of Yūhanna's error therein* (MS 2457, 10⁰, of the Bibliothèque Nationale).

(2) *A letter to Abū 'Alī Nazīf Ibn Yomn on the construction of an acute-angle triangle by means of (from ?) two unequal straight lines* (MS. 2457, 27⁰).

(3) *On the solutions of ten problems proposed to him by a certain geometer of Shīrāz* (MS. 2457,31⁰).

(4) *On lines drawn through given points in given circles* (MS. 2458,1⁰, of the Bibliothèque Nationale)

(5) *On the determination of definite mathematical rules* (MS. 2458,2⁰)

(6) *A letter containing answers to questions addressed to him concerning the solution of propositions from the Book of Lemmas of Archimedes* (MS 2458,3⁰).

(7) *On the trisection of an angle* (Leyden, 996) (Cairo, 203).

(8) *On the construction of a regular heptagon* (Cairo, 203)

(9) *Demonstration of certain propositions of Euclid, Al-Sijzi's solution of proposition 2, Book I* (India Office, 734,14)

(10) *On the measurement of spheres by means of spheres* (MS. 2457,46⁰, of the Bibliothèque Nationale)

(11) *On the attainment of the 12 proportions in the plain transversal figure by means of one operation* (Leyden, 997)

(12) *On the relation of a hyperbola to its asymptotes* (Leyden, 998)

(13) *A letter to the Shaikh, Abū'l-Husain Muhammad Ibn 'Abd Al-Jalīl, on the sections produced in paraboloids and hyperboloids of revolution* (MS. 2457,28⁰, of the Bibliothèque Nationale)

(14) *On conic sections* (Leyden, 995).

(15) *On the use of an instrument whereby extensions (distances) are known, and on the construction of this instrument* (Leyden, 999)[34]

(16) *On the astrolabe and its use* (Only in Hajji Khalifa, vol. II, p. 366).

(17) A collection of astrological works, named *Al-Jāmi'u'l-Shāhī.* (776 of the Supplement to the catalogue of Arabic MSS. in the British Museum, p. 527), containing —

1 *An introduction to astrology* (Fol. 3)

2. *Canons used by astrologers in determining fate by the stars* (Fol. 17) (British Mus. (1838) 415, 9⁰, p 198, is identical)

3. An abridgement of the *Book of Horoscopes* of Abū Ma'shar, in 33 chapters (Fol 19)[35].

4. *The book of the Zā'irjāt*, on horoscopes (Fol. 27).

5. An abridgement of the *Book of the revolution of the birth-years* of Abū Ma'shar (Fol. 30).

Uri, Bodleian, Oxford (1787), MS. 948, p 206, seems identical, but the title runs: *The revolutions of the years for the purpose of nativities*, which seems the better title Hajji Khalifa has, "The book of the revolutions (Vol. v. p 60).

6686,2 of the Bibliothèque Nationale (nouvelles acquisitions), E. BLOCHET, 1925, seems also to be identical, and the last phrase of its title, Al-sinin al-mawālid, is possible, but probably we should read, al-sinin lil-mawālid, and translate as in the Oxford MS. Another title runs — *A summary of the revolutions of the birth-years*[36].

6 *The temperaments of the planets* (tables) (Fol 58). 6686,3, of the Bibliothèque Nationale (nouvelles acquisitions) seems identical [37].

7 *On the rise and fall of prices* (Fol 70). British Mus. (1838), 415, 10⁰, p. 198, is identical

8 *On (astrological) elections* (Fol. 72), i. e., the chosing of an auspicious day on which to begin an enterprise or so as to avoid an impending evil See Hajji Khalifa, Vol. I, p. 198.

9 An abridgement of the *Book of the Thousands* of Abū Ma'shar (Fol. 81) (tables) See Hajji Khalifa, Vol. V, p. 50, and 6. above[38]

10. *The significations of "Judicial Astrology"* (or of "The decrees of the Stars") (Fol. 92)

11. *Proofs of "Judicial Astrology"* (Fol. 113). British Mus. (1838), 415,8⁰, seems identical. Its postscript reads. — "Proofs concerning the science of "Judicial Astrology".

12 *On the science of the opening of the door* (Fol. 128).

13. *The sojourning of the stars in the twelve "Houses"* (Signs of the Zodiac) (Fol. 131).

14. *Astronomical tables proving the 360 degrees of the Zodiac and showing what constellation arises in each degree.* A treatise without title (Fol. 140). 6686,4⁰, of the Bibliothèque Nationale (nouvelles acquisitions) seems identical, with the title, *"Concerning the constellations of the degrees of the Zodiac"*. E. BLOCHET says that it consists almost entirely of tables in which are found the predictions for the 360 degrees of the Zodiac.

15. *A short treatise on talismans* without title (Fol. 153). British Mus. MS. Add. 23, 400 (Corpus Astrologicus) has an excerpt from the Al-Jāmi'u'l-Shāhī.

The Gotha MS., 109, (vol. 1, p. 194) (W. PERTSCH) also probably contains an excerpt from it.

(18) *An introduction to the science of "Judicial Astrology"*, imitation of a work of the same name by Abū'l-Nasr Al-Qummī (6686,1⁰, of the Bibliothèque Nationale (nouvelles acquisitions). Cf., however, (17), 1. and 11.[39]

(19) In MS. 2458,2⁰, (Fol. 4 v⁰) of the Bibliothèque Nationale at the end, Al-Sijzī himself refers to a book of his own, which he names, *Geometrical notes* (Ta'līqāt handasiyya). See *Notices et Extraits*, t. 13, p. 143, and note 2 to p. 129.

(20) Hajji Khalifa also mentions an astrological work entitled *Ahkām Al-As'ād* (The Decrees of the Auspicious Stars?), Vol. I, p. 169, and another with the title *Burhān Al-Kifāyat* (The Sufficient Proof?), Vol. II, p. 46, a compendium of astronomy for students of astrology.

We have, moreover, in the Leyden MS. 1015 (Vol. 111, p. 64) Abū'l-Jūd's solution of Al-Sijzī's problem of trisecting an angle; and Ihtiyāru'l-Dīn Muhammad refers to Al-Sijzī in his *Judicial Astronomy* (MS. R 13, 9, of E. H. PALMER's Catalogue of the Arabic MSS. in the Library of Trinity College, Cambridge), which begins with the statement that the author has emended the astronomical tables of Ptolemy and Al-Sijzī, bringing them down to the time of writing.

These references show the scope and spheres of Al-Sijzī's influence. He was known to his successors not only as a mathematician, but also as an astronomer and astrologer; and it is safe to assume, on the basis of his extant works, that Judicial Astronomy was the field of his greatest activity.

II. THE SOURCES OF PAPPUS'S CONCEPTION OF RATIONAL QUANTITIES.

As a mathematical term, rationality has for our commentator its Euclidian signification. Incommensurability and irrationality, he says (Part 1, para. 3; cf. 4,5, & 12), belong essentially to the sphere of geometry. The numbers are all rational and commensurable, since they advance from a minimum, unity namely, by addition of the unit and proceed to infinity. They have a common measure by nature (Part 1, para. 5), for "One", as Aristotle says (Metaph. XIV. 1; 1088a, 5, 1087b, 30—35), "evidently means a measure".

The continuous quantities, on the other hand, have no minimum. They begin with a definite whole, and are divisible to infinity (Cf. Arist , Phys. 111,6; 207b, 1—5). There is, therefore, no continuous quantity which is naturally a measure, and thus continuous quantities have a common measure not by nature but only by convention (Part 1, para 5)[40]. In the case of lines, for example, some conventional common measure must be assumed; and the measure which is assumed, cannot measure all lines, since it is not a minimum, nor do lines advance from it by addition of this unit.

Rational lines, therefore, are those which are commensurable in length with the chosen unit, or the squares upon which are commensurable with the square upon that unit. Irrational lines are those which are incommensurable with the unit in both respects (Part 1, para. 18). The rationality of a magnitude

4*

depends upon its proportion to the chosen unit of measurement (Part 1, para. 14). On the other hand, the commensurability of magnitudes does not depend upon their proportion to the chosen unit, for continuous quantities are commensurable with one another, in length or in square only, by reason of a common measure, be that what it may, commensurable or incommensurable with the chosen unit (Part 1, paras. 15, 16, 17). Some continuous quantities, therefore, are irrational and at the same time commensurable. The two terms are not synonymous (Part 1, para. 15).

The commentator's conception of number and continuous quantity is, it will be observed, Aristotelian. Numbers are limited by one as their minimum, but have no maximum limit; continuous quantities have a maximum, but no minimum limit (Arist., *Phys.* III. 6; 207b, 1—5, cf. *De Caelo*, 268a, 6; *Metaph.* 1048b, 9). These notions imply Aristotle's idea of an infinite as "Not that outside of which nothing exists, but that outside of which there is always something" (*Phys.* III. 6, 207a. 1—5), infinity, for Aristotle, not being a separate, independent thing, nor even an element in things, but only an accident in something else (*Metaph.* X, 11: 1066a, 35-b, 21), with no separate existence except in thought (ibid. VIII. 6, 1048b, 15).

But our commentator, when he wishes to explain the reason why numbers have a minimum but no maximum, and continuous quantities a maximum but no minimum, i. e., are each infinite in one direction, employs the Pythagorean-Platonic notion of contraries, such as finite and infinite, that are, as Aristotle remarks (*Metaph.* I. 5; 986a, 21ff.; *Phys.* III. 4, 203a, 4—5), substances and the principles of things. "If, then", he says (Part I, para. 3), "the reason be demanded why a minimum but not a maximum is found in the case of a discrete quantity, whereas in the case of a continuous quantity a maximum but not a minimum is found, you should reply that such things as these are distinguished from one-another only by reason of their homogeneity with the finite or the infinite, some of those created things which are contraries of one-another, being finite, whereas the others *proceed from infinity*. Compare, for example, the contraries, like and unlike, equal and unequal, rest and movement. Like, equal, and rest, promote (or make for) finitude, whereas unlike, unequal, and movement, promote (or make for) infinity. And such is the case generally. Unity and plurality, the whole and the parts are similarly constituted. One and the whole clearly belong to the sphere of the finite, whereas the parts and plurality belong to the sphere of the infinite[41]". "Everything finite", he says again (Part I, para. 8 (end), "is finite by reason only of the finitude which is the *principle* of the finitudes[42]".

In Part I, paragraph 13, towards the middle, the commentator uses the Aristotelian doctrine of the two kinds of matter, sensible and intelligible (*Metaph.* 1036a, 10; 1037a, 4; 1045a, 34, 36), and the Aristotelian terms, form and matter, potential and actual. "If you wish", he says, "to understand whence incommensurability is received by the magnitudes, you must recognise that it is only found in that which can be imagined as potentially divisible into parts to infinity, and that parts originate necessarily only from matter, just as the whole from form, and that the potential in everything proceeds from matter, just as the actual from the other cause (i. e., form). The incommensurability of geometrical continuous quantities, therefore, would not have its origin in matter or anywhere, were there not, as Aristotle says, two kinds of matter, namely, intelligible matter on the one hand, and sensible matter on the other, the representation of bulk, or, in short, of extension, in geometrical figures, being by means of intelligible matter only".

The doctrine and the terms are undoubtedly Aristotelian, but the context in which they are employed is Platonic. In the first part of paragraph 13 the commentator shows that Plato in his *Parmenides* does not deny the existence of incommensurable magnitudes. For, he says, "He (i. e. Plato) has considered therein the first cause (i. e., the One) in connection with the division (or separation) of commensurable from incommensurable lines (140 c). In the first hypothesis (140 b. c. d.), namely, the equal, the greater, and the less, are discussed together, and in this case the commensurable and the incommensurable are conceived of as appearing in the imagination together with measure. Now these (i. e., the commensurable and the incommensurable — (and measure?)) cover everything which by nature possesses the quality of being divided, and comprehend the union and separation which is controlled by the God who encircles the world (Cf. the *Timaeus*, 36 c—37 c, 40 b). For inasmuch as divine number (i. e., the separate numbers of Aristotle's *Metaph.*, 1080 a, 12—b, 33; 1090 a, 2 ff.; 978 b, 31) precedes the existence of the substances of these things, they are all commensurable conformably to that cause, God measuring all things better than one measures the numbers; but inasmuch as the incommensurability of matter is necessary for the coming into existence of these things, the potentiality of incommensurability is found in them. It is, moreover, apparent that limit is most fit to controll in the case of the commensurables, since it originates from the divine power, but that matter should prevail in the case of those magnitudes which are named "incommensurable".

Here we have the Pythagorean-Platonic doctrine of the finite and the infinite as the two principles of world-creation, the Timaean doctrine of the World-Soul with its circles of the Same and the Other controlling the sensible world, and the Platonic notion of the divine numbers which are things in themselves and causes of sensible things, and which precede or are identical with the Ideas (Cf. W. D. Ross, *Aristotle's Metaphysics*, Vol. I, Introd., p. LXVI; L. ROBIN, *La Théorie platonicienne des Idées et des Nombres d'après Aristote*, Paris, 1908, p. 470).

The same Platonic background appears in the last part of the paragraph. "Where only form and limit are found", says the commentator, "there everything is without extension or parts, form being wholly an incorporeal nature. But line, figure (or plane), and bulk, and everything which belongs to the representative (or imaginative) power within us, share in a particular species of Matter (Cf. *Arist.*, *Metaph*, W. D. Ross, Vol. I, p. 199, note to 1036a, 9—10). Hence numbers are simple and free by nature from this incommensurability, even if they do not precede the incorporeal life (i. e., are the mathematical or sensible numbers, which in the Platonic scheme follow the ideas), whereas the limits (or bounds) which come thence (i. e., from the Ideal World) into the imagination and to a new existence in this representative (or imaginative) activity, become filled with irrationality and share in incommensurability, their nature, in short, consisting of the corporeal accidents".

The commentator's conception of the origin of commensurables and incommensurables in Part I, paragraph 13, is manifestly Platonic There are two principles, out of which everything proceeds, namely, the finite and the infinite; there is the Ideal World, where only limit prevails, there is the sensible world, for the existence of which matter, the indeterminate, is requisite; and between these two there lies the world of mathematical objects, which are eternal, but share in the indeterminateness of matter (Cf. Arist., *Metaph.*, 987b, 15; 1028b, 20; 1076a, 20; 1090b, 35).

The same conception is found in Part I, paragraph 9, where the commentator discusses the three kinds of irrationality. Numbers are metaphysical entities and causes of things. The World-Soul, with its mathematical ratios unified by the three means (Cf. the *Timaeus*, 34c—36d), comprehends all things, rational and irrational, distinguishes and determines them, and shapes them in every respect. The three means, the geometrical, the arithmetical, and the harmonic, are the grounds of harmony and stability throughout the universe (Cf. the Timaeus, 31c—32a; 35b ff.).

"It seems to me", says the commentator, "to be a matter worthy of our wonder, how the all-comprehending power of the Triad distinguishes and determines the irrational nature, not to mention any other, and reaches to the very last of things, the limit (or bound) derived from it appearing in all things". As Nicomachus says (see T. TAYLOR, *Theoretic Arithmetic*, p. 181), "The number, three, is the cause of that which has triple dimensions and gives bound to the infinity of number".

"The substance of the soul", proceeds the commentator, "seems to comprehend the infinity of irrationals; for it is moved directly concerning the nature of continuous quantities (cf. the Timaeus, 37a. b.) according as the ideas (or forms) of the means which are in it, demand, and distinguishes and determines everything which is undefined and indeterminate in the continuous quantities, and shapes them in every respect (Cf. the *Timaeus*, 34c—37c). These three [means] are thus bonds (cf. the *Timaeus*, 31c—32a; 35b. ff.) by virtue of which not one even of the very last of things, not to mention any other, suffers loss (or change) with respect to the ratios (or relations) which exist in it".

For our commentator, then, there is, in a metaphysical sense, nothing absolutely irrational, but only relatively so. From the point of view of an ideal system of knowledge, or, Platonically-speaking, from the point of view of the World-Soul, everything is rational. But human reason is limited, and for it some things are irrational. as, for instance, an infinite number of the continuous quantities. In the last analysis, however, even this irrationality is not absolute but only relative; for they all belong to one or other of the three classes of irrationals, and so admit of definition, have a certain form or limit.

For, says the commentator (Part I, para. 9, end), "Whatsoever irrational power there is in the Whole (or Universe), or whatsoever combination there is, constituted of many things added together indefinitely, or whatsoever Non-being there is, such as cannot be described (or conceived) by that method which separates forms, they are all comprehended by the ratios (or relations) which arise in the Soul".

III. COLLATION OF THE ARABIC TEXT WITH THE GREEK SCHOLIA.

There is some agreement between our commentary and the Greek Scholia to Book X of Euclid in J. L. HEIBERG's *"Euclidis Elementa"*, vol V. The passages where such agreement occurs, are given below. Some of the passages correspond almost word for word; in others the Arabic gives a somewhat expanded text; all these passages have been marked by an asterisk. The remainder correspond in a more general manner. *W* denotes WOEPCKE's text of the Arabic commentary*; *H* indicates HEIBERG's *Euclidis Elementa*.

Part 1.

Para. 1 (W. p. I, ll. 1—2) = H. p. 414, ll. 1—3.
* ,, 1 (W. p. I, ll. 2—3) = H. p. 415, ll. 7—8.*
* ,, 1 (W. p. 2, ll. 7—8) = H. p 414, ll. 15—16.*
* ,, 2 (W. p. 2, ll. 10—16) = H. p. 417, ll. 12—20.*
   ,, 3 (W. p. 3, ll. 4—12(15?) = H. p. 415, l. 9ff.; cf.
                                       p. 429, l 26ff. and p. 437,
                                         no. 28.
   ,, 5 (W. p 6, ll. 1—5) = H. p. 437, ll. 1—4.
* ,, 5 (W. p. 6, ll. 5—12) = H. p. 418, ll. 7—12.*
   ,, 5 (W. p. 6, ll. 12—13) = H p. 417, l. 21.
* ,, 5 (W. p. 6, ll. 13—16) = H. p. 418, ll. 12—14.*
* ,, 6 (W. p. 7, ll. 1—9) = H. p. 418, ll. 14—24.*
* ,, 9 (W. p. 9, ll. 5—15) = H. p. 484, l. 23 — p. 485, l. 7
                                         (no. 135)*.

* WOEPCKE's pagination has been indicated in this edition of the Arabic text.

Para. 10 (W. p. 10, l. 7 — p. 11, l. 2. ff.) = H. pp. 450—452,
no. 62.

The same topic, but very different presentations.

* „ 19 (W. p. 19, l. 4. ff.) — H. p. 485, ll. 8—16. Cf. also
for parts of the para., H. p. 488,
no. 146; p. 489, no. 150 (for W.,
p. 19, ll. 4—7); p. 491, no. 158.*

* „ 20 (W. p. 19, l. 16—p. 20, l. 16) = H. p. 485, l. 16 —
p. 486, l. 7.*

„ 24 (W. p. 23, ll. 15—16) = H. p. 484, ll. 8—10. ??

„ 25 (W. p. 23, ll. 17—19) = H. p. 484, no. 133, ll. 11—15.

„ 26 (W. p. 24, l. 5) = H. p. 501, ll. 11—12 (no. 189).
(W. p. 24, l. 6) = H. p. 503, ll. 3—4 ?

„ 28 (W. p. 25, ll. 15—16) = H. p. 534, ll. 13—15 (no. 290)

„ 29 (W. p. 25, ll. 20—22) = H. p. 538, ll. 7—9 (no. 309).

„ 30 (W. p. 26, ll. 3—7) = H. p. 547, l. 23—p. 548, l. 5
(no. 340).

* „ 31 (W. p. 26, ll. 8—11) = H. p. 551, ll. 21—25 (no. 353)*
* „ 32 (W. p. 26, ll. 12—21) = H. p. 553, ll. 11—18 (no. 359).*

Part 11.

Para. 2 (W. p. 29, l. 8—p. 30, l. 4) = H. p. 415, ll. 2—6.

„ 17 (W. p. 45, l. 11. ff.) = H. p. 551, ll. 2—19 ?

IV. TRANSLATION AND TEXT.

The translation is avowedly of a philological and historical
nature and does not pretend to render the thought of Pappus into
the terms and signs of modern mathematics. Whoever, therefore, would avoid the effort of imagination that is necessary, to
overcome successfully the difficulties of the style and technique
of Pappus and thereby to follow his argument, may be referred
to the Bemerkungen of Dr. JUNGE, where the chief mathematical data of the commentary will be found presented according
to modern forms and methods. It is hoped, however, that the
nature of the translation will be an advantage for the historian,

preserving, as it does, so far as is possible, the spirit and form of the original Arabic.

The technical terminology of the translation is based upon Sir T. W. Heath's translation of the tenth book of Euclid in *The Thirteen Books of Euclid's Elements*, vol. III. My indebtedness to this distinguished scholar is gratefully acknowledged; and it would be desirable that his work should be consulted before entering upon a study of the present commentary.

The Arabic text of the commentary is based upon the Paris MS., no. 2457 of the Bibliothèque Nationale, and WOEPCKE's edition printed in Paris about 1855. The emendations which have been made in WOEPCKE's text, are explained in the accompanying notes. The text is referred to throughtout as *W*.

In conclusion I would express my deep sense of gratitude to Dr. GEORGE SARTON of Harvard for much helpful encouragement and many happy suggestions, and to Professor J. R JEWETT, who has been my guide in Arabic these many years, and by whose generosity this book is published.

WILLIAM THOMSON.

NOTES.

1 No. 952, 2 of the Suppl. arabe de la Bibliothèque impériale.

2 Extrait du Tome XIV des Mémoires Présentés par divers savants a l'Académie des Sciences de l'Institut impérial de France.

3 Cf. Notes on the Text and consult Part I, notes, 19, 32, 44, 45, 98, 116, 138; Part II, notes, 2, 133, 173, 174; SUTER in order, p. 16, l. 25; p. 17, l. 3 ft and note 41; p. 20, l. 12 ff.; p. 20, ll 13—14; p 24, l. 11; p 26, ll 3—4, p. 28, note 93; p 37, l. 25; p. 56, ll. 32--33; p. 65, ll. 21—22; p. 65, l. 27 and note 241.

4 Cf. Part I, para 9 with SUTER p 20, l. 28 ff. and note 59; cf. also Part I, notes 5, 14, 22, 37, 90, 94, 98, 139, 146, 182, 210; Part II, note 5 etc; SUTER in order, p. 14, ll 2—3, p 15, note 24, p. 16, l 2 ft. and note 35; p. 18, note 47; p. 23, ll. 17—18; p 24, note 73; p. 24, l. 11; p 28, note 94; p. 29, ll. 26—28; p. 33, l 16; p 36, ll. 1—2 and note 127; p 38, note 140 etc

5 Cf. Part I, notes 85 and 123, SUTER, p 19, note 54; p. 22, note 65, p. 26, note 85.

6 See Notes on the Text, n. 1. A common practice in Arabic Calligraphy.

7 Introduction, p. 10; Conclusion, p. 73.

8 See the sketch of philosophical ideas given below. An exception perhaps is the idea of the return of all things to their source, which may be alluded to at the end of para 9, Pt I. But the text is difficult, and the translation, therefore, doubtful. Pappus may quite probably have been acquaint with the doctrines of Neoplatonism. He does not, however, show that they have influenced him much if at all.

9 De Caelo, I, 268a 11 ff See TH. GOMPERZ, *Griechische Denker*, 2nd Ed., Vol. I, p. 87.

10 Cf. Aristotle's Metaph. XII, 6; 1080b, 31; DIELS, *Doxographi Graeci*, Berlin 1879, pp. 280 (Aet. de plac. reliq., I, 3), 302 (Hipp. philosoph., 2), 555 (Epiph. Var. excerpta, Pro. I), 587 (Epiph. Haer. III, 8), 390 (Hermiae irrisio, 16)

11 See SUTER, pp. 20—21 with notes.

12 See Part I, paras 1, 10, 11, 12, 13, 17.

13 See Part I, paras. 9 and 13

14 Aristotle, Metaph, 992a, 32.

[15] See his Commentary on the first book of Euclid, ed., FRIEDLEIN, p. 5, ll. 11—14; p. 6, l. 7; p. 10, l. 15ff.; p. 11, 9—26; p. 13, l. 6ff.; p. 16, l. 4—p. 20, l. 10; p. 27, l. 27—p. 28, l. 5; p. 30 top; p. 38, l. 1ff.; p. 44, l. 25ff.; p. 51, l. 20—p. 52, l. 7; p. 57, l. 9—p. 58, l. 3ff.; p. 82, l. 7ff.; p. 84, l. 10ff.; p. 95, l. 10ff.; p. 138, l. 25; p. 213, l. 14ff.; p. 284, l. 17ff.

[16] Ibid. p. 95, l. 10ff.; p. 213, l. 14ff.; p. 284, l. 17ff

[17] See his commentary on Book I of Euclid, ed., FRIEDLEIN, p. 22, l. 11.

[18] Ibid., p. 22, l. 11ff.; p. 36, l. 12ff.; p. 90, l. 14ff.; p. 132, l. 17ff.; p. 137, l. 24ff.; p. 142, l. 8ff.; p. 146, l. 24ff.; p. 164, l. 27ff.; p. 290, l. 15ff.

[19] The *Fihrist*, pp. 177, 244; the *Ta'rikh Al-Hukama'* of Al-Qifti (J. LIPPERT, Leipzig, 1903), p. 409, l. 15.

[20] Al-Qifti, ibid. Probably these are, however, his Galen translations. See below

[21] Al-Qifti, p. 37, l. 12.

[22] It is possible that (1) and (2) refer to the same work

[23] Cf. J. BEDEZ, *Vie de Porphyre*, Leipzig, 1913, iv (Liste des Ecrits), p. 66, 5.

[24] See G. BERGSTRASSER, *Hunain Ibn Ishâq uber die Syr. u. Arab. Galen-Übersetzungen*, p 6, transl., p. 5; for no. (6), p. 49, transl., p. 40. Cf. M. MEYERHOF, *New Light on Hunain Ibn Ishâq and his period*, Isis, VIII (4), Oct, 1926, pp. 691, 700.

[25] On Al-Dimishqi cf. H. SUTER, *Die Mathematiker u. Astronomen der Araber u. ihre Werke*, Abhdl. z. Gesch. d. math. Wissensch., Heft 10, 1900, p. 49, no. 98.

[26] Sitzungsber. d Physik.-Mediz. Societät in Erlangen, 1916—17, Bd. 48 & 49. (Erlangen 1918) For Thâbit's treatise on the Paraboloids see ibid. p. 186ff.

[27] N. B. FOL 192 r⁰ is blank.

[28] The nisbah for Sijistân (cf. Kitâb *Al-Ansâb* of Al-Sam'ânî, Gibb Memorial Series, Vol. XX, p. 291). On Al-Sijzî see SUTER's *Die Mathematiker u. Astronomen d. Araber* etc, p. 80, no 185. G. SARTON, *Introduction to the History of Science*, Vol. I, p. 665.

[29] C. E. SACHAU, Leipzig, 1878.

[30] Leyden (996), Cairo (203); see F. WOEPCKE, *L'Algebre d'Omar Alkhayyami*, p. 119.

[31] Leyden (997) towards the end. See *Thabits Werk uber den Transversalensatz*, A. BJORNBO, Abhandl. z. Gesch. d. Naturwissensch. u. d. Mediz, Erlangen, Heft 7, 1924, pp. 63 & 84.

[32] See Suppl. to the Ar. MSS. in the British Mus , p. 527, no. 776; for the next see Cat. des MSS. Ar. des Nouvelles Acquis., Bibliothèque Nationale, Paris, E. BLOCHET, 1925, no. 6686.

[33] That is, in Arabic. C. SCHOY has published in Isis, VIII, pp. 21—35, 1926, a translation of the Cairo MS., 203, which discusses the construction of a heptagon in a circle as well as the trisection of an angle.

[34] The author is given as Al-Sinjari, which often occurs instead of Al-Sijzī. Cf. Hajjı Khalifa, Vol. I, pp 169, 198; Vol. II, p. 46.

[35] See SUTER's *Die Mathematiker und Astronomen der Araber* etc, p. 28, no. 53, on Abū Ma'shar; also G. SARTON, *Introduction to the History of Science*, Vol. I, p. 568.

[36] See G. SARTON's *Introduction to the History of Science*, Vol. I, p. 568; Hajjı Khalifa, Vol. I, p. 171, Vol. V, p. 60.

[37] E. BLOCHET says that this is an abridgement of the *Book of the Thousands* of Abū Ma'shar, which appears, however, hereafter in this collection. He describes it as a treatise on the astrological properties of the planets and their influences. See 9. and note thereon.

[38] Cf J. LIPPERT in the Wiener Zeitschr. f. d. Kunde d. Morgenlandes, IX, pp. 351—358, 1895 on "Abū Ma'shars Kitāb al-Ulūf". LIPPERT says that the book deals with houses of worship. But LIPPERT's judgment is based solely on four or five references to the book in other works. It may well have been for all that predominantly astrological.

[39] See SUTER's *Die Mathematiker und Astronomen der Araber* etc., p. 74, on Al-Qummī.

[40] See Die Fragmente der Vorsokratiker, H. DIELS, 3rd Ed., Berlin, 1912, Vol. 11, p. 9. for the fact that the opposition of nature to convention occurs early in Greek thought.

[41] See Arist., Metaph. 986a, 15ff ; 987a, 15ff., 987b, 19—35; cf. Metaph. 1054a, 20ff., for the Aristotelian method of dealing with the same ideas; see TH. GOMPERZ, *Griechische Denker*, 2nd Ed., Vol. I, p. 81, and the note to it on p 437, for the supposed Babylonian origin of this line of thought. Cf. Plato's Philebus 16c.ff. and Parmenides 129.

[42] The Pythagorean Monad.

TRANSLATION
PART I

Book I of the treatise of Pappus on the rational and irrational continuous quantities, which are discussed in the tenth book of Euclid's treatise on the Elements: translated by Abū ᶜUthmān Al-Dimishqī.

§ 1. The aim of Book X of Euclid's treatise on the Elements Page 1. is to investigate the commensurable and incommensurable, the rational and irrational continuous quantities. This science (or knowledge) had its origin in the sect (or school) of Pythagoras, but underwent an important development at the hands of the Athenian, Theaetetus, who had a natural aptitude for this as for other branches of mathematics most worthy of admiration. One of the most happily endowed of men, he patiently pursued the investigation of the truth contained in these [branches of] science (or knowledge), as Plato bears witness for him in the book which he called after him, and was in my opinion the chief means of establishing exact distinctions and irrefragable proofs with respect to the above-mentioned quantities For although later the great Apollonius whose genius for mathematics was of the highest possible order, added some remarkable species of these Page 2. after much laborious application, it was nevertheless Theaetetus who distinguished the *powers* (i. e. the squares)[1] which are commensurable in length, from those which are incommensurable (i. e. in length), and who divided the more generally known irrational lines according to the different means, assigning the medial line to geometry, the binomial to arithmetic, and the apotome to harmony[2], as is stated by Eudemus, the Peripatetic[3]. Euclid's object, on the other hand, was the attainment of irrefragable principles, which he established for commensurability and incommensurability in general. For rationals and irrationals he formulated definitions and (specific) differences; determined also many orders of the irrationals; and brought to light, finally, whatever of finitude (or definiteness) is to be found in them[4]. Apollonius explained the species of the ordered irrationals and discovered the science of the so-called unordered, of which he produced an exceedingly large number by exact methods.

§ 2. Since this treatise (i. e. Book X of Euclid.) has the aforesaid aim and object, it will not be unprofitable for us to consolidate the good which it contains. Indeed the sect (or school) of Pythagoras was so affected by its reverence for these things that a saying became current in it, namely, that he who first disclosed the knowledge of surds or irrationals and spread it abroad among the common herd, perished by drowning: which is most probably a parable by which they sought to express their conviction that firstly, it is better to conceal (or veil) every surd, or irrational, or inconceivable[5] in the universe, and, secondly, that the soul which by error or heedlessness discovers or reveals anything of this nature which is in it or in this world, wanders [thereafter] hither and thither on the sea of non-identity (i. e. lacking all similarity of quality or accident)[6], immersed in the stream of the coming-to-be and the passing-away[7], where there is no standard of measurement. This was the consideration which Pythagoreans and the Athenian Stranger[8] held to be an incentive to particular care and concern for these things and to imply of necessity the grossest foolishness in him who imagined these things to be of no account.

§ 3. Such being the case, he of us who has resolved to banish from his soul such a disgrace as this, will assuredly seek to learn from Plato, the distinguisher of accidents[9], those things that merit shame[10], and to grasp those propositions which we have endeavoured to explain, and to examine carefully the wonderful clarity with which Euclid has investigated each of the ideas (or definitions)[11] of this treatise (i. e. Book X.) For that which

Page 3.

we here seek to expound, is recognised as the property which belongs essentially to geometry[12], neither the incommensurable nor the irrational being found with the numbers, which are, on the contrary, all rational and commensurable; whereas they are conceivable in the case of the continuous quantities, the investigation of which pertains to geometry. The reason for this is that the numbers, progressing by degrees, advance by addition from that which is a minimum, and proceed to infinity (or indefinitely); whereas the continuous quantities begin with a definite (or determined) whole and are divisible (or subject to division) to infinity (or indefinitely)[13]. If, therefore, a minimum cannot be found in the case of the continuous quantities, it is evident that there is no measure (or magnitude) which is common to all of them, as unity is common to the numbers. But it is self-evident that they (i. e. the continuous quantities) have no minimum; and if they do not have a minimum, it is impossible that all of them should be commensurable. If, then, the reason be demanded why a minimum but not a maximum is found in the case of a discrete quantity, whereas in the case of a continuous quantity a maximum but not a minimum is found, you should reply that such things as these are distinguished from one-another only by reason of their homogeneity with the finite or the infinite, some of those created things which are contraries of one-another, being finite, whereas the others proceed from infinity. Compare, for example, the contraries, like and unlike, equal and unequal, rest and movement. [Like, equal, and rest, promote (or make for)[14]] finitude; whereas unlike, unequal, and movement promote (or make for) infinity. And such is the case generally. Unity and plurality, the whole and the parts are similarly constituted. One and the whole clearly belong to the sphere of the finite, whereas the parts and plurality belong to the sphere of the infinite. Consequently one is that which is deter- Page 4. mined and defined in the case of the numbers, since such is the nature of unity, and plurality is infinite (or indefinite); whereas

5 Junge-Thomson.

the whole is that which is determined in the case of the continuous quantities, and division into parts is, as is evident, infinite (or indefinite). Thus in the case of the numbers one is the contrary of plurality, since although number is comprised in plurality as a thing in its genus, unity which is the principle of number, consists either in its being one or in its being the first thing with the name of one. In the case of the continuous quantities, on the other hand, the contrary of whole is part, the term, whole, being applicable to continuous things only, just as the term, total, is applicable only to discrete things[15]. These things, then, are constituted in the manner which we have described.

§ 4. We should also examine the [logical] arrangement of ideas in Euclid's propositions: how he begins with that which is necessarily the beginning, proceeds, then, comprehensively and consistently, with what is intermediate, to reach, finally, without fail the goal of an exact method. Thus in the first proposition of this treatise (i. e. Book X.) the particular property of continuous things is considered together with the cause of incommensurability; and it is shown that the particular property of continuous things is that there is always a part less than the least part of them and that they can be reduced (or bisected) indefinitely. A continuous thing, therefore, is defined as that which is divisible to infinity (or indefinitely) In this proposition, moreover, he points out to us the first of the grounds of incommensurability, which we have just stated (i. e. in the two previous sentences); and on this basis he begins a comprehensive examination of commensurability and incommensurability, distinguishing by means of remarkable proofs between that which is commensurable absolutely, that which is commensurable in square and in line together, that which is incommensurable in both of these (i. e. in square and line), and that which is incommensurable in line but commensurable in square[16], and proving how two lines can be found incommensurable with a given line, the one in length only, the other in length and square[17]. Page 5. Thereupon he begins to treat of commensurability and incommensurability with reference to proportion and also with reference to addition and division (or subtraction)[18], discussing all this exhaustively and completely satisfying the just requirements of each case. Then after these propositions dealing with commensurable and incommensurable continuous quantities in common[19], comes an examination of the case of rationals and irrationals, wherein he distinguishes between those lines which are rational [straight lines commensurable] in both respects, i. e., in length and square, — and no irrationality whatsoever is conceivable with respect to these —, and those which are rational [straight lines commensurable] in square [only][20], from which is derived the first irrational line, which he calls the medial[21], and which is, then, of all [irrational] lines, the most homogeneous to the rational. Consequently in accordance with what has been found in the case of the rational lines, some medial lines are medial [straight lines commensurable] in length and square, whereas others are medial [straight lines commensurable] in square only[22]. The special homogeneity of medial with rational lines is shown in the fact that rational [straight lines commensurable] in square contain a medial area (or rectangle), whereas medial [straight lines commensurable] in square contain sometimes a rational and sometimes a medial area[23]. From these [rational and medial straight lines commensurable in square only] he derives other irrational lines many in kind, such as those which are produced by addition[24] and those which are produced by subtraction[25]. There are several points of distinction between these · in particular, the areas to which the squares upon them are equal and the relation of these areas to the rational line[26]. But, to sum up, after he has shown us what characteristics these lines have in common with one-another and wherein they are different from one-another, he finally proves that there is no limit to the number of irrational lines or to the distinctions

5*

between them[27]. That is, he demonstrates that from one irrational line, the medial, there can be derived unlimited (or infinite) irrational lines different in kind. He brings his treatise to an end at this point, relinquishing the investigation of irrationals because of their being unlimited (or infinite) in number. The aim, profit, and divisions of this book have now been presented in so far as is necessary.

Page 6.   § 5.   A thorough investigation is, however, also necessary in order to understand the basis of their distinction between the magnitudes. Some of these they held to be commensurable, others of them incommensurable, on the ground that we do not find among the continuous quantities any measure (or magnitude)[28] that is a minimum; that, on the contrary, what is demonstrated in proposition i. (Euclid, Book X.) applies to them, namely, that it is always possible to find another measure (or magnitude) less than any given measure (or magnitude)[29]. In short [they asked] how it was possible to find various kinds of irrational magnitudes, when all finite continuous quantities bear a ratio to one-another: i. e. the one if multiplied, must necessarily exceed the other, which is the definition of one thing bearing a ratio to another, as we know from Book V.[30]. But let us point out that the adoption of this position (i. e. the one just outlined) (or definition) does not enable one to find the measure of a surd or irrational[31]. On the contrary, we must recognise what the ultimate nature of this matter consists in[32], namely, that a common measure exists naturally for the numbers, but does not exist naturally for the continuous quantities on account of the fact of division which we have previously set forth, pointing out several times that it is an endless process. On the other hand it (i. e. the measure) exists in the case of the continuous quantities by convention as a product of the imaginative power[33]. We assume, that is, some definite measure or other and name it a cubit or a span or some such like thing. Then we compare this definite unit of measurement[34] which we have recognised, and

name those continuous quantities which we can measure by it,
rational, whereas those which cannot be measured by it, we
classify as irrationals To be rational in this sense is not a fact,
therefore, which we derive from nature, but is the product of
the mental fancy which yielded the assumed measure. All
continuous quantities, therefore, cannot be rational with reference to one common measure. For the assumed measure is
not a measure for all of them; nor is it a product of nature but
of the mind. On the other hand, the continuous quantities are
not all irrational; for we refer the measurement of all magnitudes
whatsoever to some regular limit (i. e. standard)[35] recognised
by us.

§ 6. It should be pointed out, however, that the term, proportion, is used in one sense in the case of the *whole*, i. e. the
finite and homogeneous continuous quantities[36], in another
sense in the case of the commensurable continuous quantities,
and in still another sense in the case of the continuous quantities
that are named rational[37]. For with reference to continuous
quantities the term, ratio, is understood in some cases only in
the sense that it is the relation of finite continuous quantities
to one-another with respect to greatness and smallness[38];
whereas in other cases it is understood in the sense that it denotes
some such relation as exists between the numbers, all commensurable continuous quantities, for example, bearing, as is evident,
a ratio to one-another like that of a number to a number; and
finally, in still other cases, if we express the ratio in terms of
a definite, assumed measure, we become acquainted with the
distinction between rationals and irrationals. For commensurability is also found in the case of the irrationals, as we learn
from Euclid himself, when he says that some medials are commensurable in length, but others commensurable in square only;
whence it is obvious that the commensurables among the irrationals also bear a ratio to one-another like that of a number to a
number, only this ratio is not expressible in terms of the assumed

Page 7.
Ms. 25. r⁰.

measure[39]. For it is not impossible that there should be between medials the ratio of two to one, or three to one, or one to three, or one to two, even if the quantity (i. e. finally, the unit of measurement) remains unknown. But this application (i. e. of the term, ratio) does not occur in the case of the rationals, since we know for certain that the least (or minimum) in their case is a known quantity. Either it is a cubit, or two cubits, or some other such definite limit (or standard). That being the case, all the finite continuous quantities bear a ratio to one-another according to one sense (i. e. of the term, ratio), the commensurables according to another sense, and all the rationals according to still another. For the ratio of the rationals is that of the commensurables also, which is the ratio of the finites. Page 8. But the ratio of the finites is not necessarily that of the commensurables, since this ratio (i. e. that of the finites) is not necessarily like the ratio of a number to a number. Nor is the ratio of the commensurables necessarily that of the rationals. For every rational is a commensurable, but not every commensurable is a rational[40].

§ 7. Accordingly when two commensurable lines are given, it is self-evident that we must suppose that they are either both rational or both irrational, and not that the one is rational and the other irrational. For a rational is not commensurable with an irrational under any circumstance. On the other hand, when two incommensurable straight lines are given, one of two things will necessarily hold of them. Either one of them is rational and the other irrational, or both of them are irrational, since in the case of rational lines there is found only commensurability, whereas in the case of irrational lines commensurability is found on the one hand, and incommensurability on the other. For those irrational lines which are different in kind, are necessarily incommensurable, because if they were commensurable, they would necessarily agree in kind, a line which is commensurable with a medial being a medial[41], and one which is commensurable with an apotome being an apotome[42], and the other lines likewise, as the Geometer (i. e. Euclid) says.

§ 8. Not every ratio, therefore, is to be found with the numbers[43]; nor do all things that have a ratio to one-another, have that of a number to a number, because in that case all of them would be commensurable with one-another, and naturally so, since every number is homogeneous with finitude (or the finite), number not being plurality, the correspondence notwithstanding, Ms. 25 v.⁰ but a defined (or limited) plurality[44]. Finitude (or the finite), however, comprehends more than the nature of number[45]; and so with respect to continuous quantities we have the ratio that pertains to finitude (or the finite), in some cases, and the ratio that pertains to number, since it also is finite, in still others. But we do not apply[46] the ratio of finite (or determinate) things to things that are never finite (i. e , are indeterminate), nor the ratio of commensurables to incommensurables. For the latter ratio (i. e., the ratio of commensurables) determines the least part (or submultiple, i.e., the minimum) and so makes everything included in it commensurable; and the former (i. e , the ratio of finite things) determines now the greatest (or greater) and now the least (or less) of the parts[47]. For everything finite is in fact Page 9. finite only by reason of the finitude which is the first (or principle) of the finitudes[48], but we for our part also give some magnitudes finitude in one way and others in another way[49]. So much it was necessary to cite in our argument concerning these things.

§ 9. But since irrationality comes to pass in three ways, either by proportion, or addition, or subtraction[50], it seems to me to be a matter worthy of our wonder (or contemplation), how, in the first place, the all-comprehending power of the Triad distinguishes and determines the irrational nature, not to mention any other, and reaches to the very last of things[51], the limit (or bound) derived from it appearing in all things[52]; and in the second place, how each one of these three kinds [of irrationals] is necessarily distinguished by one of the means, the geometric distinguishing one, the arithmetical another, and the harmonic the third. The substance of the soul, moreover, seems to comprehend the infinity of irrationals; for it is moved directly concerning the nature of continuous quantities[53] according as the ideas (or the forms) of the means which are in it, demand, and distinguishes and determines everything which is undefined and indeterminate in the continuous quantities, and shapes them in every respect[54]. These three [means] are thus bonds[55] by virtue of which not one even of the very last of things, not to mention any other, suffers loss (or change)[56] with respect to the ratios (or relations)[57] which exist in it. On the contrary, whenever it becomes remote from anyone of these ratios (or relations) naturally[58], it makes a complete revolution and possesses the image of the psychic ratios (or relations)[59]. Accordingly whatsoever irrational power there is in the whole (or in the universe), or whatsoever combination there is, constituted of many things added together Page 10. indefinitely, or whatsoever Non-being there is, such as cannot be described (or conceived) by that method which separates forms, they are all comprehended by the ratios (or relations) which arise in the Soul[60]. Consequently incommensurability is joined and united (i. e., to the whole) by the harmonic mean, when it appears in the whole as a result of the division (or separation) of forms[61]; and addition that is undefined by the units (or terms) of the concrete numbers, is distinguished by the arithmetical mean[62]; and medial irrationals of every kind that arise in the case of irrational powers, are made equal by reason of the geometric mean[63]. We have now dealt with this matter sufficiently.

§ 10. Since, moreover, those who have been influenced by speculation[64] concerning the science (or knowledge) of Plato, suppose that the definition of straight lines commensurable in length and square and commensurable in square only which he gives in his book entitled, *Theaetetus*, does not at all correspond with what Euclid proves concerning these lines, it seems to us that something should be said regarding this point[65]. After, then, Theodorus had discussed with Theaetetus the proofs of the *powers* (i. e. squares)[66] which are commensurable and incommensurable in length relatively to the *power* (square) whose measure is a [square] foot[67], the latter had recourse to a general definition of these *powers* (squares), after the fashion of one who has applied himself to that knowledge which is in its nature certain (or exact)[68]. Accordingly he divided all numbers into two classes[69], such as are the product of equal sides (i. e. factors)[70], on the one hand, and on the other, such as are contained by a greater side (factor) and a less; and he represented the first [class] by a square figure and the second by an oblong, and Ms. 26 r.º concluded that the *powers* (squares) which *square* (i. e. form into a square figure) a number whose sides (factors) are equal[71], are commensurable both in square and in length, but that those which *square* (i. e. form into a square figure) an oblong number, are incommensurable with the first [class] in the latter respect (i. e. in length), but are commensurable occasionally with one another in one respect[72]. Euclid, on the other hand, after he had examined this treatise (or theorem) carefully for some time and had determined the lines which are commensurable in length and square, those, namely, whose *powers* (squares) have to one-another the ratio of a square number to a square number, proved that all lines of this kind are always commensurable in length[73]. The difference between Euclid's statement (or proposition)[74] and that of Theaetetus which precedes it, has not escaped us. The idea of determining these *powers* (squares) by means of the square numbers is a different idea altogether from that of their having to one-another the ratio of a square [number] to a square [number][75]. For example, if there be taken, on the one hand, a *power* (square) whose measure is eighteen [square] feet, and on the other hand, another *power* (square) whose measure is eight [square] feet, it is quite clear that the one [power or square] has to the other the ratio of a square number to a square number,

Page 11.

the numbers, namely, which these two double[76], notwithstanding the fact that the two [powers or squares] are determined by means of oblong numbers. Their sides, therefore, are commensurable according to the definition (thesis) of Euclid, whereas according to the definition (thesis) of Theaetetus they are excluded from this category. For the two [powers or squares] do not *square* (i. e. do not form into a square figure) a number whose sides (factors) are equal, but only an oblong number. So much, then, regarding what should be known concerning these things[77].

§ 11. It should be observed, however, that the argument of Theaetetus does not cover every *power* (square) that there is[78], be it commensurable in length or incommensurable, but only the *powers* (squares) which have ratios relative to some rational *power* (square) or other, the *power* (square), namely, whose measure is a [square] foot. For it was with this *power* (square) as basis that Theodorus began his investigation concerning the *power* (square) whose measure is three [square] feet and the *power* (square) whose measure is five (square] feet, and declared that they are incommensurable (i. e. in length) with the *power* (square) whose measure is a [square] foot[79]; and [Theaetetus] explains this by saying: "We defined as *lengths* [the sides of the *powers* (squares)][80] which *square* (i. e. form into a square figure) a number whose sides (factors) are equal, but [the sides of the *powers* (squares)] which *square* (i. e. form into a square figure) an oblong number, we defined as *powers* (i. e. surds)[81], inasmuch as they are incommensurable in length[82] with the former [*powers* (squares)], the *power*, namely, whose measure is a [square] foot and the *powers* which are commensurable with this *power* in length, but are, on the other hand, commensurable with the areas (i. e. the squares) which can be described upon these [lengths][83]. The argument of Euclid, on the contrary, covers every *power* (square) and is not relative to some assumed rational *power* (square) or line only. Moreover, it is not possible for us to prove by any theorem (or proposition) that the *powers* (squares) which we have described above[84], are commensurable [with one-another] in length, despite the fact that they are incommensurable in length with the *power* (square) whose measure is a [square] foot, and that the unit [of measurement] which measures the lines, is irrational, the lines, namely, on which these *powers* (i. e. the squares 18 and 8) are imagined as described[85]. It is difficult, consequently, for those who seek to determine a re- Page 12. cognised measure for the lines which have the power to form these *powers* (i. e. the lines upon which these *powers* can be formed), to follow the investigation of this [problem] (i. e. of irrationals), whereas whoever has carefully studied Euclid's proof, can see that they (i. e. the lines) are undoubtedly commensurable [with one-another]. For he proves that they have to one-another the ratio of a number to a number[86]. Such is the substance of our remarks concerning the uncertainty about Plato

§ 12. The philosopher (i. e. Plato), moreover, establishes, Ms. 26 v.° among other things, that here (i e. in the *lines* of Theaetetus 148 a., which are commensurable in square but not in length) are incommensurable magnitudes We should not believe, therefore, that commensurability is a quality of every magnitude as of all the numbers, and whoever has not investigated this subject, shows a gross and unseemly ignorance of what the Athenian Stranger says in the seventh treatise of the Book of the Laws[87], [namely], "And besides there is found in every man an ignorance, shameful in its nature and ludicrous, concerning everything which has the dimensions, length, breadth, and depth[88]; and it is clear that mathematics can free them from this ignorance[89]. For I hold that this [ignorance] is a brutish and not a human state, and I am verily ashamed, not for myself only, but for all Greeks, of the opinion of those men who prefer to believe what this whole generation believes, [namely], that commensurability is necessarily a quality of all magnitudes. For everyone of them says: "We conceive that those things are essentially the same, some of which can measure the others in some way or other[90]. But the fact is that only some of them are measured by common measures, whereas others cannot be measured at all". It has also been proved clearly enough by the statement (or proposition) in the book that goes by the name of Theaetetus, how necessary it is to distinguish lines commensurable in length and square relatively to the assumed rational line, that one, namely, whose measure is a foot, from lines commensurable in square only. We have described this in what has preceded; and from what has been demonstrated in the generally-known work (i. e. Euclid)[91], it is easy for us to see that there has been described (or defined) for us a distinction that arises when two rational lines are added

Page 13. together[92]. For it says that it is possible for the sum of two lines to be either rational or irrational, even if both lines are rational, the line composed of two lines rational (and commensurable) in length and square being necessarily rational, whereas the line which is composed of two lines that are rational (and commensurable) in square only, is irrational.

§ 13. If, then, the discussion in Plato's book named after Parmenides should not contradict this (i. e. the existence of incommensurable magnitudes), [let it be observed that] he has considered therein the First Cause (i. e. The One) in connection with the division (or separation) of commensurable from incommensurable lines[93]. In the first hypothesis[94], namely, the equal, the greater, and the less are discussed together; and in this case the commensurable and the incommensurable are conceived of as appearing in the imagination together with measure[95]. Now these (i. e. the commensurable, the incommensurable, (and measure ?)) cover everything which by nature possesses the quality of being divided, and comprehend the union (combination) and separation (division)[96] which is controlled by the God who encircles the world[97]. For inasmuch as divine number[98] precedes the existence of the substances of these things, they are all commensurable conformably to that cause, God measuring all things better than one measures the numbers; but inasmuch, as the incommensurability of matter is necessary for the coming into existence of these things, the potentiality (or power) of incommensurability is found in them[99]. It is, moreover, apparent that limit is most fit to control in the case of the commensurables, since it originates from the divine power, but that matter should prevail in the case of those magnitudes which are named incommensurables[100]. For if you wish to understand whence incommensurability Ms. 27. r°. is received by the magnitudes, [you must recognise that] it is only found in that which can be imagined as potentially divisible into parts to infinity (or indefinitely); and [that] parts originate necessarily only from matter, just as the whole from form; and [that] the potential in everything proceeds from matter, just as the actual from the other cause (i. e. form)[101]. The incommensurability of geometrical continuous quantities, therefore, would not have its origin in matter or anywhere, were there not, as Aristotle says,[102] two kinds of matter namely, Page 14. intelligible matter on the one hand, and sensible matter, on the other, the representation of bulk, or, in short, of extension, in geometrical figures being by means of intelligible matter only. For where only form and limit are found, there everything is without extension or parts, form being wholly an incorporeal nature. But line[103], figure (or plane), and bulk, and everything which belongs to the representative (or imaginative) power within us, share in a particular species of matter[104]. Hence numbers are simple and free by nature from this incommensurability, even if they do not precede the incorporeal life[105]; whereas the limits (or bounds) which come thence[106] into the imagination and to a new existence in this representative (or imaginative) activity, become filled with irrationality and share in incommensurability, their nature, in short, consisting of the corporeal accidents[107].

§ 14. We must return, however, to the object of our discussion and consider whether it be possible for some lines to be rational notwithstanding their incommensurability with the lines[108] which have been assumed as rational in the first place. We must, in short, examine whether it be possible for the same magnitude[109] to be at once rational and irrational. Now we maintain that measures (i. e. in the case of the continuous quantities) are only by convention and not by nature[110], a fact which we have often pointed out before. Consequently the denotation of the terms, rational and irrational, necessarily changes according to the convential measure that is assumed[111]; and while things which are incommensurable with one another can never be commensurable in any sense whatsoever, it would nevertheless be possible for what is rational to become irrational, since the measures might be changed. But as it is desirable that the properties of rationals and irrationals should be definite and general[112], we assume some one measure and distinguish the properties of rational and irrational continuous quantities relatively to it. For if we did not

Page 15 distinguish between these relatively to some one thing, but designated a continuous quantity which the assumed measure does not measure, rational, we would assuredly not preserve the definitions of this learned scholar[113] distinct and unconfused. On the contrary, a line which we would show to be a medial, would be considered by another to have no better a claim to be a medial than a rational, since it does not lack measure[114]. But this is not a scientific method. As Euclid says, it is necessary that one line should be [assumed as] rational[115].

§ 15. Let, then, the assumed line be rational, since it is necessary to take some one line as rational; and let every line which is commensurable with it, whether in length or in square,

Ms. 27 v.⁰ be called rational. Let these be convertible terms[116]: and let it be granted, on the one hand, that the line which is commensurable with the rational line, is rational, and, on the other, that the line which is rational, is commensurable with the rational line, since

Euclid defined as irrational the line which is incommensurable with this line[117]. On these premises, then, all lines that are commensurable with one-another in length, are not necessarily proportional to the assumed line, even if they be called rational; nor are they necessarily called commensurable[118], because this line measures them. But when they are proportional to the assumed line either in square or in length, they are necessarily named rational, since every line which is commensurable with the assumed line in square or in length, is rational. The commensurability of these lines in length or in square is an additional qualification of them[119] and does not refer to their proportion to the assumed line, since medial lines, for example, are sometimes commensurable in length and sometimes commensurable in square only. He misses the mark, therefore, who says that all rational lines which are commensurable in length, are rational in virtue of their length[120]. Consequently the assumed line does not necessarily measure every rational line. For lines which are commensurable in square with the assumed rational line, are called rational without exception on the ground that if we take two square areas, one of them fifty [square] feet and the other eighteen [square] feet, the two areas are commensurable with the square on the assumed rational line whose measure is a foot, and the lines upon which they are the squares, are commensurable with one-another, although incommensurable both of them with the assumed line. There is no objection at all, then, to our calling these two lines rational and commensurable in length; rational, namely, inasmuch as the two squares upon them are commensurable with the square upon the assumed line, and commensurable in length inasmuch as even if the unit of measurement[121] which is common to them, is not the assumed rational line, there is another measure which measures them[122]. Commensurability with the assumed rational line, therefore, is the only basis of rationality[123]. Continuous quantities, on the other hand, are commensurable with one another, in length or in

Page 16.

square only, by reason of a common measure, be that what it may.

§ 16. It has been established, moreover, that the area (or rectangle) contained by two rational lines commensurable in length is rational[124]. It is not impossible, then, that the lines containing this area should be at the same time rational —, the reference in this case being to their homogeneity with the rational line, their condition, namely, compared with it in length or in square only[125] —, and also commensurable with one-another in length[126] —, where the reference is to the fact that they have necessarily a common measure. We must assume, that is, that in this case we have two lines such that containing the given area, they are named rational and are commensurable also [with one-another] in length without being measurable by the given rational line, although, on the other hand, the squares upon them are commensurable with the square upon that line. It has been demonstrated, however, that this area is rational. For it is commensurable with each of the squares upon the lines containing it; and these are commensurable with the square upon the given line; and, therefore, this area is also necessarily

Ms. 28 r.⁰ commensurable with it and thus rational[127] if, however, we take the two given lines as commensurable [with one-another] in length but incommensurable both in length and square with the line which is rational in the first place, we cannot prove in any way that the area contained by them is rational. On the contrary if you apply the length to the breadth[128] and find the measure of the area, it will not be an extension such as you can

Page 17. prove to be rational. For example, if the ratio to one-another of the two lines containing it be three to two, then the area of the rectangle (or area) must be six times something-or-other[129]. But this something-or-other is an unknown quantity, since the half and the third of the lines themselves are irrational[130]. It is not correct, however, for anyone to maintain that there are two kinds of rational lines, those, namely, which are measured by the line which is rational in the first place, and those which are measured by another line which is not commensurable with that line. On the other hand lines commensurable in length are of two kinds, those, namely, which are measured by the line which is rational in the first place, and those which are commensurable with one-another, although they are measured by another line which is incommensurable with that line. Euclid never names those lines which are incommensurable with the given rational line in both respects (i. e. in length and in square) rational. And what would have prevented him doing so, if instead of determining rational lines by reference to that line alone, he had also determined them by adopting some other measure from those lines which are called rational and referred them to it?[131]

§ 17 Plato gives even rational lines diverse names. We know that he calls the line which is commensurable with the given rational line, *length*[132], and that he names that one which is commensurable with it in square only, *power*[133], adding on that account[134] to what he has already said, the explanation, "Because it is commensurable with the rational line in the area to which the square upon it is equal"[135]. Euclid, on the other hand, calls the line which is commensurable with the rational line, however commensurable[136], rational, without making any stipulation whatsoever on that point: a fact which has been a cause of some perplexity to those who found in him some lines which are called rational, and are commensurable, moreover, with each other in length but incommensurable with the given rational line (i e. in Page 18. length) But perhaps he did not mean to measure all rational lines by the line which was assumed in the first place, but intended to give up that measure, despite the fact that in the definitions he proposed to refer the rationals to it, and to change to another measure incommensurable with the first, naming such lines[137], then, without noting it[138], rational because they were commensurable with the given rational line in one respect that is, in square only, but referring their commensurability in length to another measure, subscribing in this instance to the opinion that they were commensurable (i. e. with another) in both respects, but not rational in both respects (as, e. g., $\sqrt{2}$ and $\sqrt{8}$).

§ 18. We maintain, therefore, that some straight lines are wholly irrational and others rational. The irrational are those whose lengths are not commensurable with the length of the rational line nor their squares with its square. The rational are those which are commensurable with the rational line in either respect (i. e. in length or in square only). But some of the rationals are commensurable with one-another in length, others in square only, and some of those which are commensurable with one-another in length, are commensurable with the rational line in length, others are incommensurable (i. e. in length, but commensurable in square) with it. In short, all lines which are rational and commensurable in length with the rational line, are commensurable with one-another (i. e. in length), but all rational [lines] which are commensurable with one-another in length, are not commensurable with the rational line (i. e. in length)[139]. Some of the lines, again, which are commensurable with the rational line in square, for which reason, indeed, they also are named rational[140], are commensurable with one-another in length, but not relatively to that line; others are commensurable in square only (i. e. with the rational line and with one-another). The following example will make this clear. If, namely, we take an area (or rectangle) contained by two rational lines which are commensurable in square with the given line, but with one-another in length, then this area is rational. If, on the other hand, the area is contained by two lines which are commensurable with one-another and with the rational line in square only, it is medial[141]. That is the sum and substance of what we have to say concerning such things[142]. It should be evident now, however, that if [it be stated that] an area is contained by two lines rational and commensurable in square [only], [this means that] the two rational lines are commensurable with one-another and with the given rational line in square only[143]; whereas if [it be stated that] an area is contained by two lines rational and commensurable in length, [this may mean either (i) that] the two rational lines are commensurable with one-another and with the rational line in length, or [(2) that] they are commensurable with the rational line in square only, but with one-another in another respect (i. e. in length).

Page 19

§ 19. We must also consider the following fact. Having found by geometrical proportion that the medial line is a mean proportional between two rational lines commensurable in square only and, therefore, that the square upon it is equal to the area (or rectangle) contained by these two lines[144] —, the square upon a medial line being one which is equal to the rectangle contained by the two assigned lines as its adjacent sides[145] —, he (i. e. Euclid) always assigns the general term, medial, to a particular species (i. e. of the medial line)[146]. For the medial line the square upon which is equal to the rectangle contained by two rational lines commensurable in length, is necessarily a mean proportional to these two rationals; and the line the square upon which is equal to the rectangle contained by a rational and an irrational line, is also of that type (i e a mean proportional); but he does not name either of these medial, but only the line the square upon which is equal to the given rectangle[147]. Moreover since in every case he derives the names of the *powers* (i. e. the square-areas) from the lines upon which they are the squares, he names the area on a rational line rational[148] and that on a medial line medial.

§ 20. Comparing, furthermore, the medials theoretically to the rational lines[149], he says that the former resemble the latter inasmuch as they are either commensurable in length or commensurable in square only, and the area (or rectangle) contained by two medials commensurable in length is necessarily medial, just as the area contained by two rationals commensurable in

6*

length is, on the other hand, rational[150]. The area, moreover, contained by two medials commensurable in square only is sometimes rational and sometimes medial[151]. For just as the square on a medial line is equal to the area contained by two rationals commensurable in square, so the square on a rational line is equal sometimes to the area contained by two medial lines commensurable in square. There are thus three kinds of medial areas. the first contained by two rational lines commensurable in square, the second by two medials commensurable in length, and the third by two medials commensurable in square; and there are two kinds of rational areas: the one contained by two rational lines commensurable in length, and the other by two medial lines commensurable in square[152]. It appears, then, that the line which is taken in [mean] proportion between two medial lines commensurable in length, is, together with that one which is taken in mean proportion between two rational lines commensurable in square, in every case medial[153], but that the line which is taken in mean proportion between two medials commensurable in square[154], is sometimes rational and again medial, so that the square upon it is now rational and now medial. Thus we may have two medial lines commensurable in square only, just as we may have two rational lines commensurable in square only, and the ground of distinction (or variance) between the areas contained by the two sets of lines[155] must be the line which is the mean proportional between these two extremes, namely, either a medial between two rationals or a medial between two medials, or a rational between two medials[156]. In short, sometimes the bond (i. e. the mean) is like the extremes, and sometimes it is unlike. But we have discussed these matters sufficiently.

§ 21. Subsequent to his investigation and production of the medial line, he (i. e. Euclid) began, after careful consideration, an examination of those irrational lines that are formed by addition and division (i. e. subtraction) on the basis of the examination which he had made, of commensurability and incommensurabil-

Ms. 29 r.⁰
Page 20.

ity[157], commensurability and incommensurability appearing also in those lines that are formed by addition and subtraction[158]. The first of the lines formed by addition is the binomial (binomium)[159]; for it also [like the medial with respect to all irrational Page 21. lines[160]] is the most homogeneous of such lines to the rational line, being composed of two rational lines commensurable in square. The first of the lines formed by subtraction is the apotome[161]; for it also is produced by simply subtracting from a rational line another rational line commensurable with the whole[162] in square. We find, therefore, the medial line by assuming a rational side and a given diagonal[163] and taking the mean proportional between these two lines; we find the binomial by adding together the side and the diagonal, and we find the apotome by subtracting the side from the diagonal[164]. We should also recognise, however, that not only when we join together two rational lines commensurable in square, do we obtain a binomial, but three or four such lines produce the same thing. In the first case a trinomial (trinomium) is produced, since the whole line is irrational, in the second a quadrinomial (quadrinomium); and so on indefinitely. The proof of the irra- Ms. 29 r.[0] tionality of the line composed of three rational lines commensurable in square is exactly the same as in the case of the binomial[165].

§ 22. It is necessary, however, to point out at the very beginning that not only can we take one mean proportional between two lines commensurable in square, but we can also take three or four of them and so on ad infinitum, since it is possible to take as many lines as we please, in [continued] proportion between two given straight lines. In the case of those lines also which are formed by addition, we can construct not only a binomial, but also a trinomial, or a first, or second trimedial, or that line which is composed of three straight lines incommensurable in square, such that, taking one of them with either of the [remaining] two[166], the sum of the squares[167] on them is rational,

Page 22. but the rectangle contained by them is medial, so that in this case a major results from the addition of three lines. In the same way the line the square upon which is equal to a rational and a medial area, can be produced from three lines, and also the line the square upon which is equal to two medial areas[168]. Let us take, for example, three rational lines commensurable in square only. The line which is composed of two of these, is irrational, namely, the binomial. The area, therefore, contained by this line and the remaining line is irrational. Irrational also is the double of the area contained by these two lines The square, therefore, on the whole line composed of the three lines is irrational. Therefore the line is irrational; and it is named the trinomial. And, as we have said, if there are four lines commensurable in square, the case is exactly the same; and so for any number of lines beyond that. Again, let there be three medial lines commensurable in square, such that one of them with either of the remaining two contains a rational rectangle. The line composed of two of these is irrational, namely, the first bimedial, the remaining line is medial, and the rectangle contained by these two is irrational[169]. The square on the whole line, therefore, is irrational [and therefore the line also]. The same facts hold with respect to the rest of the lines. Compound lines, therefore, formed by addition are infinite in number[170].

§ 23. In like manner we need not confine ourselves in the case of those irrational straight lines which are formed by division (i. e. subtraction), to making one subtraction only, obtaining thus the apotome, or the first, or second apotome of the medial, or the minor, or that [line] which produces with a rational area a medial whole, or that which produces with a medial area a medial whole[171]; but we can make two or three or four subtractions. For if we do that, we can prove in the same way [as in these] that the lines which remain, are irrational, and that each of them is one of the lines which are formed by subtraction. If from a rational line, for example, we cut off another rational line commensurable with the whole line in square, we obtain, for remainder, an apotome, and if we subtract from that line which has been cut off[172], and which is rational, and which Euclid calls the *Annex*[173], another rational line which is commensurable with it in square, we obtain, as remainder, an apotome; and if we cut off from the rational line which has been cut off from that line[174], another line commensurable with it in square, the remainder is likewise an apotome. The same thing holds true in the case of the subtraction of the rest of the lines[175]. There is no possible end, therefore, either to the lines formed by addition or to those formed by subtraction. They proceed to infinity, in the first case by addition, in the second by subtraction from the line that is cut off (i. e. the annex). It seems, then, that the infinite number of irrationals becomes apparent by such methods as these, so that [continued] proportion does not cease at a definite multitude (i. e. number) of means, nor the addition of compound lines come to an end, nor subtraction arrive at some definite limit or other[176]. With this we must be content so far as the knowledge of rationals[177] is concerned.

Page 23. Ms. 30 r.°

§ 24. Let us begin again and describe its parts (i. e. the parts of Book X)[178]. We maintain, then, that the first part deals with the commensurable and incommensurable continuous quantities. For he (i. e. Euclid) establishes in it that in this instance (i. e. in the case of continuous quantities) incommensurability is a fact[179], [shows] what continuous quantities are incommensurable[180] and how they should be distinguished, and [explains] the nature of commensurability and incommensurability as regards proportion[181], the possibility of finding incommensurability in two ways, either with reference to length and square or with reference to length only[182], and the mode of each of them with respect to addition and subtraction[183], increase and diminution. That is, in all these propositions, fifteen in number, he instructs us concerning commensurable and incommensurable continuous quantities[184].

§ 25. In the second part he discusses[185] rational lines and medials such as are commensurable with one-another in square and length, the areas that are contained by these lines, the homogeneity of the medial line with the rational, the distinction between them, the production of it (i. e. of the medial), and such like subjects[186] For the fact that it is possible for us not only to find two rational lines commensurable in length but also to find two such lines commensurable in square [only], shows that we can obtain two lines incommensurable with the assigned line, the one in square and the other in length only[187]. If, then, we take a rational line incommensurable in length with a given line, we obtain two rational lines commensurable in square only. And if we take the mean proportional between these, we obtain the first irrational line[188].

§ 26. In the third part he provides the means for obtaining the irrationals that are formed by addition, by furnishing for that operation two medial lines commensurable in square only which contain a rational rectangle, two medial lines commensurable in square which contain a medial rectangle[189], and two straight lines neither medial nor rational, but incommensurable in square, which make the sum of the squares upon them[190] rational, but the rectangle contained by them medial, or, conversely, which make the sum of the squares upon them medial, but the rectangle contained by them rational, or which make both the sum of the squares and the rectangle medial and incommensurable with one-another[191]. These propositions, namely, and everything that appears in the third part, were selected by him for the sole purpose of finding the irrational lines which are formed by addition. For if those lines which have been obtained (i. e. in the third part) be added together, they produce these irrational lines.

§ 27. In the fourth part he makes known to us the six irrational lines that are formed by addition[192]. These are composed either of two rational lines commensurable in square[193], — two [rational] lines commensurable in length forming when added

Page 24.

Ms. 30 v.⁰

together a whole line that is rational —, or of two medial lines commensurable in square[194], — two medials commensurable in length forming when added together a medial line —, or of two lines, unqualified[195], which are incommensurable in square. Three are irrational for the reason we have given[196]; two are composed of two medials commensurable in square; and one of two rationals commensurable in square[197]: six lines altogether, the [lines in the] third part having been produced in order to Page 25. establish these [six lines] in the fourth part In this fourth part, then, he shows us the composition of these six irrational lines by forming some of them, namely, the first three, from lines commensurable in square, and the others, that is to say, the second three, from [lines] incommensurable in square[198], in the case of the three latter [propositions] either making the sum of the squares upon them (i. e. upon the two lines incommensurable in square) rational but the rectangle contained by them medial[199], or, conversely, making the sum of the squares upon them medial but the rectangle contained by them rational, or, finally, making both the sum of the squares upon them and the rectangle contained by them medial and incommensurable with one-another. For were they commensurable with one-another (i. e., the sum of the squares and the rectangle), the two lines which have been added together, would be commensurable in length[200]. He proves also the converse of these propositions in some form or other, namely, that each of these six irrationals is divided at one point only[201]. For he demonstrates that if the two lines are rational and commensurable in square, then the line composed of them is a binomial; and that if this line be a binomial, then it can be composed of these two lines only and of no others; and so analogously with the rest of the lines. In this part, therefore, we have two series of six propositions, the first six putting together these six irrational lines, and the second six demonstrating the converse propositions.

§ 28. After these parts[202] the binomial line is [at last] found in the fifth part, the first, namely, of those lines which are formed by addition[203]. Six varieties of this line are set forth[204]. And I do not think that he did this (i. e. found the six binomials) without a [definite] purpose, but provided them[205] as a means to the knowledge of the difference between the six irrational lines formed by addition, by means of which (i. e. the binomials) he might make known a particular property of the areas to which the squares upon these (i. e. upon the six irrationals formed by addition) are equal[206].

§ 29. This [fifth] part, consequently, is followed by the sixth part in which he examines these areas and shows that the square on the binomial is equal to the area contained by a rational line and the first binomial, that the square on the first bimedial is

Page 26. equal to the area contained by a rational line and the second binomial, and so forth[207]. These lines, therefore, (i. e. the six irrationals formed by addition) produce six areas contained [respectively] by a rational line and one of the six binomials[208].

§ 30. In the seventh part he discusses the incommensurability [with one-another] of the six irrational lines that are formed by addition, proving that any line which is commensurable with

Ms. 31 r.⁰ anyone of these, is of the same order as it[209]. Applying, then, the squares upon them to rational lines he examines the breadths of the areas [thus produced] and finds six other [propositions], the converse of the six mentioned in the sixth part[210].

§ 31. In the eighth part he demonstrates the difference between the six irrationals that are formed by addition, by means of the areas to which the squares upon them are equal[211]. In addition he gives a clear proof of the distinction between these irrational lines that are formed by addition, by adding together a rational and a medial area, or, again, two medial areas[212].

§ 32. Thereafter in the ninth part he describes the six irrational lines that are formed by subtraction[213], in a way analogous to that in which he has described the six that are formed by addition, making the apotome to correspond to (or the contrary of)[214] the binomial, in that it is obtained by the subtraction of the less from the greater of the two lines which when added together, form the binomial; and the first apotome of a medial to correspond to (or the contrary of) the first bimedial; and the second apotome of a medial to the second bimedial; and the minor to the major; and that which produces with a rational area a medial whole, to that the square upon which is equal to a rational plus a medial area; and that which produces with a medial area a medial whole, to that the square upon which is equal to two medial areas. The reason for the application of these names to them is obvious. And just as he proves in the case of [the irrational lines that are formed by] addition[215], that each of them can be divided at one point [only], so he shows immediately after these [propositions concerning the irrational lines][216] which are formed by subtraction, that each of them has one *Annex* [only][217].

§ 33. In the tenth part in order to define these six irrational lines he sets forth some apotomes that are to be found in a manner analogous to that in which the binomials were found[218].   Page 27.

§ 34. This is followed in the eleventh part by the demonstration of the six irrational lines that are formed by subtraction[219], the squares upon which are equal [respectively] to a rectangle contained by a rational line and one of the apotomes, also numbering six, taken in their order.

§ 35. After examining this matter in the eleventh part, in the twelfth part he describes the incommensurability with one-another of these six irrationals, proving that any line which is commensurable with anyone of these, belongs necessarily to the same kind (or order) as it[220]. He points out also wherein they differ from one-another, showing this by means of the areas which, when applied to a rational line, give different breadths[221].

§ 36. When he comes to the thirteenth part he proves [in it] that the six irrational lines that are formed by addition, are different from the lines that are formed by subtraction[222], and that those which are formed by subtraction are different from one-another[223]. He distinguishes these also by the subtraction of areas just as he did the lines that are formed by addition, by means of the addition [of areas][224]. For subtracting a medial area from a rational, or a rational from a medial, or a medial from a medial, he finds the lines the squares upon which are equal to these areas, namely, the irrationals which are formed by subtraction. Thereafter, wishing to demonstrate the infinite number of irrationals, he finds lines unlimited (or infinite) in number, different in kind (or order), all arising from the medial line[225]. With this indication he brings this treatise to an end, relinquishing the investigation of irrationals, since they are infinite in number[226].

End of the first book of the commentary on Book X.

NOTES.

[1] See paragraphs X & XI of Part I and Appendix A for the fact that *Powers* in this connection means *Squares*. See also WOEPCKE's *Essai*, p. 34, and note 3. The reference is to *Theaetetus*, 147 d.—148 a. For the first two sentences of the paragraph see J. L. HEIBERG, *Euclidis Elementa*, Vol. V, p. 414, ll. 1—3 and p. 415, ll 7—8.

[2] In Part II, paragraphs 17—20, the author develops this discovery of Theaetetus further and proves that the irrationals that are formed by addition, can be produced by means of arithmetical proportion, and those that are formed by subtraction, by means of harmonic proportion. The medial line is, of course the geometric mean between two rational lines commensurable in square only.

[3] See PROCLUS, *Commentary on the first book of Euclid's Elements*. Basle, 1533, p. 35, l. 7: p. 92, l. 11: p. 99, l. 28: *The Commentary of Eutocius*, p 204 of the Oxford edition of the Works of Archimedes; Frabicii *Bibliotheca Graeca*, 4th edition, Hamburg, 1793, Vol. III, p 464 & 492.

[4] WOEPCKE translates: "And, finally, he demonstrates clearly their whole extent", remarking that the author alludes to prop. 116 (115) of Book X. But the Arabic word *Tanāhi* does not mean *Extent*, but *End, Limit*, or *Finitude*; and the allusion is most probably to propositions 111—114, 111 showing that a binomial line cannot be an apotome, whereas 112—114 show how either of them can be used to rationalise the other. (W. p. 2, l. 6.) For the last sentence of para. I see J. L. HEIBERG, *Euclidis Elementa*, Vol. V, p. 414, ll. 15—16.

[5] See J. L. HEIBERG, *Euclidis Elementa*, V, p. 417, l 15, where ἄλογον and ἀνείδεον are used together in the same way; also p. 430, ll. 10—11, where ἄλογος and ἄρρητος are so used; see H. VOGT, *Die Entdeckungsgeschichte des Irrationalen....*, Biblioth. Mathem. 10, 1909/1910, p. 150, n. 1. See *Euclidis Elementa*, V, p. 417, ll. 19—20, for the translation: "The sect (or school) of Pythagoras was so affected by their reverence etc." (W. p. 2, ll. 13 & 10.)

[6] That is, the world of generation and corruption, the sensible world, a brief statement of the Platonic position as, e. g., in *Phaedo* 79 c (cf. *Symp.* 202 a, *Republic* 478 d, and *Tim.* 51 d.) The sensible world is

in a state of continual change; there is no identity of quality in it; therefore no standard of judgment; and consequently no real knowledge of it or through it. The Arabic word, *Tashābuh*, means *Identity of quality or accident* (See *A Dict. of Technical Terms* etc., A. SPRENGER, Calcutta, 1862, Vol. I, p 792, Dozy, Vol. I, p. 726, col. 1). It is probably a translation of the Greek word ὁμοιότης, which Pappus uses (See FR. HULTSCH, *Pappus*, Vol. III, Index Graecitatis, p. 22) (W. p. 2, l. 15)

⁷ The Arabic word, *Al-Kawn*, means *The coming-to-be, or, The coming-to-be and the passing-away* (See *A Dict. of Technical Terms*, Vol. II, p. 1274). The Arabic word, *Marūr*, probably renders the Greek word ῥοή, Stream or Flow (W. p. 2, l. 16).

⁸ See Plato, *De Legibus*, Lib. VII, 819, beginning.

⁹ The Arabic phrase, *Mumayyizu-l-Aḥdāth*, is evidently an epithet for Plato, although I have not been able to find the Greek phrase upon which it is based (W. p. 2, l. 20).

¹⁰ The Arabic phrase, *Al-Mustahiqqatu-lil-'ār*, qualifies *Al-amūr* (things) and not *Al-Ahdāth* (accidents) as in SUTER's translation (W. p. 2, l. 20)·

¹¹ The Arabic word, *Qawl*, may mean *Enunciation* or *Proposition* (cf. Glossary for references to the text; see BESTHORN & HEIBERG, *Eucl. Elem.*, Al-Hajjāj, 1 (p. 34, last line; p. 36, l. 16; p. 40, l. 4). *Ma'na* may mean *Definition* (cf. Glossary for references to the text).

¹² I interpret the Arabic phrase, *Ḥāṣṣatu-l-Maqūmati*, according to Wright's Grammar, 3rd Ed., Vol. II, p. 232, C, etc The Arabic word, *Al-Maqūm*, occurs again in the next paragraph (Part. I., Para. 4., WOEPCKE's text, p. 4, l. 14) with *Al-Muthbat* as an interlinear gloss. According to this gloss *Al-Maqūm* means *Established, Known, Proved, or Belonging as a property or quality to* (W. p. 3, l. 3).

¹³ Aristotle says that numbers are limited by *one* as their minimum, but that they have no maximum limit; whereas exactly the opposite is true of the continuous quantities In consequence of the finiteness of the world they are limited as to their maximum, but have no minimum (See Arist. *Phys.* III. 6, 207b, 1—5; cf. J. L. HEIBERG, *Euclidis Elementa*, Vol. V, p. 415, l. 9ff., 24ff.; p. 429, l. 26ff ; *Nicomachus of Gerasa*, University of Michigan Studies, Humanistic Series, Vol. XVI, Part II, p. 183, ll. 7—10.)

¹⁴ SUTER's statement that „Hier befindet sich im MS. eine nicht lesbare, verdorbene Stelle" (p. 15, n. 24), based apparently on WOEPCKE's note 7 to page 3, that "Verba 'w-al-wuqūf' etc, usque ad 'Al-Musāwi', in texta omissa, margini adscripta, sed rescisso postea margine ex

parte peremta sunt", is misleading. The part of the text which has
been omitted and then given in the margin, can be read with the
exception of one word; and that word of which two letters can still be
deciphered, can be reconstructed from the context. What has hap-
pened, is a curious case of haplography, and I have reconstructed the
text. (See text and notes on the text.) (W. p. 3, ll. 18—19.)

For the philosophical notion expressed in these sentences compare
The Commentary of Proclus on Book I of Euclid, ed., FRIEDLEIN,
p. 87, l. 19ff.; p. 314, l. 16ff. It follows the Pythagorean doctrine
that the principles of things are such contraries as *Limit and Unlimited*
(the Finite and the Infinite), *Odd and Even* etc (cf. ARIST, *Metaph.*, A.
I; 986a, 22ff.). In Platonism the Finite and the Infinite became the
two principles out of which everything arose (Cf. Plato's *Philebos*
16c ff.).

[15] See Arist., *Metaph.* 1024a, 6. On the opposition of Unity and Plurality
see Arist., *Mesaph.*, 1054a, 20ff., 1056b, 32, 1057a, 12. On Plurality
as the genus of Number see Arist., *Metaph.*, 1057a, 2, and for the fact
that One means a measure, i. e., is One, the arithmetical unit, or the
first thing with the name of One, e. g., one foot, see Arist., *Metaph.*,
1052a, 15—1053b, 4; 1087b, 33—1088a, 4.

[16] See Euclid, Bk. X., props. 5—9. For "Commensurable absolutely",
cf. Def. I.

[17] See Euclid, Bk. X., prop. 10.

[18] See Euclid, props. 11—18, esp 11, 15, 17, 18.

[19] See Euclid, props. 11, 14, 17, 18. WOEPCKE's judgment on the text
here is unsound, and SUTER, following it, misses the sequence of
thought (See text and notes on the text,) (W. p. 5, l. 3ff.).

[20] See Euclid, prop. 18, Lemma.

[21] See Euclid, prop. 21.

[22] The Arabic phrases, *Mantiqatun fī-l-amraini* and *Mantiqatun fī-l-
quwwati*, which, rendered literally, give *Rational lines in both respects*,
i. e. in square and length, and *Rational lines in square*, mean, as is clear
from prop. 21, *Rational lines commensurable in square and length* and
Rational lines commensurable in square. The following phrases, therefore, *mawsitatun fī-ṭ-ṭuli wa-l-quwwati*, and *mawsitatun fī-l-quwwati*,
literally, *Medial lines in length and square* and *Medial lines in square*,
must mean *Medial lines commensurable in length and square* and *Medial
lines commensurable in square*, as given above. Further confirmation
of this fact may be found in the sentence which follows this one, where
props. 21 & 25 are alluded to in the text. WOEPCKE's correction of

mantiqatun to *mawsitatun* is, therefore, to be accepted. SUTER's translation and note 35 are based on a misunderstanding of the text. The full phrase is given, Part I, para. 18. (W. p. 5, l. 6ff.)

23 See Euclid, Bk. X., props. 21 & 25.

24 See Euclid, Bk X., props. 36ff.

25 See Euclid, Bk. X., props. 73ff.

26 See Euclid, Bk. X., props 54ff. & 92ff.

27 See Euclid, Bk X., prop. 115

28 That is, a measure or magnitude which is common to all magnitudes as unity is common to the numbers, and which must be, therefore, the minimum measure or magnitude as One is the minimum number. The Arabic word, *Qadr*, means strictly *a Measurable Quantity or Magnitude*, and is then used, as in paragraph 3, Part I., in the sense of *a Measure or a Unit of Measurement* (See the Glossary for references to the text). (W. p. 6, l. 3; cf p. 3, l 10). Cf J. L. HEIBERG, *Euclidis Elementa*, Vol. V, p. 437, ll. 1—4.

29 Or, "To find another measure or magnitude less than the lesser of two given measures or magnitudes", if we adopt the marginal addition to the text, which seems unnecessary, however, and may have been added to make the statement conform more literally with the enunciation of proposition 1. The literal translation of the longer statement is: "That there can always be found another measure or magnitude less that any given measure or magnitude which is less than some measure or magnitude or other" (W. p. 6, ll. 4—5).

30 Book V., Def. 4. Cf. J. L HEIBERG, *Euclidis Elementa*, Vol. V., p. 418, l. 7ff. for this sentence in the Greek Scholia to Book X.

31 Or, "An irrational measure", i. e., unit of measurement. As SUTER points out, Pappus probably means that it is not possible to prove by means of the propositions of Book V. alone that, e. g, $\sqrt{8}$ and $\sqrt{18}$ have a common measure, i. e. $\sqrt{2}$ (Page 17, note 40.)

32 WOEPCKE's reading of the text is false at this point, and SUTER naturally gives up in despair (See text and notes on the text.) Cf. for the following sentence J. L. HEIBERG, *Euclidis Elementa*, Vol. V, p. 418, l. 10ff. (W. p. 6, l. 10).

33 Cf. J. L. HEIBERG, *Euclidis Elementa*, Vol. V., p 417, l. 21. Τὰ μὲν μαθήματα φανταστικῶς νοοῦμεν, τοὺς δὲ ἀριθμοὺς δοξαστικῶς. That is, as a hypothesis accepted for practical purposes, based on generalizations from sense-perception, but not supported by any rational principle.

34 *Al-ʿadad*, which is most probably the original reading of the text,

means in the first place *Quantity (Al-Kammiyyatu*; see *A Dict. of Technical Terms* etc", A. SPRENGER, Vol. II, p. 949), and is here used in the sense of a quantity recognised as a unit of measurement. It is employed as a gloss for *Al-Qadr*, Measure, Unit of Measurement (cf. the previous note 28) in the MS. in the next paragraph, 6, and in paragraphs 11, 14, and 15 the two words are used as synonyms. (see Glossary for references to the text). The Greek word behind *Al-'adad* is probably ἀριθμὸς used as in Plato's *Philebus*, 25a, b; 25e, in the sense of that which numbers. On the argument of this paragraph up to this point cf J. L. HEIBERG, *Euclidis Elementa*, Vol. V, p. 418, l. 13 ff. (W. p. 6, l. 14)

[35] That is, the Platonic πέρας. Cf. p. ara 9 and the third note to para. 9 for this meaning of *hadd* (W. p. 6, last line).

[36] The original text of the MS., as given by WOEPCKE, p 7, notes 1, 2, and 3, is to be prefered. *Al-Muṭlaq* is used in arithmetic to denote a *Whole* Number (See *A Dict. of Technical Terms* etc, A. SPRENGER, Vol. II, p 921; Dozy, Vol. II, p. 57, right column) and is used here probably by analogy in the same sense. WOEPCKE's text runs: — "It is also necessary to point out that the term "proportion" can in general be used to denote one thing in the case of etc." For this and succeeding sentences cf. J. L. HEIBERG, *Euclidis Elementa*, Vol. V, p. 418, l. 17 ff.

[37] SUTER's note 47, p. 18, seems contrary to the whole argument of the paragraph. See especially the last sentence. Commensurable and rational magnitudes are not contraries, but neither are they identical.

[38] The Arabic phrase translated, "With respect to greatness and smallness", renders the Greek, κατὰ τὸ μεῖζον καὶ ἔλαττον — (Cf. J. L HEIBERG, *Euclidis Elementa*, Vol. V, p. 418, l. 19), i. e., "According to the great and small". The reference is probably to Euclid, Bk. V, Def 4: — "Magnitudes are said to have a ratio to one-another which are capable, when multiplied, of exceeding one-another"; which, as T. L. HEATH remarks, excludes the relation of a finite magnitude to a magnitude of the same kind which is either infinitely great or infinitely small and serves to show the inclusion of incommensurables. See para. 8, note 47.

b) This is the Platonic expression for continuous change. See, however, para. 8, note 47. G. J.

[39] See Euclid, Bk. X. props 23, 27 & 28 SUTER (See p 19, notes 49 & 50) cites the two medials, $\sqrt[4]{5}$ & $\sqrt[4]{80}$, which are incommensurable with unity, but have the ratio to one-another of 1 to 2

[40] See SUTER, *Beiträge zur Geschichte der Mathematik bei den Griechen und Arabern*, Abhandlungen zur Geschichte der Naturwissenschaften und der Medizin, Heft IV, Erlangen, 1922, p. 19, Note 52, and Appendix 2. Irrationals as has been stated, may be commensurable with one-another.

[41] Euclid, Bk. X. prop. 23.

[42] Euclid, Bk. X., prop. 103.

[43] Literally, within Number.

[44] WOEPCKE substitutes the supralinear gloss for the MS. reading, but the latter should be restored to the text, since the whole argument of the paragraph is based upon the idea of finitude. The Arabic phrase given in the MS. and translated, "A defined plurality" is a rendering of the Greek definition of number, πλῆθος ὡρισμένον (Eudoxus in "*Jambl. in Nicom. Arith*"., Introd., 10, 17: cf. the Aristotelian definition, πλῆθος τὸ πεπερασμένον, *Metaph.* 1020a, 13; 1088a, 5, whereas the supralinear gloss gives the Greek definition, "A progression (and retrogression) of multitude", προποδισμός, ἀναποδισμός. SUTER does not appear to have grasped the sense of the Arabic nor the syntax either, the matter is hardly philosophical (W. p. 8, 1 17 and note 5).

[45] WOEPCKE substitutes the supralinear gloss for the MS. reading. The Arabic word rendered by "Comprehends more than" should be read *Mujāwizatun*, not *Muhāwiratun* or *Mujāwiratun*, as WOEPCKE suggests. The supralinear gloss, *Arja'u min*, is an explanation of this term. The meaning is that finitude is a more comprehensive term than number, or, according to the gloss, is of a higher category, number being just one of its kinds and not therefore, exhausting its content, so that the ratio pertaining to number does not cover everything included under the ratio pertaining to finitude (W. p. 8, 1. 17 and note 6).

[46] Literally, "We exclude the ratio of finite things from ....".

[47] Magnitudes are commensurable when they can be measured by some unit or other which is the least part or minimum. This minimum, therefore, is determined ultimately by the ratio of the magnitudes to one-another. The ratio of the finites, on the other hand, is defined (Euclid, Bk. V, Def 4) so as to exclude the relation of a finite magnitude to a magnitude of the same kind *which is either infinitely great or infinitely small*, and to show the inclusion of incommensurables (See note 38 above).

b) Perhaps an allusion to Plato's *Parmenides*, 140c. See Introduction, p. 6 or a reference to the idea of continuous change; see para. 6. G J.

[48] That is, presumably, the Pythagorean Monad. Cf. Part I, para 13 (W. p 13, l. 11) where it is stated that God measures all things better than one measures the numbers.

[49] Human reason, however, is limited and can find no natural unit of measurement for continuous quantities, as for numbers. For them, therefore, it uses various conventional units of measurement, which do not, therefore, apply to all finite things.

[50] For the para. see J. L. HEIBERG, *Euclidis Elementa*, Vol. V, p. 484, l. 23—p. 485, l. 7. That is, medials, binomials, and apotomes.

[51] That is, the things furthest removed from their causes, the ideas or forms in the Universal Soul, and which are, then, only very dim reflextions or very poor images of these, devoid for the most part of form, or limit, or definiteness.

[52] That is, as the whole argument of this paragraph goes to prove (cf. also § 13), there is nothing absolutely irrational but only relatively so. From the point of view of an ideal system of knowledge, or, Platonically speaking, from the point of view of the World-Soul, everything is rational, but for human reason there are things which are relatively irrational, as, e. g., an infinite number of the continuous quantities. But these are, even for human reason, relatively rational, inasmuch as they all belong to one or other of the three classes of irrationals, and so admit of definition, have a certain form or limit. For the Platonist, and likewise the Neopythagorean and the Neoplatonist, the cause of this, that everything consists of three parts, is the number *three* conceived of as a metaphysical entity. "The Triad", says Nicomachus (in Photius), "is the cause of that which has triple dimensions and gives bound to the infinity of number". (Cf. T. TAYLOR, *Theoretic Arithmetic*, London, 1816, p. 181). The doctrine is derived from the Platonic speculation concerning the *separate* as distinct from the mathematical and sensible numbers. (Cf. Aristotle, *Metaph* 1080a, 12—1083a, 14.) The *separate numbers* were not only the formal but also the material causes of everything Even the universal soul, it should be observed, is threefold, being formed from same (τὸ ταυτόν), other (τὸ Θάτερον), and being (ἡ ὀυσία) (Cf. PLATO's *Timaeus*, 37a; *Proclii Diodachi in Platonis Timaeum Commentaria*, E. DIEHL, Leipzig, 1903, Vol. II, p 295 (on Timaeus, 37a), p. 125, l. 23ff., p. 157, l. 27ff., p. 272, l. 21ff., p. 297, l. 17ff, p. 298, l. 2ff.). On the threeness of things see Aristotle, *De Coel.*, I. 1.

[53] The Greek corresponding to this passage in the Arabic is found in J. L. HEIBERG's *Euclidis Elementa*, Vol. V, p 485, l. 3ff. The Arabic,

7*

Tushabbahu an ("seems to"), gives the Greek ἔοικεν; the Arabic, *Min qurbin* ("directly"), gives the Greek προσεχῶς; so far as the Arabic is concerned, the latter phrase might be translated. "By affinity". For the notion of the soul's being moved concerning the nature of the continuous quantities, see Plato's *Timaeus,* 37a b.. "Therefore since she (the soul) is formed of the nature of same and of other and of being, of these three portions blended, in due proportion divided and bound together, and turns about and returns into herself, whenever she touches aught that has manifold existence or aught that has undivided, *she is stirred through all her substance,* (κινουμένη διὰ πάσης ἑαυτῆς) and she tells that wherewith the thing is same and that wherefrom it is different etc. (R. D. ARCHER-HIND's translation). Cf. also the commentary of Proclus on the Timaeus, E. DIEHL, Vol. II, p. 298, l. 2 ff. & pp. 302—316 on Timaeus 37a b., esp. p. 316, ll. 24—25 (W. p. 9, l. 11 ff.).

54 For the interpretation of this sentence cf. Plato's *Timaeus,* 34c.—37c., where Plato describes the composition of the soul out of same, other, and being, goes on then (35b ff) to give an account of the mathematical ratios pertaining to the soul, to state, finally (36e ff.), that God fashioned all that is bodily, within her; that from the midst even unto the ends of heaven she was woven in everywhere and encompassed it around from without; and that she can tell that wherewith anything is same and that wherefrom it is different, and in what relation or place or manner or time it comes to pass both in the region of the changing and in the region of the changeless that each thing affects another and is affected. See the commentary of Proclus on the Timaeus, E. DIEHL, Vol. II, p 47, l 28ff : "Again the Soul is one and contains in itself that which is divine (τὸ θεῖον) and that which is irrational (τὸ ἄλογον), and in the divine part of itself it comprehends (περιέχει) rationally the irrational powers (τὰς ἀλόγους δυνάμεις) by which it governs the irrational and arranges it in a becoming manner" Cf. also Vol. II, p. 106, ll. 9—15, p. 108, l. 29ff., p. 160, l. 26ff., p. 208, l. 5ff. Cf. J. L HEIBERG, *Euclidis Elementa,* Vol. V, p 485, l 3ff. for the Greek.

55 The basis of this view is again to be sought in the *Timaeus,* 31c.—32a. & 35b.ff. In the first passage Plato shows how the mean term of three numbers makes the three an unity and how the material world is a harmony through the proportion of its elements. In the second the harmony or unity of the soul is established by the three means. Cf. the commentary of Proclus, Vol. II, p. 198, l. 9ff.: "The three

means may be said to be the sources of union (ἐνωτικὰι) and connection (συνεκτικὰι) to the Soul or in other words to be unions, proportions, and bonds (δεσμὸυς). Hence also Timaeus names them, |bonds. For prior to this he had said that the geometric mean is the most beautiful of bonds and that the other means are contained in it. But every bond is a certain union." Cf. also Vol. II, pp. 16, 18, 21 (on Timaeus 31c.— 32a.), p. 131, l. 30ff.; Vol. III, p. 211, l. 28ff. That is, the three means are the basis of the unity of the soul and of everything, there-fore, rational or irrational.

[56] Or, "Is deprived of the ratios etc " The reading of the ms. is *Yughlaba*, and the marginal gloss is *Yuqlaba* The idea to be conveyed is evidently that of loss or change of property or relation (W., p. 9, l. 14).

[57] I have adopted with WOEPCKE the marginal reading, *Al-Nisabi*, instead of the text's *Al-Sababi*, because *Al-Mawjūdati* (Which exist) seems to require this change. Observe also that *Al-Nisabi* (ratios) is used in the next sentence manifestly with reference to the same object as here The argument, moreover, deals with the ratios of the soul and those of continuous quantities, and how the three means are the causes of union therein (W., p. 9, l. 15).

[58] The clause is difficult; and a marginal gloss, instead of helping to solve the difficulty, adds to it. The gloss reads, *Lākin* (not *Lākinnahu*, as with WOEPCKE) *shai'un (shai'an ?) ba'da shai'in minha*, instead of *Lākinnahu matā ba'ada* (not instead of *Lākinnahu matā ba'ada 'an wāhidin minha*, as with WOEPCKE). The meaning to be attached to this is obscure, to say the least; it can only be conjectured that it should mean that one thing after another of these last things returns and becomes the image of the psychic ratios. "Naturally" gives the Arabic *Min til-qā'i tabī'atin*, i e., from, for, or on the part of any nature, *Min til-qā'i* meaning the same as *Min 'indi*, or *Min qibali*, or *Min ladun Ya'ud* might be read instead of *Ba'ada*, i. e "Whenever it turns back from anyone of these ratios" (W p. 9, ll. 14—15).

[59] The clause is again obscure. The meaning of the Arabic phrase, *Min al-rās ilā ghairihi* is not clear I suspect that some Greek phrase such as ἐς πόδας ἐκ κεφαλῆς is the basis of the Arabic. The meaning of the sentence as a whole is, however, doubtless that given above. The last things are those furthest removed from their psychic prototypes, things almost devoid of form or limit. Even these, however, are sub-ject to the ratios that govern their psychic prototypes, can never indeed, change or lose these. There is a limit, therefore, beyond which they cannot go, since, then, they would lose these ratios and change

their nature. They can only return whence they came The Platonic doctrine of the harmony of the world (cf. the Timaeus) and the Neo-Platonic doctrine of the return of all things to their source give a basis for the solution of the passage.

[60] So stands the text of this sentence, which has apparently a metaphysical signifance Things irrational are divided into three classes. (1) Irrational powers, as, e, g., the two psychic powers, anger and desire, (cf. the citation from Proclus in note 54 above).

(2) Infinite series of things, as, e, g., species.

(3) Not-being, τὸ μὴ ὄν, i. e., Matter (ὕλη) or Space (χώρα) which has not yet received any form, is still formless (ἄμορφον) or without shape (ἀχημάτιχον) (cf. *Timaeus* 50b—52c; Arist., *Met.*, W D. Ross, Vol. 1, Comm. p. 170), forms probably being conceived of as mathematical figures in this instance, concerning which idea see the *Timaeus* 53c. and ZELLER's *Pre-Socratic Philosophy* (Trans., S. F ALLEYNE, 1881), Vol. 1, p. 436, on Philolaus (W. p. 9, l. 17—p. 10, l 2).

[61] As in the case of apotomes, for example. Harmonic proportion is such that the difference between the middle term and the first is to the first as the difference between the middle term and the last is to the last.

[62] As in the case of the binomials, for example. The arithmetical mean separates three or more terms by the same term, but with irrationals this term is an unknown quantity

[63] As in the case of the medials, for example. The geometric mean unites three or more terms by the same ratio. Mathematically the paragraph informs us that there are three kinds of irrationals, and that to each kind one of the three means pertains. See Part 11, para 17ff., where the author shows how the three kinds of irrationals are produced by the three kinds of proportion.

[64] Or, "Those who have influenced speculation", reading *Al-Mu'tharina* or *Al-Mu'aththirina* (W. p. 10, l. 6).

[65] See *Theaetetus*, 147d.—148b. For the Greek cf. J. L. HEIBERG, *Euclidis Elementa*, Vol. V, pp. 450—452, no. 62.

[66] See Appendix A for a discussion of the use of the term, *Quwwah* (power = square) in paragraphs X & XI (W. p. 10, l. 10). Sometimes it would have been more convenient and practical to translate "powers" (= square-roots), the point being that $\sqrt{5}$ and $\sqrt{3}$, e. g., are incommensurable with 1 (= $\sqrt{1}$) in length, whereas $\sqrt{4}$ is commensurable But the use of "Quwwatun" (= power) throughout paras. 10 and 11 proves that it means square and square only; and the awkwardness of

the argument will be excused, it is hoped, for the sake of its historical accuracy.

[67] Whose lineal measurement is, therefore, a foot. Cf. Appendix A.

[68] That is, conceptual knowledge dealing with forms or genera which are not subject to change, and knowledge of which is, therefore, by its very nature real knowledge. I read *Al-Muntabih* not *Al-Mutanabbih* (W. p. 10, l. 11).

[69] *Theaetetus*, 147e.—148a.

[70] The Arabic is an exact rendering of the Greek ἴσον ἰσάκις, *Al-Mutasāwiyan mirāran mutasāwiyatan* (W. p. 10, l. 12).

[71] That is, they form the number into a square figure as in the problem of the quadrature of a circle. Cf. Appendix A on *Rabba'a*. If "Quwwatun" is taken as "power" (= square-root), then "Rabba'a (to square) must be translated, "Whose square is", and so throughout wherever this change is made

[72] There is no mention of the fact referred to in this last clause in *Theaetetus*, but it is a pet idea of the commentator. G. J.

[73] Cf. Book X, prop. 9. I read with SUTER *Abadan* not *Aiḍan* (W. p. 10, l 19).

[74] See note 11 of this Part for the meaning of "Qawl".

[75] Or, "The definition that determines these "powers" (squares) by means of the square numbers is different altogether from that which makes them have to one-another the ratio of a square number to a square number".

[76] That is, the ratio of 9 to 4, the halves of 18 and 8.

[77] I have adopted the reading of the MS. WOEPCKE preferred the supralinear gloss (see text and notes on the text.) (W. p. 11, ll. 7—8, note 5.)

[78] As SUTER says (p. 22, note 62), the definition of Theaetetus was not universally valid, whereas that of Euclid was.

[79] *Theaetetus*, 147d. And in the next clause it is evident that Theaetetus must be the subject of the verb, *explains*, since the reference is to 148a.—b. (W p. 11, l 13).

[80] The Arabic is a free rendering of the Greek of *Theaetetus* 148a.—b. I have taken the *Ha* of *Annahā tulun* and of *Annahā qiwan* as referring to the *Sides (Al-Adlā'u)*, although the form of the sentence would lead one to suppose that it referred to the antecedent of *Allatī*, i. e. *Power* or *Powers (quwwatun or qiwan)*. But if the Greek on which the Arabic is based, is taken into account, the antecedent of *Allatī* would be some phrase equivalent to ὅσοι μὲν γραμμαί. The fact, then, that in the

Greek the subject of discussion is the *lines* or *sides of the squares*,
points to *sides (Al-Adlā'u)* as the most probable antecedent to *Hā*
(W. p. 11, ll. 14—15)

81 That is, the sides of squares commensurable in square but not in length

82 That is, as the side of a square.

83 That is, the squares upon these *powers (surds)* are commensurable
with the squares upon the lines called *lengths*. SUTER omits this
sentence the Greek behind it is evidently [συμμετρος] τοῖς δ'ἐπιπέδοις
ἀ δύνανται *Theaetetus* 148b. *Length* and *power* here denote, as
SUTER says, rational and irrational respectively (W p 11, l 17).

84 That is, as SUTER says, the squares of 18 square feet and of 8 square
feet mentioned in the previous paragraph, 10

85 Cf the previous note, 34, on the meaning of *Al-'adad* SUTER's note,
65, rests on a misconception, due to his not recognising the real meaning
of *Al-'adad* and its use in the sense of *Unit of Measurement* His note 54
also rests on a misconception of the sense of the paragraph. And
Pappus had in all probability the same conception of irrationality as
Euclid. I have translated the last clause according to the reading of
the MS. The marginal gloss given by WOEPCKE would run: "On which
these *powers* are [described] (i. e. which are the sides of these squares)
The original text adds the important point that these lines are ima-
ginary, so far, that is, as measure is concerned (W. p. 11, l 21)

86 SUTER's change of subject *(lines to squares)* and the consequent
change of *number* to *square number* is unnecessary. The lines are
commensurable in length according to Book X, prop 9, and have,
therefore the ratio of a number to a number according to Book X,
prop. 5. (W. p. 12, ll. 2—3) There is' a Latin translation of the
treatise up to the end of this paragraph in the Paris MS. 7377 A,
fol 68—70b., apparently by GERHARD of Cremona. See STEIN-
SCHNEIDER in Z. D M G , Bd. 25, Note 2. (Cf. SUTER, p. 23, note 67)

87 PLATO's *De Legibus*, Bk VII, 817 (end)--820.

88 Cf. *De Legibus* VII, 819 (STALLBAUM, 1859, Vol. X, Sect II, p. 379,
ll 1—5) The Arabic, *Wa ba'da hadhihi-l-Ashya'i*, gives the Greek
μετὰ δε ταῦτα. In the Arabic, *Bi-l-Tab'i* (= Greek φύσει) qualifies
Qabihun (shameful); and it is to be observed that H. MUELLER (1859)
and OTTO APELT (1916) both make φύσει to qualify *ludicrous* and not
ignorance, as most of the commentators do (See JOWETT). WOEPCKE's
reading, *Yadhaku minhu jami'a* etc., is a marginal reading. The MS.
reads *Fadahika minhu bijami'i* etc. *Bijami'i* is certainly correct,
although *Jahila* can take the accusative. *Fadahika minhu* is possible,
but the *F* may just be a Y thickly written (W. p. 12, ll. 7—9)

[89] Cf. *De Legibus* VII, 819d. (STALLBAUM, p. 379, l. 5.) (W. p. 12, ll. 9—10.)

[90] For this passage beginning, "For I hold", cf. *De Legibus* 819d. (STALLBAUM, p. 379, ll. 9—12), 820a (STALLBAUM, p. 381, ll. 1—2), 820b. (STALLBAUM, p. 381, ll 3—9). SUTER's note 70, is based on a mistranslation. His translation, p. 23, l. 15, would demand instead of *Man taqaddama (yuqaddimu?)*, *Mimman taqaddama min al-Nāsi*. Moreover the verb *Istahā* needs a complement, and *Min Zanni man taqaddama* etc. is that complement. This phrase is not, therefore, the *Man zanna* of SUTER's translation (W p. 12, ll. 11—12.)

[91] According to WOEPCKE and SUTER we have here in the phrase, *Al-Kitābi-l-ma'rūfi b...*, a repetition of a phrase of the preceding sentence, namely, *Al-Kitābi-l-ma'rūfi bi-Thi'ā titus*, i e "The book that goes by the name of Theaetetus", except that unfortunately the last word is illegible. In my opinion, however, the last word of the phrase is undoubtedly *Thabatan*, an accusative of respect modifying *Qila*, i. e., "From what has been said by way of support or demonstration in the . . book". The complement of *Al-ma'rūf* has, therefore, either been omitted, or *Al-ma'rūf* is used here absolutely with the meaning of *Mashhūr*, i. e., *Well-known, Standard* (Cf. Lane's Arabic Dict., I. V, p. 2017, col. I). The latter supposition finds support in the fact that Euclid was generally known to his successors as *The* Στοιχειωτής simply, and that they took a knowledge of his works for granted (Cf. M CANTOR, *Vorlesungen über Geschichte der Mathematik*, 3rd Ed., 1907, p. 261, the reference to Archimedes, *De sphaera et Cylindro* (Ed. HEIBERG, I. 24), also J. L. HEIBERG, *Litterargeschichtliche Studien über Euclid*, Leipzig, 1882, p. 29 (foot) and his reference to Proclus). The propositions in Euclid referred to are evidently 15 and 36 of Book X. (W. p. 12, l. 20.)

[92] Or, "Applied to one-another".

[93] *Parmenides* 140c.

[94] *Parmenides* 140b., c., d. *Al-Wad'u* is the Greek ἡ ὑπόθεσις of Parmenides 136, for example. SUTER's note 73 is based on a false rendering of *Al-Wad'u*. *Al-Mawdi'u* also is quite correct and means *case* as translated above (W. p. 13, l 6).

[95] That is, the three ideas are interdependent.

[96] The Greek words behind *Al-Ijtimā'u* (union) and *Al-Iftirāqu* (separation) are probably ἡ σύγκρισις and ἡ διάκρισις as used, e. g., in Aristotle's *Metaph.*, 988b. 32—35, cf. Plato's use of συγκρίνεσθαι and διακρίνεσθαι in *Parmenides* 156b. The sensible world is the

product of union and division, which are themselves the results of the movements of the circles of the same and the other in the World-Soul. Cf. *Timaeus* 36 c.—37 c and the commentary of Proclus on the Timaeus, E. DIEHL, Vol. II, p. 158, ll. 18—19, p 252 ff. (W. p. 13, l 9).

⁹⁷ That is, the World Soul of *Timaeus* 34 b. c., 36 c. d. e., 40 b., which through the revolutions of the circles of the same and the other controlls the world. Observe the use of κράτος in 36 c for the sense of the Arabic word *qawā* (controlls). Cf. also the commentary of Proclus, E. DIEHL, Vol I, p. 414, l 13, where the soul is said to be ἀνακυκλοῦσαν τὸ πᾶν; cf. also Vol. II, p. 286, l. 21, p. 292, l. 10 ff., p. 316 ll. 24—25 (W p. 13, l. 9).

⁹⁸ *Al-'adad* is the reading of the MS *Al-Qadr* is a marginal reading to be taken in the sense of *measure*, not *will*, as SUTER supposes, *number* being *that which measures* in this case. *Divine number* is the Platonic *separate numbers*, conceived of as separate substances and first causes of existing things (See Arist., *Metaph.*, 1080 a. 12—b. 33, 1090 a. 2 ff., 987 b. 31). All things are, therefore, commensurable by divine number, since it is their formal cause. But matter is also necessary for their existence; and it is indefinite; therefore they can be incommensurable (W. p. 13, l 10)

⁹⁹ Matter is here conceived of Platonically. It is the *Indefinite Dyad* (Cf Arist., *Metaph.*, 1081 a. 14; cf. also 1083 b., 34), or *The Great and Small* (Cf Arist. *Metaph.*, 987 b. 20; cf also 1085 a 9), which as the material principle of sensibles is, as the *Timaeus* clearly enough says (52 a.), space not yet determined by any particular figure and capable of indefinite increase and indefinite diminution

¹⁰⁰ *Limit* is the Platonic τὸ πέρας. It is imposed on matter, *the unlimited* (τὸ ἄπειρον), by the Ideas or the divine numbers.

¹⁰¹ Cf. Arist. *Metaph.*, 1—9, esp 8; Z. 1034 b. 20—1035 b. 31, esp. 1035 a. 25. The Arabic words translated, *Part, Whole, Matter, Form, Potentiality, Actuality*, give the Greek words, μέρος, ὅλον, ὕλη, εἶδος, δύναμις, ἐνέργεια. (W. p. 13, l 18).

¹⁰² See W. D. Ross, *Aristotle's Metaphysics*, Vol. II, p. 199 (note to 1036 a. 9—10). "The words, ὕλη νοητή", says Mr Ross in part, "occur only here and in 1037 a. 4, and 1045 a. 34, 36. Here it is something which exists in individuals (1037 a. 1, 2), in non-sensible individuals (1036 b. 35) or in sensible individuals not regarded as sensible (1036 a. 11), and the only instances given of these individuals are mathematical figures (1036 a. 4, 12; 1037 a. 2). It seems to be equivalent to ἡ τῶν μαθηματικῶν ὕλη of K 1059 b. 15. ALEXANDER, there-

fore, indentifies it with extension (510. 3, 514. 27), which is satisfactory for Z (1036). But in H (1045a) it is the generic element in a definition and, therefore, (1) is present in the nature of a species, and (2) has no limitation to mathematical objects. The instance given in H is a mathematical one: "Plane figure is the ὕλη νοητή of the circle". So ὕλη νοητή in its widest conception is the thinkable generic element which is involved both in species and in individuals, and of which they are specifications and individualizations". "Matter" says Mr. Ross again (Vol. II, p. 195 to 1036a. 8), "is sensible and (changeable), or else intelligible, viz, the matter which exists in sensibles not qua sensible, i. e. mathematical figures". (W. p. 14, l. 1—l. 5) Cf. The Commentary of Proclus on Book I of Euclid, ed., FRIEDLEIN, p. 51, l. 13ff.; p. 57, l 9ff.

[103] *Rasmun*, meaning *Line*, is unusual. *Khattun* is the common word. *Rasmun* means usually *Mark, Sign, Trace, Impression*. But undoubtedly *Rasmun, Shaklun*, and *Hajmun* give here the Greek γραμμή, ἐπίπεδος, and σῶμα, and to be observed is the fact that *Rasmun* and γραμμή correspond in several of their meanings, e. g., *Writing, Drawing*, or *Sketching*. It might mean a mathematical diagram, but that is the meaning of *Shaklun*. Perhaps the three terms represent the μῆκος, ἐπίπεδος, ὄγκος of Arist., *Metaph.* M 1085a ll. 10—12. Then *Rasmun* would give μῆκος (W. p. 14, l. 5).

[104] Cf. W. D. Ross, *Aristotle's Metaphysics*, Vol. II, p. 199, note to 1036a. 9—10 (towards the end) "It is evident", says Mr. Ross, "from line 11 that in Aristotle's view everything which has sensible matter has intelligible matter, but not vice-versa. We get a scale of matters, each of which implies all that precedes: (1) ὕλη νοητή; (2) ὕλη αἰσθητή including, (a) ὕλη κινητή (τοπική), (b) ὕλη ἀλλοιωτή, (c) ὕλη αὐξητὴ καὶ φθιτή, (d) ὕλη γεννητὴ καὶ φθαρτή, which is ὕλη μάλιστα καὶ κυρίως (*De Gen. et. Corr.*, 320a 2).

[105] That is, sensible and mathematical numbers, which in the Platonic system follow the ideas (the incorporeal life), are free from incommensurability no less than the ideal numbers which precede the ideas (L ROBIN, *La Théorie platonicienne des Idées et des Nombres d'après Aristote*, Paris, 1908, p. 470), or are identical with them (W. D. Ross, *Arist., Metaph.* Vol. I, Introd., p. LXVI). They possess only limit and form (W. p. 14, ll. 6—8).

[106] That is, from the incorporeal life, the ideal world, the Plotinian τὸ ἐκεῖ.

[107] E. g., Length, breadth, and thickness (W p 14, l. 8).

[108] The MS. reading, *The lines which have* etc., is correct, and not the marginal reading, *The line which etc.*, as WOEPCKE suggests. This may be seen from the fact that the author in the next sentence but one speaks of *measures*. Cf. also para. 5, near the middle, where it is asserted that one may assume a line a cubit long, or a line a span long, or some line or other, to be the rational unit of measurement (W. p. 14, l. 12)

[109] Cf. note 28 of Part I. of the translation for this sense of *Qadr* (W. p. 14, l. 14).

[110] Cf. para. 5, near the middle (W. p 6, ll 10—13), (W. p. 14, l. 14).

[111] That is, the rationality or irrationality of a magnitude depends upon the given rational unit of measurement. Cf. note 34 of this Part of the translation for the meaning of ʿadad. It is *number* as *measure* (W. p. 14, l. 15).

[112] The marginal reading, adopted by WOEPCKE, *Muhaṣṣalatun* might mean *determinate*, as in para. 3, near the end. In all probability, however, it is a gloss on the MS reading, *Mujmalatun*, meaning *general*, in the sense that the properties sum up the species of rationals and irrationals (W. p 14, l. 18)

[113] That is, presumably, Euclid The marginal reading which WOEPCKE adopts, *Al-ʿilmi*, would run, "*Of his science*" On *La*, as marking the apodosis of a conditional sentence, cf. Wright's *Arabic Grammar* 3rd Ed, Vol. II, p. 349A (W. p 14, last line).

[114] That is, it can be measured by some unit of measurement or other (W. p. 15, l. 2).

[115] As SUTER says, this means that some line or other must be taken as the rational unit of measurement (W. p. 15, l. 3).

[116] That is, the subject and predicate of the previous clause-viz., "*Every line which is commensurable*", i. e., *commensurable and rational*; as may be seen from the next two sentences. The Arabic runs literally: "And let the one of the two of them be convertible into the other". I read, of course, *Yaʿkasu*, and not *Bi-l-ʿaksi*, as WOEPCKE. I read also *Yusamma* and *Yudaʿu*, and not *Nusammi* and *Nadiʿ u*. (W. p. 15, ll. 6—7).

[117] Cf. Book X, Definitions 3 & 4.

[118] Commensurable, that is, in length or in square; since lines are said to be commensurable in length, although not commensurable with the assumed line. See the end of this paragraph and the succeeding one.

[119] Literally, "Is a something added to them from without". But the Arabic phrase, *Min khārijin*, probably gives some such Greek phrase as ἐκτὸς τούτων (ἐκτός?, ἔξω?), meaning, *besides* (praeterquam), as in Plato's *Gorgias*, 474 d. The Commentator means that in the two phrases, *rational lines commensurable in length* and *rational lines commensurable in square*, *commensurable in length* and *commensurable in square* do not modify the idea, *rational line*, i. e., as the next clause says, do not refer to the proportion of the lines to the assumed rational line, but modify the idea, *line*, i. e., refer to the proportion of the lines to one-another (W. p. 15, ll. 14—15).

[120] Since lines can be rational and commensurable in length, although not commensurable with the assumed rational line in length. See the end of this paragraph and the next paragraph.

[121] Cf. note 34 of Part I of the Translation for the meaning of *Al- adad*. The unit of measurement in this case is $\sqrt{2}$.

[122] WOEPCKE omits the phrase, *Yaqdiru-l-khatta-l-mafrūda aidan*, from the text of the MS. at this point, since it is impossible that this measure ($\sqrt{2}$) should "measure the assumed line also". Perhaps we should read "*Biqadri-l-khatti* etc", meaning, "With the measure of an assumed line also" (W. p. 16, l. 4, note 3).

[123] Literally, "There is not anything, then, which makes a rational except commensurability with the assumed rational line". SUTER's notes 84 & 85 rest on a misapprehension of the meaning of the text. Pappus had undoubtedly the same conception of rationality as Euclid, as has already been pointed out in note 85 above (W. p. 16, l. 1 ff.).

[124] Euclid, Book X, prop. 19.

[125] In short, "What ratio they have to the rational line", or, "What is the mode of their relation to the rational line".

[126] But not commensurable in length with the given rational line. The Arabic is slightly involved in this sentence. But observe that the Arabic, *Amma . . . .amma*, renders the Greek μὲν.... ..δὲ. Cf. Wright's *Arabic Grammar*, 3rd Ed., Vol. I, p. 292 B (W. p. 16, ll. 9—12).

[127] Book X, prop 19 and Definition 4.

[128] That is, if you multiply the length by the breadth.

[129] Literally, "Then the area of the rectangle must be six *somethings-or-other*. But what the six somethings-or-other are, is not known".

[130] As SUTER says (Appendix 3), the lines containing the rectangle would be, e. g , $3\sqrt[4]{2}$ and $2\sqrt[4]{2}$, which are commensurable in length, but the product of which is $6\sqrt{2}$, a medial, irrational rectangle.

[131] Not very clear, as already SUTER has observed.   G. J.

[132] Cf. *Theaetetus*, 148a.; ı. e. μῆχος. (W p. 17, 1 15).

[133] Cf. *Theaetetus*, 148a. b ; ı. e. δύναμις. (W p. 17, 1 16).

[134] That ıs, to explain the use of the name 'power' (square) for these lines.

[135] Cf. *Theaetetus*, 148b.

[136] That ıs, in length or ın square.

[137] That ıs, the lınes commensurable wıth thıs other measure but incommensurable wıth the fırst

[138] The MS. readıng ıs "*Wahuwa la yash'iru*". The meanıng ıs that Euclıd wıthout giving notice of the basis of hıs procedure, named these lınes ratıonal on the ground that they were commensurable wıth the gıven lıne ın square, and named them commensurable ıh length on the ground that they had a common measure, although that measure was not the gıven line (W. p. 18, l. 2).

[139] Which they are not, accordıng to defınitıon.   See Defınitıon 3, Book X. SUTER's note 94 rests on a mısapprehensıon of the text (W. p. 18, l. 3).

[140] Cf. the prevıous paragraph towards the end.

[141] SUTER remarks (Appendix 4): Thıs last proposition ıs not wholly correct. If, for example, the gıven ratıonal lıne is 10 and the two lınes containıng the area 5 and $\sqrt{3}$, the aıea, $5\sqrt{3}$, ıs medıal, but one of the sıdes, 5, ıs commensurable wıth the gıven ratıonal lıne, 10.   That ıs, both sides need not be ıncommensurable wıth the gıven lıne ın length.

[142] SUTER supposes (note 96) that thıs sentence should stand at the end of the paragraph, or else that the rest of the paragraph is a later additıon The latter supposıtıon seems to him the more lıkely, sınce what comes hereafter is to hım self-evident, even naive. It is, however, pertinent, if somewhat tautologous The commentator poınts out in thıs paragraph that ratıonal lınes are; —

(1) commensurable ın lengtlı wıth the given lıne and theıefore wıth one-another.

(2) commensurable ın square only wıth the gıven lıne Of these
   (a) some are commensurable wıth one-another ın length, but not with the gıven lıne,
   (b) others are commensurable ın square only wıth the gıven line and wıth each other.

Therefore ın thıs last part of the paragraph he poınts out that ıt ıt be stated that an area ıs contained by two lines ratıonal and commensuıable ın square only, this means that the two ratıonal lınes are commensurable wıth one-another and with the given ratıonal lıne in square only Etc. (See Translatıon.)

[143] WOEPCKE' conjecture that the reading should be "*In square only*" and not "*In length only*" is correct. The use of *only* determines the use of *square* (W. p. 18, last line, note 6).

[144] Cf. Book X, props. 21 & 22; J. L. HEIBERG, *Euclidis Elementa*, Vol. V, p. 488, no. 146; p. 489, no. 150. On the paragraph cf. ibid., p. 485, ll. 8—16.

[145] Book X, prop. 21   That this clause seems to repeat the previous clause, is due to the exigences of translation.   The former clause translated literally would run somewhat as follows: "And, therefore, can have a square described on it equal in area to the rectangle etc. "The use of *Janbatun* (Side) is unusual.   The ordinary word for side is *Ḍil'un*.   The dual of *Janbatun* may emphasize the fact that the sides are adjacent sides.   The two lines are, of course, the extremes, τὰ ἄκρα, but this in Arabic is *Ṭarafāni* (W p. 19, l. 7).

[146] Cf. J. L. HEIBERG, *Euclidis Elementa*, Vol. V, p. 485, ll. 8—9; p. 491, no. 158, for the Greek of this clause   *Juz'iyyatun* (Particular) is an adjective qualifying *Ṭabi'atun* (nature or species), not a noun as SUTER takes it.   *'alā tabi'atin juz'iyyatin* gives the Greek ἐπὶ μερικωτέρας φύσεως (W. p. 19, ll. 7—8).

[147] That is, the rectangle contained by two rational lines commensurable in square only.

[148] Cf. Book X, Def. 3. As this definition shows, this phrase includes not only the square upon the line but all areas which are equal to the square upon the line.

[149] Cf. for this paragraph J. L. HEIBERG, *Euclidis Elementa*, Vol. V, p. 485, l. 16—p. 486, l. 7. Cf. also para. 4 above in the translation. As SUTER says (note 98), this resemblance is nowhere expressly stated in Euclid   The short lemma before proposition 24 does not carry the comparison so far as Pappus does here.   Pappus seems to have based his comparison on props. 21—25.

[150] See Book X, prop. 23, Porism; props. 24 and 19.

[151] See Book X, prop. 25.

[152] Cf. SUTER, Appendix 6, who gives the following examples of these areas in the order of the text: (1) $\sqrt{3}\cdot\sqrt{5}=\sqrt{15}$, (2) $2\sqrt[4]{5}\cdot 3\sqrt[4]{5}$ $=6\sqrt[4]{5}=\sqrt[4]{180}$, (3) $\sqrt[4]{20}\cdot\sqrt[4]{45}=\sqrt[4]{900}=\sqrt{30}$; (1) $3\cdot 5=15$, or $\sqrt{18}\cdot\sqrt{8}=12$, (2) $\sqrt[4]{27}\cdot\sqrt[4]{48}=\sqrt[4]{1296}=6$

[153] The Greek of this sentence is given in J. L. HEIBERG's *Euclidis Elementa*, Vol. V, p. 485, ll. 23—25: — καὶ ἔοικεν ἡ μὲν τῶν μήκει συμμέτρων μέσων ἀνάλογον μεταξὺ ληφθεῖσα καὶ ἡ τῶν δυνάμει συμμέτρων ῥητῶν ἐκ παντὸς εἶναι μέση. (W. p. 20, l. 5).

154 WOEPCKE's emendation of the text is correct, as may be seen from the context. We must read "*Commensurable in square,*" not "*Commensurable in length.*" The error occurs, however, in the Greek text, cf. J. L. HEIBERG's *Euclidis Elementa* Vol V, p. 485, ll. 25—27: — ἡ δὲ τῶν ῥητῶν μήκει συμμέτρων τότε μὲν ῥητή, τότε δὲ μέση. — The Arab translator probably did not notice the error and translated mechanically (W. p 20, l. 8).

155 That is, the two rationals or the two medials commensurable in square.

156 The Greek is given in J. L. HEIBERG, *Euclidis Elementa*, Vol V, p. 486, ll. 3—6. — ἀιτιατέον οὖν τὴν ἀναλογίαν τῆς τῶν περιεχομένων χωρίων διαφορᾶς τὴν μεταξὺ τῶν ἄκρων etc. — The primary meaning of *Ikhtilātun* is *Mixture, Confusion*, but here it renders the Greek ἡ διαφορά Cf. *Khiltun*, meaning *Kind, Species* (DOZY, *Supplément*, Vol. 1, p 394, col. 1). *Al-Ṭarajāni* is the technical Arabic term for the *extremes* and does not mean, as SUTER supposes, the length and breadth of the area, although they are here that also. The Greek gives only the first and last of the three types of means given by the Arabic text (W. p. 20, ll. 12—13).

157 Cf Book X, props 1—18 (20). Cf. Para. 4 above (W. p 5)

158 Cf. Book X, props 36ff., 73ff.

159 Cf. Book X, prop. 36.

160 Cf. Para. 4 above near the middle (W. p. 5, l. 7).

161 Cf. Book X, prop. 73.

162 That is, with the minuendus. G. J.

163 SUTER quite rightly remarks (note 103): "Clearer would have been the expression, "And the diagonal of the square described on the rational line". WOEPCKE, however, (*Extrait du Tome XIV des Mémoires présentés . à l'Academie des Sciences de l'Institut imperial de France Essai d'une Restitution de Travaux perdus d Apollonius*, p. 37, note 1) takes the diagonal as *a* in his example. The side is, then, as SUTER says, $= \sqrt{\frac{a^2}{2}}$ WOEPCKE also points out that the Arabic word translated, *diagonal*, also means *diameter*, and shows how this meaning of the word might be interpreted geometrically. But the meaning, *diagonal*, gives the simpler and the better idea (W. p. 21, l. 5).

164 SUTER says (Appendix 7): According to WOEPCKE the three lines are, the medial line $= \sqrt{a\sqrt{\frac{a^2}{2}}}$, the binomial $= a + \sqrt{\frac{a^2}{2}}$, the apotome $= a - \sqrt{\frac{a^2}{2}}$; but in my opinion they are, the medial line $= \sqrt{a\sqrt{2a^2}}$, the binomial $= \sqrt{2\,a^2} + a$, the apotome $= \sqrt{2\,a^2} - a$. — Both conceptions are justified, so far as Euclid's definitions are concerned.

[165] a) WOEPCKE's conjecture that *irrationality (Asammu)* must be supplied is undoubtedly correct; cf. Book X, prop. 37 and the next paragraph (W p. 21, l. 12).

b) That $a + \sqrt{b} + \sqrt{c}$ is not "rational", $= \sqrt{d}$, can be proved as follows. It would follow that $a + \sqrt{b} = \sqrt{d} - \sqrt{c}$, i. e., a binomial would be equal to an apotome, which according to Euclid X, 111, is impossible. G. J.

[166] WOEPCKE's conjecture, *"One of them" (Aḥaduhā)*, instead of *"One of the two of them" (Aḥaduhumā)* is supported by the reading of the text later in the paragraph (W. p. 22, l. 9). "Again, let there be three medial lines commensurable in square, such that one of them *(Aḥaduhā)*". The following *Ma'a* may have caused the intrusion of the *M* between the *H* and the *A* (W. p. 21, l. 21).

[167] The Arabic is *Majmū'a-l-murabba'i*, i e., *the sum of the square [areas] that is produced by the two of them.* — But the reference is to prop. 39 of Book X, and the phrase is best rendered into English by *"The sum of the squares on them"* Cf. note 190 for this and "synonymous" Arabic phrases. SUTER thinks that Pappus applied this extension wrongly to irrationals which he had not discussed. But this is only a question of method of treatment (W. p 21, l. 21).

[168] Cf. Book X, props. 40 and 41.

[169] a) "Namely, the first bimedial . . . .. irrational", may be a gloss. The paragraph is most concise in statement and omits many steps in the argument. See prop. 37, Book X (W p. 22, ll. 10—11).

b) The previous sentence presupposes something impossible Three medials commensurable in square are of the form $\sqrt{a}\ \sqrt[4]{m}$, $\sqrt{b}\ \sqrt[4]{m}$, $\sqrt{c}\ \sqrt[4]{m}$. If now each with either of the remaining two form a rational rectangle, the product of the first two is rational, viz $\sqrt{a\,b\,m} = r$, Likewise $\sqrt{a\,c\,m} = r_2$; $\sqrt{b\,c\,m} = r_3$. The three multiplied together give $a\,b\,c\,m\,\sqrt{m} = r, r_2 r_3$. That is, a square root is equal to a rational number, which is nonsense. G. J.

[170] That is, binomials, bimedials etc On the mathematical implications of the paragraph see WOEPCKE's *Essai*, notes to pp. 37—42; T. L. Heath's *"The Thirteen Books of Euclid's Elements"* (1908), Vol. III, pp. 255—258.

[171] Cf. Book X, props. 73—78.

172 Or, "Which is to be cut off", taking the participle in its gerundial sense and the clause in a general sense.

173 a) On the "Annex" cf T. L. Heath's "*The Thirteen Books of Euclid's Elements*" (1908), Vol III, p. 159. The Greek is ἡ προσαρμόζουσα. The Arabic *(Al-Lifqu)* means *To join and sew together the two oblong pieces of cloth of a garment*, i. e. in its primary sense (W. p. 22, last line).

b) *Annex* or ἡ προσαρμόζουσα is = *Subtrahendus*. Euclid's apotome, a—b, is formed from two rational lines If from the sub-trahendus, b, something be subtracted, c, a new apotome arises, a — (b — c). The difficulty mentioned by WOEPCKE (Essai p. 43 = 700) is thus resolved. G. J.

174 That is, the annex of the apotome last arrived at

175 That is, not only apotomes but also first and second apotomes of a medial, minors etc. can be produced by the same method of subtraction.

176 Compound lines are those formed by addition.

177 SUTER adds logically enough in his translation, "And irrationals".

178 *Jumlatun* means a *part* or a *chapter* of a book (See Dozy, *Supplément*, Vol. 1, p. 219, col. 1), not a *Class* in this case, as SUTER translates it (W. p. 23, l. 10).

179 Book X, prop. 1.

180 Book X, prop. 2.

181 Cf. Book X, props. 3—9, esp 5—9; cf. also props 11 & 14.

182 Cf. Book X, prop. 10, and Definitions 1 & 2. That is, the incommensur-ability of lines may be based upon their lineal measurements only or upon their lineal and square measurements. SUTER translates, "In square only", taking "*In length*" *(Fi-l-tûli)* in the second case to be an error for „*In square*" (With reference to the square: *Fi-l-Quwwati)* (W. p. 23, l. 14).

183 Cf. props. 15—18. The "*Them*" are the commensurable and incom-mensurable continuous quantities.

184 Prop. 16 of our Euclid is manifestly referred to in the previous clause; cf. the previous note. Cf. J. L. HEIBERG, *Euclidis Elementa*, Vol. V, p. 484, ll. 8—10.

185 *Dhakara* here gives the Greek διδάσκει (J. L HEIBERG, *Euclidis Elementa*, Vol. V, p. 484, l. 13), and later, para. 30, first line, it renders the Greek διαλέγεται δεικνύων (Ibid, p 547, l. 24). "*To Discuss*" has much the same connotation (W. p. 23, l. 17).

186 Props. 19—26. Prop. 21 is referred to in the phrase, "The production of it" or "The finding of it" The *Annahā* after the third *Dhakara* of this paragraph may be an interpolation. The Greek has nothing

corresponding to it (J. L. Heiberg, Ibid., p. 484, ll. 11—15; no. 133, esp. l. 14) (W. p. 23, l. 18).

[187] Prop. 10 of our Euclid. Cf. the lemma to prop. 18, and Heath's note to prop. 10 (Vol. III, p. 32).

[188] Prop. 21.

[189] Props 27 & 28 respectively. For the first clause cf J. L Heiberg, *Euclidis Elementa*, Vol. V, p. 501, no. 189 (cf. p. 503, ll. 3—4).

[190] The reference is to prop. 33. The Greek is τὸ μὲν συγκείμενον ἐκ τῶν ἀπ' ἀυτῶν τετραγώνων. For this the Arabic uses several phrases: *Majmu'u-l-Murabba'ı-l-kā'ıni mınhumā* (para. 22); *Al-Murabba'u-lladhi mınhumā ma'an* (para. 26, twice); *Al-Murabba'u* (Same paragraph, a line later, but manifestly depending for its sense on the previous phrase; *Al-Murabba'u-l-murakkabu mın murabba'aıhımā* (para. 27), *Al-Murabba'u-lladhı min murabba'aihımā* (para. 27); *Al-Murabba'u-lladhı mınhumā* (para. 27) This last phrase is shown by its context to be identical in meaning with the two previous phrases and thus proves that all the phrases given here have one and the same meaning (W p 25, l. 5).

[191] Book X, props. 33—35 respectively. Suter (note 111) gives as examples, $\sqrt{8 + \sqrt{32}}$ and $\sqrt{8 - \sqrt{32}}$; both are incommensurable in square; the sum of their squares is rational (16); their product medial ($\sqrt{32} = 4\sqrt{2}$).

[192] Book X, props 36—41.

[193] That is, the binomial, prop. 36.

[194] That is, the first and second bimedials, props 37 and 38.

[195] That is, the major, the side of a rational plus a medial area, and the side of the sum of two medial areas These two lines are not qualified as either rational or medial. Cf. paragraph 25, where they are described as "Neither rationals nor medials". The reference is to props. 39—41. Woepcke's conjecture is, therefore, correct. We must read "Incommensurable in square" and not "Commensurable in length". The error is probably a copyist's mistake. The phrase, *"Commensurable in length"* occurs in the MS. directly above on the previous line and again two lines before at the end of the line (W. p. 24, ll. 19—20).

[196] That is, in the previous paragraph, 26: "And two straight lines, neither medial nor rational, but incommensurable in square, which make the sum of the squares upon them rational, but the rectangle contained by them medial etc ".

8*

197 And, therefore, irrational. The two last clauses might be translated as follows: — "Two because of the two medials etc.; and one because of the two rationals etc.". But the preposition, *Min*, can hardly convey both the sense given it in the translation and that given it in this note, as in SUTER's translation, even if, ultimately, such is the meaning to be attached to the text (W. p. 24, ll. 21—22).

198 Book X, props. 36—38 & 39—41 respectively.

199 The phrase, *Fi kulli wāhidi min hadhihi* (in the case of each one of these), translated above: "In the case of the three latter propositions", refers evidently to props. 39—41, in which these irrationals are formed from lines incommensurable in square (W. p. 25, l. 3).

200 a) The text is incorrect. It should run: — "The whole line would be medial". Proof · —

$$x^2 + y^2 = \sqrt{a},$$ i. e., the sum of the squares is medial.

$$xy = n\sqrt{a},$$ i. e., the rectangle is medial and commensurable with $\sqrt{a}$.

$$x^2 + 2xy + y^2 = \sqrt{a}(1 + 2n)$$

The whole line $\quad x + y = \sqrt{\sqrt{a}} \ \sqrt{1 + 2n} = $ medial

$$x - y = \sqrt{\sqrt{a}} \cdot \sqrt{1 - 2n} = \text{medial.}$$

$$x = \tfrac{1}{2}\sqrt{\sqrt{a}} \ (\sqrt{1 + 2n} + \sqrt{1 - 2n}) = \text{2nd bimedial.}$$

$$y = \tfrac{1}{2}\sqrt{\sqrt{a}} \ (\sqrt{1 + 2n} - \sqrt{1 - 2n}) = \text{2nd apo-}$$

tome of a medial; x and y are not commensurable in length. G. J.

b) This is undoubtedly, however, the text of the MS., and there is no just reason for supposing a scribal error. The only question is whether the error is one of translation or a slip of the original author.

201 Book X, props 42—47.

202 The Arabic word, *Ma'a*, usually meaning "*With*" "*Along with*" probably renders here the Greek μετά ("After") (W. p. 25, l. 15)

203 Book X, prop. 48

204 Props. 48—53 Cf. for these two sentences J. L. HEIBERG, *Euclidis Elementa*, Vol V, p. 534, no. 290. The Arabic phrase, *Wa huwa musarrafun 'ala sittati anhā'in*, gives the Greek ἐξαχῶς διαποικιλλομένην (W. p. 25, l. 16).

205 The *Hu* (it) in *Ista'addahu* (he provided it (these)) refers back to the *Hu* (it) in *Fa'alahu* (he did it (this)), which refers back to *Amrun*,

which is the finding of the six binomials. In the next clause *Alladhi* and *'alaihi* (by means of which) also refer back ultimately to *Amrun*. I have, therefore, translated the *Hu* in *Ista'addahu* by *"These"* for the sake of clarity (W. p. 25, ll. 16—17).

[206] That is, that the squares upon these six irrationals formed by addition are equal to the rectangle contained by a rational line and one of the six binomials respectively.

[207] Book X, props 54, 55, 56—59.

[208] For this paragraph cf. J. L. HEIBERG, *Euclidis Elementa*, Vol. V, p. 538, no. 309.

[209] Book X, props. 66—70.

[210] Book X, props. 60—65. SUTER has not grasped the meaning of the text The Greek runs (J. L. HEIBERG, etc., p 547, 1 23—p. 548, l. 5 for the paragraph, and for the last sentence, p. 548, ll. 2—5): — καὶ ἔτι τὰς δυνάμεις αὐτῶν παρὰ τὰς ῥητὰς παραβάλλων ἐπισκέπτεται τὰ πλάτη τῶν χωρίων ἀντίστροφον ἑτέραν ἑξάδα τῇ ἐν τῷ ε̄ κεφαλαίῳ παραδοθείσῃ ταύτην εὑρών. — The Arabic does not say that these propositions belong to part seven. As a matter of fact they form the first group mentioned in part eight. Did propositions 60—65 come after propositions 66—70 in Euclid? (W. p 26, ll 6—7).

[211] Book X, props 60—65 Cf. the previous note

[212] Book X, props. 71—72. WOEPCKE omits the phrase, *Allati li-ba'dihā 'inda ba'din*, given in the MS., without comment. It is true that this phrase is not necessary in the Arabic for the sense of the clause. But it gives the Greek: — ἣν ἔχουσιν αἱ κατὰ σύνθεσιν ἄλογοι πρὸς ἀλλήλας —, which is represented, therefore, in the Arabic not only by the status constructus, but also by this clause. For the paragraph in the Greek cf. J. L. HEIBERG, *Euclidis Elementa*, Vol. V, p. 551, no. 353; for the clause cited, ibid., l. 23 (W. p. 26, l. 11, note 2).

[213] Book X, props. 73—78.

[214] Cf. Part II of the translation, para 12, towards the end and the note on *Naẓīr* given there. Cf also the following paras., 13, 14, and 15

[215] WOEPCKE's conjecture is unnecessary. The meaning of the Arabic phrase, *Fi-l-Tarkibi*, is quite clear (W. p. 26, l. 20, note 5).

[216] I think that it would be better to adopt the marginal reading, *Fi-*, and translate the clause in full as above (W. p. 26, l. 21, note 6).

[217] Book X, props. 79—84. On *annex* cf. note 173 above. For the paragraph in the Greek cf. J. L. HEIBERG, *Euclidis Elementa*, Vol. V, p. 553, no. 359.

[218] Book X, props. 85—90. Cf. para. 27 above. The Arabic has the singular, "The binomial was found" (W. p. 27, l. 1).

[219] Book X, props. 91—96.

[220] Book X, props. 103—107.

[221] Book X, props. 97—102. That is, the squares on the various irrationals applied to a rational line give as breadths the various apotomes.

[222] Book X, prop. 111, first part.

[223] Book X, prop 111, second part.

[224] Book X, props. 108—110 Cf. para 30 above.

[225] Book X, prop 115.

[226] Literally, "Abandoning irrationality, on the ground that it proceeds without end". Cf. paragraph **4,** above, (end): — "*Wa taraka-l-Naẓara fī-l-ṣummi li-khurūjihā ilā mā lā nihāyata*". "*Tamurru bila nihāyatin*" is a circumstantial clause (a *mafʿūlun li-ajlihi*) giving the reason for the relinquishing of the investigation. Observe that props. 112—114 are not referred to at all. But cf. note 4 above (W. p. 27, l. 18).

PART II

Book 11 of the commentary on the tenth book of Euclid's Ms. 31 v.⁰ treatise on the elements[1].

§ 1. The following is, in short, what should be known con- Page 29. cerning the classification of the irrationals. In the first place Euclid explains to us the ordered [irrationals], which are homogeneous with the rationals. Some irrationals are unordered, belonging to the sphere of matter, which is called the *Destitute*[2] (i. e., lacking quality or form), and proceeding ad infinitum; whereas others are ordered, in some degree comprehensible, and related to the former (i. e., the unordered) as the rationals are to themselves (i. e., the ordered). Euclid concerned himself solely with the ordered [irrationals], which are homogeneous with the rationals and do not deviate much [in nature] from these. Apollonius, on the other hand, applied himself to the unordered, which differ from the rationals considerably.

§ 2. In the second place it should be known that the irrationals are found in three ways, either by proportion, or addition, or division (i. e., subtraction[3]), and that they are not found in any other way, the unordered being derived from the ordered in these [three] ways only. Euclid found only one irrational line Page 30. by proportion, six by addition, and six by subtraction; and these form the sum total of the ordered irrationals[4].

§ 3. In the third place we should examine all the irrationals with respect to the areas to which the squares upon them are equal, and observe every distinction between them with respect to these [areas], and investigate to which of the areas the squares upon each one of them are [respectively] equal, when these [areas] are "parts" (or "terms")[5], and to which the squares upon

them are equal, only when these [areas] are "wholes"[6] In this
way we find that the square upon the medial [line] is equal to a
rectangle contained by two rational lines commensurable in
square, and each of the others we treat in like manner. Accordingly he (i. e., Euclid) also describes the application of the
squares [upon them to a rational line] in the case of each one of
them and finds the breadths of these areas[7]. Whereupon,
zealous to make his subject clear, he adds together the areas
themselves, producing the irrationals that are formed by addition[8]. For when he adds together a rational and a medial area,
four irrational lines arise; and when he adds together two medial
areas, the remaining two lines arise. These lines, therefore, are
also named *compound lines* with reference to the adding together of the areas; and those that are formed by subtraction
are likewise named *apotomes* (or *remainders)*[9] with regard to the
subtraction of the areas to which the squares upon them are
equal[10]; and the medial is also called *medial,* because the square
upon it is equal to the area (or rectangle) contained by two
rational lines commensurable in square [only][11]

§ 4. Having advanced and established[12] these facts, we should
then point out that every rectangle is contained either by two
rational lines, or by two irrational lines, or by a rational and an
irrational line, and that if the two lines containing the rectangle

Page 31. be rational, then they are either commensurable in length or
commensurable in square only, but that if they be both irrational,
then they are either commensurable in length (i. e., with one-
another), or commensurable in square only (i. e., with one-
another), or incommensurable in length and square, and, finally,
that if one be rational and the other irrational, then they are
both necessarily incommensurable. If the two rational lines
containing the given rectangle are commensurable in length,
the rectangle is rational, as the Geometer (i. e., Euclid) proves-,
viz.: — "The rectangle contained by two rational lines commensurable in length is rational"[13], if they are commensurable

in square only, the rectangle is irrational and is called *medial*, and the line the square upon which is equal to it, is medial, a proposition which the Geometer also proves-, viz: — "The rectangle contained by two rational lines commensurable in square only is irrational, and the line the square upon which is equal to it, is irrational: let it be [called] *medial*[14]". If the two lines containing the rectangle are, on the other hand, irrational, the rectangle can be either rational or irrational. For if the two lines are commensurable in length (i. e., with one another), the rectangle is necessarily irrational, as he (i. e., the Geometer, Euclid) proves in the case of medial lines[15], which method of proof applies to all irrationals. But if the two lines are commensurable in square only (i. e., with one-another), the rectangle can be rational or irrational; for he shows that the rectangle contained by two medial lines commensurable in square [only] is either rational or irrational[16]. And, finally, if the two lines are wholly incommensurable (i. e., in length and square), the rectangle contained by them is either rational or irrational. For he finds two straight lines incommensurable in square containing a rational [rectangle][17]; and he finds likewise two others containing a medial [rectangle][18]; and the two lines (i. e., in each case) are incommensurable in square, which is what is meant by lines being wholly incommensurable, since lines incommensurable in square are necessarily incommensurable in length also[19].

§ 5. Thus he finds by geometric proportion that the medial line has described upon it a square equal to a medial rectangle, which rectangle is equal to that contained by two rational lines commensurable in square. That is his reason for calling it[20] by this name.

§ 6. The six irrationals that are formed by addition[21] are explained by means of the addition of the areas to which the squares upon them are equal, which areas can be rational or medial[22]. For just as we find the medial line by means of the rationals alone, so we find the irrational lines that are formed by

Ms. 32 r.⁰

Page 32.

addition, by means of the two former, i. e., the rationals and medials, since the irrationals that are nearer [in nature][23] to the rationals, should always yield to us the principles of the knowledge of those that are [in nature] more remote[24]. Thus the lines that are formed by subtraction, are also found only by means of the lines that are formed by addition[25]: but we will discuss these later. The lines that are formed by addition, however, are found by taking two straight lines. Two straight lines must be either commensurable in length, or commensurable in square only, or incommensurable in square and length[26]. If they are commensurable in length, they cannot be employed to find any of the remaining irrationals[2] . For the whole line that is composed of two lines commensurable in length, is like in kind (or order) to the two lines which have been added together[28]. If, therefore, they are rational, their sum is also rational; and if they are medial, it is medial. For when two commensurable continuous quantities are added together, their sum is commensurable with each of them, and that which is commensurable with a rational, is rational, and that which is commensurable with a medial, is medial[29].

§ 7. The two lines, therefore, that are added together, must be necessarily either commensurable in square only, or incommensurable in square and length. In the first place let them be commensurable in square: and to begin with let us imagine the possible cases[30] and point out that either the sum of their squares is rational and the rectangle contained by them medial, or both of these are medial, or, again, the sum of their squares is medial and the rectangle contained by them rational, or both of these are rational. But if both of them be rational, the whole line is rational[31]. Let them both (i. e., the sum of the squares and the rectangle) be rational, and let us apply to the rational line AB the rectangle AC equal to the square upon the whole line LN and let us cut off from it (AC) the rectangle AF equal to the sum of the squares upon LM and MN, so that the remaining

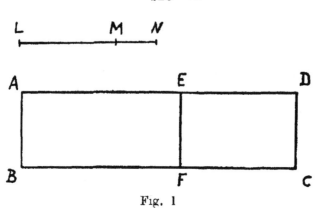

Fig. 1

rectangle FD is equal to twice the rectangle contained by LM
and MN. Then because both the rectangles applied to the
rational line AB are rational, therefore both the lines, AE and
ED, are rational and commensurable with the line AB in length
and, therefore, with one-another. The whole line AD is, therefore, commensurable with both of them and with the line AB,
and, therefore, the rectangle AC is rational. The square upon
LN is, therefore, of necessity also rational. Therefore the line
LN is rational. We must not, therefore, assume both of them, Ms. 32 v.°
i. e., the sum of the squares upon LM and MN and the rectangle
contained by them, to be rational. — There remain, then, [the
three possible cases]: either the sum of the squares upon them is
rational and the rectangle contained by them medial, or the
converse of this, or both of them are medial. — If the sum of
their squares be rational and the rectangle contained by them
medial, the whole line is a *binomial*, the square upon it being
equal to a rational plus a medial area, where the rational is
greater than the medial[32]. For it has already been shown that
when a line is divided into two unequal parts, twice the rectangle
contained by the two unequal parts is less than the sum of the
squares upon them[33]. Conversely, i. e., if the rectangle contained
by the two given lines which are commensurable in square only,
be rational and the sum of their squares medial, the whole line
is irrational, namely, *the first bimedial*, the square upon it being

equal to a rational plus a medial area, where the medial is greater than the rational[34]. If, however, to state the remaining case, both of them, i. e , the sum of their squares and the rectangle contained by them, are medial, the whole line is irrational, namely, *the second bimedial*, the square upon it being equal to two medial areas, these two medial [areas] being, let me add, incommensurable [with one-another][35]. — If they be not so, let them be commensurable [with one-another]. Then the sum of the squares upon LM and MN[36] is commensurable with the rectangle contained by LM and MN. But the sum of the squares upon LM and MN is commensurable with the square upon LM, the square upon LM being commensurable with the square upon MN, since the two lines, LM and MN, were assumed to be commensurable in square, and when two commensurable lines are added together, their sum is commensurable with each of them[37]. The square upon LM, therefore, is commensurable with the rectangle contained by LM and MN. But the ratio of the square upon LM to the rectangle contained by LM and MN is that of the line LM to the line MN. The line LM, therefore, is commensurable with the line MN in length. But this was not granted (i. e., in the hypothesis): they were commensurable in square only[38]. The sum of the squares, therefore, upon LM and MN is necessarily incommensurable with the rectangle contained by these lines. Such, then, are the three irrational lines which are produced when the two given lines are commensurable in square.

§ 8. Three other [lines] are produced when they (i. e., the two given lines) are incommensurable in square. Let LM and MN be incommensurable in square. Then either both the sum of their squares and the rectangle contained by them are rational; or these are both medial; or one of them is rational and the other medial, which gives two alternatives as in the case of the two lines commensurable in square[39]. But if both the sum of the squares upon LM and MN and the rectangle contained by them be rational, the whole line [LN] is rational[40]. — Take the rational

Page 34.

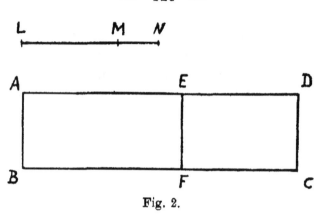

Fig. 2.

line [AB], and let there be applied to it the rectangle [AC] equal
to the square upon LN, and let there be cut off from this rectangle [AC] the rectangle AF equal to the sum of the squares upon
LM and MN, so that the remaining [rectangle] FD is equal to
twice the rectangle contained by LM and MN. AF, then, and
FD are rational and have been applied to the rational line AB.
Both of them, therefore, produce a breadth rational and commensurable with the line AB. Therefore AE and ED are
commensurable [with one-another], and AD is commensurable
with both of them and is, therefore, rational and commensurable Page 35.
in length with the line AB. But the rectangle contained by two
rational lines commensurable in length is rational[41]. Therefore
the rectangle AC is rational. Therefore the square upon LN is
rational. Therefore LN is rational; since the line the square
upon which is equal to a rational (i. e., is rational), is rational. —
Since, therefore, we desire to prove that the whole line (i. e., LN) Ms. 33 r.⁰
is irrational, we must not assume both of the areas (i. e., the sum
of the squares upon LM and MN and the rectangle LM·MN) to
be rational, but either that both of them are medial, or that one
of them is rational and the other medial, which latter instance
gives two alternatives For either the rational [area] or the
medial is the greater; since if they were equal [to one-another],
they would be commensurable with one-another, and the rational
would be a medial and the medial a rational. — If the sum of the

squares upon LM and MN be rational, but the rectangle contained by LM and MN medial, let [the whole line] LN be [called] the *major*, since the rational [area] is the greater[42]. Conversely, if the sum of the squares upon LM and MN be medial, but the rectangle contained by LM and MN rational, let LN be [called] the *side of a square equal to a rational plus a medial area*[43], since its name must be derived from both the areas, from the rational, namely, because it is the more excellent in nature, and from the medial, because it is in this case the greater. If, however, both the areas are medial, let the whole line (i. e., LN) be [called] the *side of a square equal to two medial areas*[44]. Euclid in this case also adds in his enunciation that the two medial areas are incommensurable[45].

§ 9. We need not, therefore, conceive of the irrationals that are formed by addition, as [resulting from] the adding together of lines in two ways[46], but rather as [the result of] the adding together in two ways of the areas to which the squares upon these lines (i. e., The six irrationals by addition), are equal[47]. Euclid makes this fact all but clear at the end of this section[48], where he proves that if a rational and a medial area be added together, four irrational lines arise, and that if two medial areas be added together, the two remaining [lines] arise. It is obvious, then, in our opinion, that if the two lines are commensurable in square, of necessity three lines arise, and that if they are incommensurable in square, three [lines also] arise; since it is impossible that they should be commensurable in length. — Enquiry must be made, however, into the reason why when describing the [lines] commensurable in square, he (i. e., Euclid) also mentions their kind (or order), saying, namely, [in the enunciation], "Two rationals commensurable in square or two medials"[49], whereas when positing (or describing) the incommensurable in square, he does not name them rational or medial[50]. He ought, [as a matter of fact], to have given the enunciation in the former cases the same form which it has in the latter, as, for example: — "When

Page 36.

two straight lines commensurable in square [only] which make the sum of the squares upon them medial, but the rectangle contained by them rational[51], be added together, the whole line is irrational: let it be called the first bimedial"; and in like manner [should have been stated the proposition dealing] with the second bimedial. For this is the form of enunciation which he gives in the case of the [lines which are] incommensurable in square, naming them neither medial nor rational, but making such an assumption in the case of the areas only, i. e., the sum of the squares upon these lines and the rectangle contained by them, positing either that both are medial, or that one is rational and the other medial, with either the rational or the medial the greater[52]. — Let me point out, then, that I consider Euclid to assume that when two lines are commensurable in square, the square upon each of the lines is rational, if the sum of the squares upon them is rational, and medial, if the sum of the squares upon them is medial; but that when two lines are incommensurable in square, the square upon each of them is not rational, when the sum of the squares upon them is rational, nor medial, when the sum of the squares upon them is medial. Accordingly when he posits [lines] commensurable in square[53], he names them rational or medial, since lines the squares upon which are equal to a rational area, are rational, and lines the squares upon which are equal to a medial area, are medial. But when he posits [lines] incommensurable in square, there is no basis[54] for his naming them rational or medial, since only lines the squares upon each one of which are equal to a rational area, should be named rational, not those the sum of the squares upon which is rational, but the squares upon which are not [each] rational. For a rational area is not necessarily divided into two rational areas. He names medial also those lines the squares upon which are each equal to a medial area, not those the sum of the squares upon which Page 37. is medial, but the squares upon which are not [each] medial. For Ms. 33 v. a medial area is not necessarily divided into two medial areas.

§ 10. Such was his (i. e., Euclid's) idea. But proof is required of the fact that two lines[55] are rational or medial, when they are commensurable in square and the sum of the squares upon them rational or medial, and that this statement (or enunciation) does not hold concerning them, when they are incommensurable in square. — Let the two lines, LM and MN, be commensurable in square, and let the sum of the squares upon them be rational I maintain, then, that these two lines are rational. For since the line LM is commensurable with the line MN in square, therefore the square upon LM is commensurable with the square upon MN. Therefore the sum of the squares upon the two of them is commensurable with [the square upon] each of them. But the sum of the squares upon the two of them is rational. Therefore [the square upon] each of them is rational. Therefore the lines, LM and MN, are rational and commensurable in square. — Let, now, the sum of the squares be medial. I maintain, then, that these two lines are medial. For since LM and MN are commensurable in square, therefore the squares upon them are commensurable. Therefore the sum of the squares upon them is commensurable with [the square upon] each one of them. But the sum of the squares is medial. Therefore the squares upon LM and MN are medial. Therefore they (i. e., the two lines, LM and MN) are also medial For that which is commensurable with a rational, is rational, and that which is commensurable with a medial, is medial; and the line the square upon which is equal to a rational [area], is rational, and the line the square upon which is equal to a medial [area], is medial. If, then, the squares upon LM and MN are medial, their sum (i. e., the line LN) is medial; and if the sum of the squares upon them is medial, then they (i. e., the lines, LM and MN) are medial, since LM and MN are commensurable in square[56]. — Let the two lines, however, be incommensurable in square. I maintain, then, that they are not rational, when the sum of the squares upon them is rational, nor medial, when it (i. e., the sum of the squares) is medial.

Assume this to be possible, and let the squares upon LM and MN be rational, and let there be applied to the rational line AB Page 38. the rectangle AC equal to the sum of the squares upon LM and MN, and let there be cut off from it the rectangle AF equal to the square upon LM, so that the remaining rectangle EC is equal to the square upon MN. Then because the square upon LM is incommensurable with the square upon MN, since these are incommensurable in square, it is obvious that AF is incom-

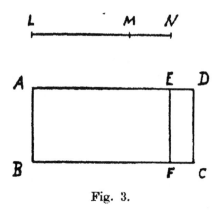

Fig. 3.

mensurable with EC. The line AE, therefore, is incommensurable with the line ED in length. But because the squares upon LM and MN are rational, therefore the rectangles, AF and EC, are rational; and they have been applied to the rational line AB; therefore the lines, AE and ED, are rational and commensurable in square only. But since the rectangle AF is incommensurable with the rectangle EC, therefore the line AE is incommensurable with the line ED in length. The line AD, therefore, is a binomial and, therefore, irrational[57]. But the rectangle AC is rational, since it is equal to the sum of the squares upon LM and MN, which is rational, and it has been applied to the rational line AB. Therefore the line AD is rational. The same line is, therefore, both rational and irrational[58]. The squares upon LM and MN are not, therefore, rational. — Again, let the sum of the squares upon LM and MN, which [lines] are incommensurable

9 Junge-Thomson.

in square, be medial. I maintain, then, that the squares upon
LM and MN are not medial. Assume this to be possible, and
let AB be rational, but let the same two rectangles (i e., AF and
EC) be [in this case] medial[59]. The lines, AE and ED, are, then,
both rational and commensurable in square only[60]. AD, there-
Ms 34 1,0 fore, is a binomial and, therefore, irrational But it is [also]
rational, since the sum of the squares upon LM and MN is medial,
and it has been applied to the rational line AB producing a
rational breadth (i e., AD). The squares upon LM and MN are,
therefore, not medial It has been proved, therefore, that two
lines incommensurable in square are not also rational or medial,
when the sum of the squares upon them is rational or medial[61]
Since, then Euclid has shown this (i e , the proposition concerning lines being rational or medial, when the sum of the
squares upon them is rational or medial) to be true in the case of
[lines] commensurable in square, but not true in the case of
[lines] incommensurable in square[62], he names the commen
surable in square rational or medial, but does not name the latter
so He names them *incommensurable in square* simply[63].

§ 11 Since, then, [Euclid's] division [of lines] assumes, to
Page 39 begin with, only lines commensurable in square and lines incommensurable in square[64], he finds the irrational lines therewith
by adding rational areas with medial areas, or by adding together
medial areas which are incommensurable with one-another[65],
these two kinds of areas being convenient, inasmuch as they are
produced by rational lines For when the lines containing an
area are rational, they are either so (and therefore also commensurable) in length, in which case the area contained by them is
rational, or they are so (and therefore also commensurable) in
square, in which case the area contained by them is medial[66]
Consequently he finds the six irrationals that are formed by
addition, by means of the fact that rational lines contain one [or
other] of these two [kinds of] areas — Let this description which
we have given of the irrationals that are formed by addition,

suffice, since we have already shown their order and number with respect to this division (i e., of lines into those that are commensurable and those that are incommensurable in square)[67]

§ 12. We find the six [irrationals] that are formed by subtraction, by means of those that are formed by addition For if we consider each one of the irrational lines which we have discussed[68] and treat one of the lines (i e , one of the terms) of which it is composed as a whole line and the other as a part of that then the remainder which is left over from it (i e , the remainder left after taking the term treated as a part from that one treated as a whole line) constitutes one of these six irrationals[69] When *the whole straight line and a part of it*[70] produce [by addition] the binomial, [by subtraction] the apotome arises When they produce [by addition] the first bimedial, [by subtraction] the first apotome of a medial arises When they produce [by addition] the second bimedial, [by subtraction] the second apotome of a medial arises. When they produce [by addition] the major, [by subtraction] the minor arises. When they produce [by addition] the side of a square equal to a rational plus a medial area, [by subtraction] that (the line) which produces with a rational area a medial whole arises When they produce [by addition] the side of a square equal to two medial areas, [by subtraction] that which produces with a medial area a medial whole arises Thus it is clear that the latter [six irrationals] are produced from the former six, that they are their *likes* (or *contraries*)[71], and that those [irrationals] that are formed by subtraction, are homogeneous with those that are formed by addition, the apotome being homogeneous with the binomial, the first apotome of a medial with the [first] bimedial [the two terms of which, two medial straight lines commensurable in square only,] contain a rational rectangle. the second apotome of a medial with the [second] bimedial [the two terms of which etc.,] contain a medial rectangle, the others being the likes (or contraries) of one-another in like manner

Page 40

9*

§ 13. That we name the irrationals that are formed by subtraction, *apotomes*[72], only because of the subtraction of a part of the line from the whole [line], need no more be supposed than that we named the six [irrationals] that are formed by addition, *compound lines*, because of the addition of the lines On the contrary we name them [so] only with respect to the areas that are subtracted and subtracted from, just as we named those irrationals that are formed by addition, *compound lines*, Ms. 34 v. only with respect to the areas to which when added together, the squares upon them (i. e, the six irrationals formed by addition) are equal. — — Let the line AB produce with [the line]

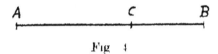

Fig 4

BC a binomial [73]. Now the squares upon AB and BC are equal to twice the rectangle contained by AB and BC plus the square upon AC[74] But the sum of the squares upon AB and BC is rational, whereas the rectangle contained by them is medial[75] Subtracting, then, a medial area (i. e, twice AB·BC) from a rational area (i. e, $AB^2 + BC^2$), the line the square upon which is equal to the remaining area (i e.. AC^2), is the apotome (namely, AC)[76] Consequently just as the binomial can be produced by adding together a medial and a rational [area], where the rational is the greater, so if a medial [area] be subtracted from a rational, the line the square upon which is equal to the remaining [area], is the apotome We designate the binomial, therefore, *by addition* (or *The line formed by addition*) and the apotome *by subtraction* (or *The line formed by subtraction*), because in the former case we add together a medial [area], which is the less, and a rational, which is the greater, whereas in the latter case we subtract the very same medial [area] from the very same rational, and because in the former case we find the line the square upon which is equal to the whole [area] (i. e.. the sum of the two areas), whereas in the latter case we find the line the square upon which is equal to the remaining [area] (i. e., after subtraction of the medial from the rational). The apotome and the binomial are, therefore, homogeneous, the one being the contrary of the other[77] — Again if the two lines, AB and BC, are commensurable in square, and the sum of the squares upon them is medial, but the rectangle contained by them rational[78], the medial [area] (i. e., $AB^2 + BC^2$) is equal to twice the rational (i. e., twice $AB \cdot BC$ plus the square upon the remaining line AC). Conversely to the former case, then, subtracting here a rational area (i. e., twice AB BC) from a medial (i. e., $AB^2 + BC^2$), the line the square upon which is equal to the remaining [area] (i. e., AC^2), is the first apotome of a medial (i. e., AC)[79] Consequently just as we produce the first bimedial by adding a medial [area] with a rational, granted that the rational is the less and the medial the greater, so, we maintain, the first apotome of a medial is the line the square upon which is equal to the remaining [area] after the subtraction of that rational from that medial — Again if AB and BC produce, [when added together], the second bimedial[80], so that the sum of the squares upon them is medial [and also the rectangle contained by them][81], and the sum of the squares upon AB and BC is greater than twice the rectangle contained by them, by the square upon the line AC[82], subtracting then, a medial [area] (i. e. twice AB BC) from a medial (i. e., $AB^2 + BC^2$), where the lines containing the medial and subtracted area[83] are commensurable in square, the line the square upon which is equal to the remaining [area] (i. e., AC^2), is the second apotome of a medial[84] For just as the line the square upon which is equal to these two medial areas when added together, was named the second bimedial, so the line the square upon which is equal to the area which remains after subtraction of the less of the two medial [areas] from the greater, is called the second apotome of a medial — Again when the two lines, AB and BC, are incommensurable in square, the sum of the squares

Page 41

upon them rational but the rectangle contained by them medial, subtracting, then, twice the medial area (i e., twice $AB \cdot BC$) from the rational (i. e., $AB^2 + BC^2$), the square upon AC remains, and it (i e, the line AC) is named here the minor, just as it was named there (i e., in the case of the addition of these two areas) the major[85]. For the square upon the latter is equal to the [sum of the] two areas, whereas the square upon the former is equal to the area that remains after subtraction (i e., of the less of these areas from the greater). Consequently he names the latter the minor, because it is the like (or contrary) of that which he names the major. — Again if the sum of the squares upon AB

Ms 35 r.⁰ and BC be medial, but the rectangle contained by them rational[86], and twice the rational area (i e, twice AB BC) be subtracted from the medial, which is the sum of the squares upon them (i e, $AB^2 + BC^2$), then the line the square upon which is equal to the area that remains after subtraction, is the line AC; and it is named the line which produces with a rational area a medial

Page 42. whole, since it is obvious that the square upon it plus twice the rectangle contained by the two lines. AB and BC, which is rational, is equal to the sum of the squares upon AB and BC[87] — Again if the two lines, AB and BC, be incommensurable in square, the sum of the squares upon them and the rectangle contained by them medial but incommensurable with one-another, subtracting, then, twice the rectangle contained by them (i e, twice $AB \cdot BC$) from the greater medial area, namely, the sum of the squares upon them (i e, $AB^2 + BC^2$), the line the square upon which is equal to the remaining area (i. e., AC^2), is the line AC, and it is named the line which produces with a medial [area] a medial whole, since the square upon it and twice the rectangle contained by AB and BC are together equal to the sum of the squares upon AB and BC, which is medial[88]

§ 14 If, then rational areas[89] be added with medial [respectively], or medial areas with one-another. it is clear that the irrational lines the squares upon which are equal to the sum of

two such areas, are those which receive their name in view of this
addition   But if medial areas be subtracted from rational, or
rational from medial, or medial from medial, it is obvious that
we have the irrational lines that are formed by subtraction   In
the case of the latter areas we do not subtract a rational from a
rational, since, then, the remaining area would be rational.   For
it is evident that a rational exceeds a rational by a rational[90] and
that the line the square upon which is equal to a rational area,
is rational.   If, then. the line the square upon which is equal to
the area that remains after subtraction. is to be irrational
and the square upon it to be equal to another area, which from
this specification of it is irrational the area subtracted from a
rational area cannot be rational   Three possibilities remain.
therefore · either to subtract a rational from a medial, or a medial
from a rational, or a medial from a medial   But when we subtract
a medial area from a rational, the two lines[91] which we produce.
the two squares upon which are equal to the two remaining areas.
are irrational.   For if the two lines containing the medial area
are commensurable in square. the apotome arises, but if they are
incommensurable in square. the minor arises   And when we
subtract a rational area from a medial, we likewise produce two
other [irrational] lines.   For if the two lines containing the
rational and subtracted area are commensurable in square, the
first apotome of a medial arises; but if they are incommensurable
in square, that which produces with a rational area a medial Page 43
whole, arises   And, finally. when we subtract a medial area from
a medial, if the two lines containing the medial [and subtracted[92]]
area are commensurable in square, the line [the square upon
which is equal to] the remaining [area] is [the second apotome of
a medial, but if they are incommensurable in square], that which
produces with a medial area a medial whole, [arises][93]   For, in
the case of addition, when we joined medial areas with rational.
or rational with medial, or medial with medial, we produced six
irrational lines only, [two] in each case[94], whence the method of

positing [in the enunciations] the addition of lines containing the less areas, the squares upon which are equal to the greater areas where we assume the lines in certain cases to be commensurable in square and in others incommensurable in square[95]

§ 15 To sum up. [Firstly], when a medial area is added to a rational, the line the square upon which is equal to the sum, is a binomial; when it is subtracted from it, the line the square upon which is equal to the remaining area, is an apotome, granted that it (i. e the medial area) is contained by two lines commensurable in square[96]. — [Secondly,] when a rational area is added to a medial the line the square upon which is equal to the sum is a first bimedial, when it is subtracted from a medial, the line the square upon which is equal to the remaining area is a first apotome of a medial, granted that it (i e , the rational area) is contained by two lines commensurable in square[97] — [Thirdly], when a medial area is added to a medial, the line the square upon which is equal to the sum, is a second bimedial, when it is subtracted from a medial, the line the square upon which is equal to the remaining area, is a second apotome of a medial, granted that it (i e , the first mentioned medial area) is contained by two lines commensurable in square[98] — [Fourthly], when a medial area is added to a rational, the line the square upon which is equal to the sum, is a major when it is subtracted from a rational, the line the square upon which is equal to the remaining area, is a minor granted that it (i. e , the medial area) is contained by two lines incommensurable in square which make the sum of the squares upon them rational[99] — [Fiftly,] when a rational area is added to a medial, the line the square upon which is equal to the sum, is the side of a square equal to a rational plus a medial area, when it is subtracted from a medial, the line the square upon which is equal to the remaining area, is the line which produces with a rational area a medial whole, granted that it (i e., the rational area) is contained by two lines incommensurable in square which make the sum of the squares

Ms. 35 v.[0]

Page 44.

upon them medial[100] — [Sixthly,] when a medial area is added to a medial, the line the square upon which is equal to the sum, is the side of a square equal to two medial areas; when a medial is subtracted from a medial, the line the square upon which is equal to the remaining area, is the line which produces with a medial area a medial whole, granted that the less area itself is contained by two lines incommensurable in square, the sum of the squares upon which is equal to the greater[101] — The areas may be taken, therefore, in three ways: either a medial is joined with a rational, or a rational with a medial, or a medial with a medial. A rational is never joined with a rational as has already been shown[102]. The lines containing these areas may be of two kinds either commensurable in square or incommensurable in square. That they should be commensurable in length is impossible. The areas may be either added together or subtracted from one-another.

§ 16. The irrational lines, therefore, (i e those formed by addition and subtraction) are twelve. They are the contraries of one-another: firstly, with respect to the manner in which the areas (i e , the rationals and medials) are taken, since [for example,] we sometimes add a medial to a rational, and sometimes we subtract a medial from a rational[103]: secondly, with respect to the lines containing the less areas, the squares upon which are equal to the greater, since these are sometimes commensurable in square and sometimes incommensurable in square[104]; and thirdly, with respect to the areas taking the place of one-another, since, for example, we sometimes subtract a rational from a medial and sometimes a medial from a rational, and sometimes a rational and less area is added to a medial and sometimes a medial and less area is added to a rational[105]. The lines, therefore, that are formed by addition are respectively the contraries of those that are formed by subtraction so far as concerns the manner in which the areas are taken (i e , whether they are to be added together or subtracted from one-another)

With reference to the lines which contain the less areas, the first three of the lines formed by addition and of those formed by subtraction are respectively the contraries of the following three And with respect to the areas taking the place of one-another, the ordered irrationals are the contraries of one-another taken in threes[106] Such, according to the judgment of Euclid, is the manner in which the irrationals are classified and ordered.

Ms 36 r °
Page 45

§ 17 Those who have written concerning these things (i e., of irrationals), declare that the Athenian, Theaetetus, assumed two lines commensurable in square and proved that if he took between them a line in ratio according to geometric proportion (the geometric mean), then the line named the *medial* was produced, but that if he took [the line] according to harmonic proportion (the harmonic mean), then the *apotome* was produced[107]. We accept these propositions, since Theaetetus enunciated them, but we add thereto, in the first place, that the geometric mean [in question] is [and only is] the mean (or medial) line between two lines rational and commensurable in square[108], whereas the arithmetical mean is one or other of the [irrational] lines that are formed by addition, and the harmonic mean one or other of the [irrational] lines that are formed by subtraction, and, in the second place, that the three kinds of proportion produce all the irrational lines Euclid has proved

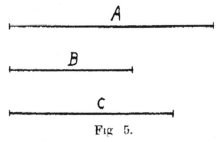

Fig 5.

quite clearly that when two lines are rational and commensurable in square, and there is taken between them a line proportional to them in geometric proportion (i e., the geometric mean), then the line so taken is irrational and is named the *medial*[109] We will now show the remaining [two kinds of] proportion[110] in the case of the remaining irrationals. — Take two straight lines, A and B, and let C be the arithmetical mean between them The lines, A and B, when added together, are, then, twice the line C, since this is the special characteristic of arithmetical proportion If, then, the two lines, A and B, are rational and commensurable in square, the line C is a binomial For, when added together, they are twice C. But when added together, they produce a binomial Since, then, the line C is their half [and so commensurable with them][111], therefore this line (i e , C) is also a binomial — But if the two lines, A and B, are medial and commensurable in square and contain a rational rectangle their sum (A + B), which is the double of the line C is a first bimedial. The line C, therefore, is also such, since it is the half of the two extremes (i e , A and B) — If, however, they (A and B) are Page 46 medial and commensurable in square and contain a medial rectangle, their sum (A + B) is a second bimedial It is also commensurable with the line C, since C is its half Therefore the line C is also a second bimedial — If, on the other hand, the lines, A and B, are incommensurable in square, and the sum of the squares upon them is rational, but the rectangle contained by them irrational (i e , medial), the line C is a major For the sum of the two lines, A and B, is a major: it is also the double of the line C, therefore the line C is a major — But if, conversely, the two lines, A and B, are incommensurable in square, and the sum of the squares upon them is medial, but the rectangle contained by them rational the line C is the side of a square equal to a rational plus a medial area. For it is commensurable with the sum of the two lines, A and B, and their sum is the side of a square equal to a rational plus a medial area. — If, however, the two lines, A and B, are incommensurable in square, and both the sum of the squares upon them and the rectangle contained by them are medial, the line C is the side of a square equal to two medial areas. For the sum of the two lines, A and B, is the

double of C and is the side of a square equal to two medial areas.
Therefore the line C is the side of a square equal to two medial

M-. 36 v⁰ areas The line C, therefore, when it is the arithmetical mean,
produces all the irrational lines that are formed by addition

§ 18   Let the enunciations [of these propositions], therefore,
be stated as follows — (1) If there be taken a mean (or medial)
line between two lines rational and commensurable in square
according to arithmetical proportion (i e , the arithmetical
mean), the given line is a binomial. — (2). If there be taken the
arithmetical mean[112] between two lines medial, and commensurable in square, and containing a rational rectangle. the given line
is a first bimedial. — (3) If there be taken the arithmetical mean
between two lines medial, and commensurable in square, and
containing a medial rectangle. the given line is a second bimedial
— (4) If there be taken the arithmetical mean between two
straight lines incommensurable in square, the sum of the squares
upon which is rational, but the rectangle contained by them
medial, the given line is irrational and is named the major —

Page 47 (5) If there be taken the arithmetical mean between two straight
lines incommensurable in square the sum of the squares upon
which is medial, but the rectangle contained by them rational,
the given line is the side of a square equal to a rational plus
a medial area — (6) If there be taken the arithmetical mean
between two straight lines incommensurable in square the sum
of the squares upon which is medial and also the rectangle contained by them, the given line is the side of a square equal to two
medial areas. The proof common to all of them[113] is that since
the extremes, when added together, are double the mean and
produce the required irrationals, therefore these (i e , the
means[114]) are commensurable with one order [or another] of
these irrationals

§ 19. We must now examine how the irrational lines that are
formed by subtraction, are produced by the harmonic mean
But first let us state that the special characteristic of harmonic

proportion is that the rectangles contained by each of the extremes in conjunction respectively with the mean, are together
equal to twice the rectangle contained by the extremes[115], and,
in addition, that if one of the two straight lines containing a
rational or a medial rectangle be anyone of the irrational lines
that are formed by addition, then the other is one of the [irra-
tional] lines that are formed by subtraction, the contrary,
namely, of the first[116] For example, if one of the two lines
containing the rectangle be a binomial, the other is an apotome,
if it be a first bimedial, the other is a first apotome of a medial
if it be a second bimedial, the other is a second apotome of a
medial if it be a major, the other is a minor, if it be the side of
a square equal to a rational plus a medial area, the other is that
(i e the line) which produces with a rational area a medial
whole, and if it be the side of a square equal to two medial areas,
the other is that which produces with a medial area a medial
whole — Assuming these propositions for the present[117], let us
take the two lines AB and BC, and let BD be the harmonic mean

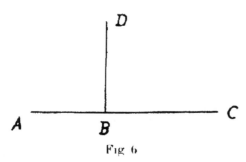

Fig 6

between them. Then if the two lines, AB and BC, are rational
and commensurable in square[118], the rectangle contained by them
is medial, and, therefore, twice the rectangle contained by them
is medial But twice the rectangle contained by them is equal to
the rectangle contained by the two lines, AB, BD, plus the rectangle contained by the two lines, BC BD Therefore the sum
of the rectangles contained respectively by AB·BD and BC BD
is also medial. But the sum of the rectangles contained re-

Page 48

spectively by AB·BD and BC·BD is equal to the rectangle
Ms. 37 r.° contained by the whole line AC and the line BD. Therefore
the rectangle contained by the two lines, AC and BD, is medial.
But it is contained by two straight lines, one of which, AC namely,
is a binomial Therefore the line BD is an apotome — But if
the two lines, AB and BC, be medial, and commensurable in
square, and contain a rational rectangle, and we proceed exactly
as before, then the rectangle contained by the two lines, AC and
BD, is rational But the line AC is a first bimedial. Therefore
the line BD is a first apotome of a medial. — If, however, the
two lines, AB and BC, are medial, and commensurable in square
and contain a medial rectangle, then, for exactly the same
reasons, the rectangle contained by AC and BD is medial. But
the line AC is a second bimedial. Therefore the line BD is a
second apotome of a medial. — If, on the other hand, the two
lines, AB and BC, are incommensurable in square, and the sum
of the squares upon them is rational, but the rectangle contained
by them medial, then twice the rectangle contained by them is
medial, and, therefore, the rectangle contained by AC and BD
is medial. But the line AC is a major. Therefore the line BD
is a minor. — But if the two lines AB and BC, are incommensurable in square, and the sum of the squares upon them is
medial, but the rectangle contained by them rational, then the
rectangle contained by the two lines, AC and BD, is rational But
the line AC is the side of a square equal to a rational plus a
medial area Therefore the line BD is that (i. e. the line)
which produces with a rational area a medial whole — If,
however, the two lines AB and BC, are incommensurable in
square, and both the sum of the squares upon them and the
rectangle contained by them are medial, then the rectangle
contained by the two lines, AC and BD, is medial But the line
AC is the side of a square equal to two medial areas Therefore
the line BD is that which produces with a medial area a medial
whole When, therefore, the arithmetical mean is taken between

the lines that are added together (i e., to form the *compound lines*), one of the irrational lines that are formed by addition (i. e., a *compound line*) is produced; whereas when the harmonic mean is taken, one of the [irrational] lines that are formed by subtraction, is produced; and the latter is the contrary of the line formed by the addition of the given lines.

§ 20   Let the enunciations of these [propositions] be also stated as follows — (1) If the harmonic mean be taken between two lines which [added together] form a binomial, the given line is an apotome — (2) If the harmonic mean be taken between two lines which [added together] form a first bimedial, the given line is a first apotome of a medial — (3) If the harmonic mean be taken between two lines which [added together] form a second bimedial, the given line is a second apotome of a medial — (4) If the harmonic mean be taken between two lines which [added together] form a major, the given line is a minor — (5) If the harmonic mean be taken between two lines which [added together] form the side of a square equal to a rational plus a medial area, the given line is that (i e., the line) which produces with a rational area a medial whole. — (6) If the harmonic mean be taken between two lines which [added together] form the side of a square equal to two medial areas, the given line is that which produces with a medial area a medial whole   The geometric mean, therefore, produces for us the first of the irrational lines namely, the medial: the arithmetical mean produces for us all the lines that are formed by addition, and the harmonic mean produces for us all the lines that are formed by subtraction — It is evident, moreover, that the proposition of Theaetetus is hereby verified[119]   For the geometric mean between two lines rational and commensurable in square is a medial line, the arithmetical mean between them is a binomial, and the harmonic mean between them is an apotome[120]   This is the sum and substance of our knowledge concerning the thirteen irrational lines so far as the classification and order of them is concerned

Page 49

Ms. 37 v.⁰ together with their homogeneity with the three kinds of proportion, which the ancients extolled

§ 21 But we must now prove by the following method the proposition that if one of the two lines containing a rational or a medial rectangle is anyone of the irrational lines that are formed by addition, then the other is its contrary of the lines that are **Page 50** formed by subtraction Let us first, however, present the following proposition Let the two lines, AB and BC, contain a rational rectangle, and let AB be greater than BC. On the line AC describe the semicircle ADC, and draw the line BD at

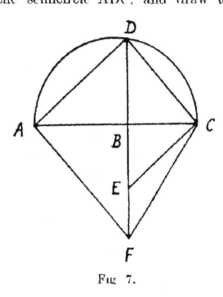

Fig 7.

right angles [to AC]. The line BD, then, is also rational, since it has been proved that it is a mean proportional between the lines AB and BC, and if we join DA and DC, the angle at D is a right angle, since it is in a semi-circle. Draw the line AF at right-angles to the line DA; produce the line DB, so that it meets the line AF at the point F and draw a line at right-angles to DC [at the point, C] This line, then, I maintain, will not meet the line DF at the point F nor will it pass outside DF, but touch within it[12] If possible, let it meet [the line DF] at F Then the area DAFC is a [rectangular] parallelogram,

since all its angles are right angles But the line DA is greater
than the line DC Therefore the line CF is greater than the line
AF, since the opposite sides [of a parallelogram] are equal
Therefore the squares upon BC and BF (BC² + BF²) are greater
than the squares upon AB and BF (AB² + BF²) Therefore BC
is greater than AB which is contrary (i e , to the hypothesis)
for it was [given as] less than AB — The following proof would
be, however pieferable Because the angles at A and C are
right angles and the lines, AB and BC, perpendiculars [to DF],
therefore the rectangle contained by DB and BF is equal to the
square upon BC But it is also equal to the square upon AB
Therefore the square upon AB is equal to the square upon BC
But we have assumed the line AB to be greater than the line
BC — In the same way we can prove that this line (i e , the line
at right-angles to DC) does not meet DF beyond the point F. —
Let it meet DF, therefore, between D and F at the point E
I maintain, then, that the rectangle contained by FB and BE is
equal to the square upon DB, which is rational For DCE is a
right-angled triangle, and the line CB a perpendicular [to DE]
Therefore the two triangles (CBE and CBD) are similar triangles
(i e , of the same order) Therefore the angle at E is equal to the
angle DCE. But for the very same reason the angle DCB is Page 51
equal to the angle BDA, and the angle BDA to the angle
BAF, since the angles at C, D, and A, are all right angles Therefore the angle at E is equal to the angle BAF But the two
angles at B (i. e , CBE and ABF) are right angles Therefore the
angles of the triangle BCE are equal [respectively] to those of
the triangle BAF. Therefore the ratio of the line BF to the
line BA is that of the line BC to the line BE, since they subtend
equal angles. Therefore the rectangle contained by FB and BE
is equal to the rectangle contained by AB and BC But the
rectangle contained by AB and BC is equal to the square upon
DB Therefore the rectangle contained by FB and BE is
rational

10 Junge-Thomson.

§ 22   Having first proved these propositions, we will now prove what we set out to prove[122]   Let the two lines, AB and BC, contain a rational rectangle.   Euclid has proved that a rational rectangle applied to a binomial produces as breadth an apotome of the same order as the binomial[123]   If, then, the line AB is a binomial, the line BC is an apotome   If it is a first binomial BC is a first apotome. If it is a second binomial, BC is a second apotome   If it is a third [binomial], BC is a third [apotome], and so on[124]   Suppose, now. that the line AB is a first bimedial.   Proceeding, then, as before[125], we can prove that 'the line BC is a first apotome of a medial For[126] the line BF is a second binomial, since the square upon a first bimedial applied to a rational line produces as breadth a second binomial And the line BE is a second apotome, since the rectangle contained by $FB \cdot BE$ is rational, and a rational area applied to a second binomial produces as breadth a second apotome.   Therefore the line BC is a first apotome of a medial, since the side of a square equal to an area contained by a rational and a second apotome is a first apotome of a medial — Let now the line AB be a second bimedial and contain with BC a rational rectangle I maintain, then, that the line BC is a second apotome of a medial For proceeding exactly as before, because the line AB is a second bimedial, and the line DB a rational, therefore the line BF is a third binomial, since the square upon a second bimedial applied to a rational straight line produces as breadth a third binomial   And the line BE is a third apotome, since the rectangle contained by $FB \cdot BE$ is rational and if one of the two lines containing a rational rectangle be a binomial, the other is an apotome of the same order as the binomial   But the line BF is a third binomial   Therefore BE is a third apotome   But the line BD is rational, and the side of a square equal to a rectangle contained by a rational line and a third apotome is a second apotome of a medial, therefore the line BC is a second apotome of a medial, since the rectangle contained by $BE \cdot BD$ is equal

Ms. 38 r°

Page 52.

to the square upon BC, the angle at C being a right angle —
Again, let the line AB be a major. I maintain, then, that the
line BC is a minor. For proceeding exactly as before, because
the line AB is a major, and the line BD rational, therefore the
line BF is a fourth binomial, since the square upon a major
applied to a rational line produces as breadth a fourth binomial.
But the rectangle contained by FB·BE is rational. Therefore
the line BE is a fourth apotome, since the line BF is of exactly
the same order as the line BE, the rectangle contained by them
being rational. Because, then, the line BD is rational and the
line BE a fourth apotome, the line BC is a minor, since the
side of a square equal to a rectangle contained by a rational
and a fourth apotome is a minor. — Again, let the line AB be
the side of a square equal to a rational plus a medial area. I
maintain, then, that the line BC is that (i. e., the line) which
produces with a rational area a medial whole. For proceeding
exactly as before, because the line AB is the side of a square
equal to a rational plus a medial area, and the line BD rational,
therefore the line BF is a fifth binomial since the square upon
the side of a square equal to a rational plus a medial area when
applied to a rational line, produces as breadth a fifth binomial.
And because the rectangle contained by FB·BE is rational, Page 53
therefore the line BE is a fifth apotome. Since, then the line Ms 38 v°
BD is rational, the line BC is that which produces with a
rational area a medial whole. For this line is that the square upon
which is equal to a rectangle contained by a rational line and a
fifth apotome. — Finally let the line AB be the side of a square
equal to two medial areas. I maintain then, that the line BC
is that which produces with a medial area a medial whole. For
proceeding exactly as before, because the line BD is rational,
and the line AB the side of a square equal to two medial areas,
therefore the line BF is a sixth binomial. But the rectangle
contained by FB·BE is rational. Therefore the line BE is a
sixth apotome. But the line BD is rational. Therefore the

10*

square upon BC is the square upon a line which produces with a medial area a medial whole   Therefore BC is that which produces with a medial area a medial whole — If, therefore, one of the two straight lines containing a rational rectangle be anyone of the irrational lines that are formed by addition, the other is its contrary of the lines that are formed by subtraction   Our discussion has proved this.

§ 23 It will be obvious, moreover from the following propositions that if one of the two lines containing a medial rectangle be anyone of the irrational lines that are formed by addition,

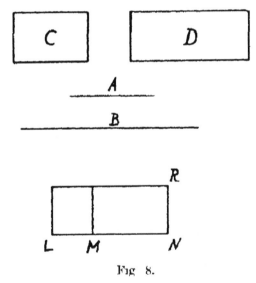

Fig 8.

then the other is its contrary of those that are formed by subtraction   But first let us present [the proposition] that if the ratio of two straight lines to one-another be that of a rational to a medial rectangle or of two medial rectangles to one-another which are incommensurable with one-another, then the two lines are commensurable in square. — Let the ratio of the line A to the line B be that of the rectangle C to the rectangle D, one of which is rational and the other medial, or both of which are medial but incommensurable with one-another   Let the line NR be rational, and let us apply to it the rectangle RM equal

to the rectangle C, and also the rectangle RL equal to the rectangle D. The two lines, MN and NL, are, therefore, rational and
commensurable in square, since the two rectangles applied to the
rational line (NR) are either rational and medial respectively, or Page 54.
both medial but incommensurable with one-another. Because,
then, the ratio of the line MN to the line LN is that of the
rectangle RM to the rectangle RL that is, of the rectangle C
to the rectangle D, and the ratio of the rectangle C to the
rectangle D is that of the line A to the line B, therefore the
ratio of the line MN to the line LN is that of the line A to the
line B. But the lines, MN and LN, are commensurable in
square Therefore the line A is commensurable with the line
B in square — Having demonstrated this, let us now proceed to
prove what we set out to do, namely that if one of the two
straight lines containing a medial rectangle be anyone of the

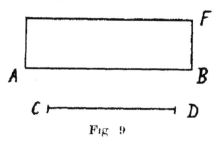

Fig 9

irrational lines that are formed by addition, the other is its contrary of the lines that are formed by subtraction Let the two
lines, AB and CD, contain a medial rectangle, and let AB be
one of the lines that are formed by addition[127] I maintain, then,
that the other line, CD, is not only one of the lines that are formed
by subtraction, but also the contrary of that line (AB) Apply
to the line AB a rational rectangle, namely, that contained by AB
and BF. The line BF, then, as we have already proved[128], is one
of the irrational lines that are formed by subtraction, the contrary, namely, of the line AB, since they contain a rational
rectangle. But because the rectangle contained by AB and CD
is medial and that contained by AB and BF is rational, therefore

the ratio of the line FB to the line CD is that of a rational to a medial rectangle. Wherefore they are commensurable in square, as we have just proved[129] Consequently whichever of the irrational lines formed by subtraction the line CD is, the line AB is its like (or contrary)[130], since the line FB is exactly similar (i. e. in order) to CD, the two rectangles to which the squares upon them are equal, being commensurable[131]. Therefore when one of the two straight lines containing either a rational or a medial rectangle is anyone of the irrational lines that are formed by addition, the other is the line which is its like (or contrary) of those that are formed by subtraction. — Having demonstrated these propositions, it is clear, then, that all the irrational lines that are formed by subtraction are produced from the lines that are formed by addition by means of harmonic proportion in the manner previously described[132] since we have assumed nothing that cannot be proved

§ 24 Following our previous discussion, we will now set forth the essential points of difference between the binomials and also between the apotomes, their contraries[133]. The binomials, as also the apotomes, are of six kinds The reason why they are six in kind is obvious The greater and less terms of the binomial, namely, are taken, and the squares upon them distinguished For it is self-evident that the square upon the greater term is greater than the square upon the less either by the square upon a line that is commensurable with the greater, or by the square upon a line that is incommensurable with it[134] But in the case of the square upon the greater term being greater than the square upon the less by the square upon a line commensurable with the greater, the greater [term], or the less, can be commensurable with the given rational line, or neither of them Both of them cannot be commensurable with it. since then, they would be commensurable with one-another, which is impossible And in the case of the square upon the greater term being greater than the square upon the less by the square upon a line incom-

mensurable with the greater, it follows likewise that the greater
term, or the less, can be commensurable with the given rational
line, or neither of them   Both of them cannot be commensurable
with it for exactly the same reason [as is given above]   There
are, therefore, three binomials, when the square upon the greater
term is greater than the square upon the less by the square upon
a line commensurable with the greater: and there are likewise
three when the square upon the greater term is greater than the
square upon the less by the square upon a line incommensurable
with the greater   And since we have pointed out that when the
ratio of the whole line to one of its [two] parts is that of the [two
terms of a] binomial, then the other part of the whole line is an
apotome[135] and since it is self-evident that the square upon the
whole line is greater than the square upon the first-mentioned
part either by the square upon a line that is commensurable
with the whole line, or by the square upon a line that is incommensurable with it, and that in both cases either the whole line
can be commensurable with the given rational line or that part
of it which has the ratio to it of the [two terms of a] binomial. or Page 56
neither. but not both, just as in the case of the binomial, therefore necessarily the apotomes are six in kind and are named the
first apotome, the second, the third, and so on up to the sixth

§ 25   By design he (i e , Euclid) discusses the six apotomes
and the six binomials only in order to demonstrate completely
the different characteristics of those irrational lines that are formed by addition and those that are formed by subtraction   For
he shows that they vary from one-another in two respects, either
with regard to the definition of their form[136] or with regard to
the breadths of the areas to which the squares upon them are
equal, so that the binomial. for example. differs from the first
bimedial not only in form, since the former is produced by two
rationals commensurable in square and the latter by two medials
commensurable in square and containing a rational rectangle.
but also in the breadth produced by the application of the areas

of the squares upon them to a rational line. The breadth so
produced in the case of the former is a first binomial, in the case
of the latter a second binomial. In the case of a second bimedial
it is a third binomial, in the case of a major a fourth, in the case
of the side of a square equal to a rational plus a medial area, a
fifth, and in the case of the side of a square equal to two medial
areas, a sixth. The binomials are equal in number to the irrational lines that are formed by addition, each group numbering
six, the binomials in order being the six breadths produced by
applying the areas of [the squares upon] the latter to a rational
line, the first in the case of the first, the second in the case of the
second, and so on in the same fashion up to the sixth, which is the
breadth of the area of the square upon the side of a square equal
to two medial areas when applied to a rational line. — In
exactly the same way he appends the six apotomes in order to
demonstrate the difference between the six irrationals that are
formed by subtraction, which is not a mere matter of difference
of form alone. For the apotome differs from the first apotome of
a medial not only in that it is produced by the subtraction of a
line (part) the ratio of which to the whole line from which it is
subtracted, is that of the [two terms of a] binomial, whereas the
latter is produced by the subtraction of a line the ratio of which
to the whole line from which it is subtracted, is that of the [two
terms of a] first bimedial, but also in that the square upon an
apotome, when applied to a rational line, produces as breadth
a first apotome, whereas the square upon a first apotome of a
medial produces as breadth a second apotome. And the rest of
the lines proceed analogously. The apotomes, therefore, are
equal in number to the irrational lines that are formed by subtraction. The squares upon the latter, when applied to a rational
line, produce as breadths the six apotomes in order, the square
upon the first producing as breadth the first apotome, the square
upon the second the second apotome, the square upon the third
the third apotome, the square upon the fourth the fourth apo-

Ms. 30 v°

Page 57

tome, the square upon the fifth the fifth apotome, and the square upon the sixth the sixth apotome, the sum total of both kinds [of lines], i. e., of apotomes and of the irrational lines that are formed by subtraction And they correspond in order, the first with the first, the intermediate with the intermediate, and the last with the last.

§ 26. We should, however, discuss the following propositions The square upon one of the irrational lines formed by addition produces, when applied to a rational line, one of the binomials as breadth, and the square upon one of the irrational lines formed by subtraction produces, when applied to a rational line, one of the apotomes as breadth apply now these same squares not to a rational but to a medial line, and it can be shown that the breadths [produced] are first or second bimedials in the case of

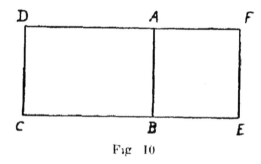

Fig 10

[the irrational lines that are formed by] addition, and first or second apotomes of a medial in the case of those lines that are formed by subtraction[137]. We must begin our proof of this, however, [with the following proposition] If a rational rectangle be Page 58 applied to a medial line, the breadth [so produced] is medial. Let the rectangle AC be a rational rectangle applied to the medial line AB I maintain, then, that the line AD is medial. Describe on AB the square ABEF, which is, therefore medial and has to the rectangle AC the ratio of a medial to a rational area. The ratio of AF to AD is, therefore, that of a medial to a rational area Therefore the lines, AF and AD, are commensurable in square. But the square upon AF is medial, since the square upon AB is medial. Therefore the square upon AD is medial. Therefore the line AD is medial.

§ 27. Having first proved this [proposition], I now maintain that if the square upon a binomial or the square upon a major be applied to a medial line, it produces as breadth a first or a second bimedial. Let the line AB be a binomial or a major, the line CD a medial, and the rectangle DG equal to the

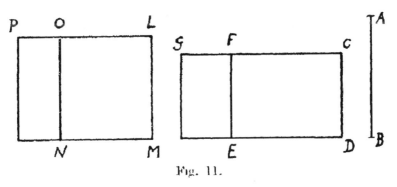

Fig. 11.

square upon AB. Take a rational line LM, and let the rectangle MP equal the square upon AB — If, then, the line AB be a binomial, the line LP is obviously a first binomial[138], but if the line AB be a major, then LP is a fourth binomial[139], as has already been proved with respect to the application of the specified areas[140] to a rational line. Divide LP into its two terms at the point O. Then in the case of both of these binomials (First and fourth) the line LO is commensurable with the given rational line LM, the rectangle MO is rational, and the rectangle PN is medial[141], since the two lines, LM and LO, are commensurable in length, but the two lines NO and OP, rational and commensurable in square [only]. Cut off [from DG] the rectangle DF equal to the rectangle MO. The remaining rectangle NP[142] is, then, equal to the rectangle EG, since the rectangle DG is equal to the rectangle MP. The rectangle EG is, therefore, medial — But the rectangle DF is a rational rectangle applied to the medial line CD. The line CF, therefore, is medial,

as has been shown above[143]   And the square upon CD, then,
since it is medial, being the square upon the medial line CD, can
be regarded (or taken) as either commensurable with the rectangle EG, or incommensurable with it   In the first place let it
be commensurable with it   But, then the ratio of the square
upon CD to the rectangle EG is that of the line CD to the line
FG, since they have exactly the same height. The line CD is,
therefore, commensurable with the line FG in length   The line
FG is therefore medial   Therefore the lines, CF and FG, are
medials — The rectangle contained by the two lines (i e , CF
and FG) is also, I maintain, rational   For[144] since the line CD
is commensurable with the line FG in length , and the ratio
of the line CD to the line FG is that of the rectangle contained
by CD and CF to that contained by CF and FG, if then, you
place the two lines CD and FG, in a straight line, and make the
line CF the height, the rectangle DF is commensurable with
the rectangle contained by CF and FG[145]   But the rectangle
DF is rational. Therefore the rectangle contained by CF and
FG is also rational. Therefore the line CG is a first bimedial[146]
— Let now the square upon CD be incommensurable with the
rectangle EG. The ratio of the line CD, then, to the line FG
is that of a medial area to a medial area incommensurable with
it. This will be obvious, if we describe the square upon CD
For the square so described and the rectangle EG have exactly
the same height (CD, namely). wherefore their bases, the lines,
FG and CD, namely have to one-another the same ratio exactly
as they have, the latter line (i e CD) being equal to the base of
the area (i e the square) described upon it   CD, therefore, is
commensurable in square with FG as has been shown above
The square upon FG, therefore, is medial   Therefore the line
FG itself is medial   Therefore the two lines. CF and FG, are
medial — And the rectangle contained by them is. I maintain,
medial For since the rectangle DF is rational, but the rectangle
EG medial, therefore the ratio of CF to FG is that of a rational

to a medial area   Therefore CF and FG are commensurable in square, as has already been proved. Since, then, the line CD is incommensurable in length with the line FG, the rectangle DF incommensurable with the rectangle contained by CF and FG, and the rectangle DF rational, therefore the rectangle contained by CF and FG is not rational, and the two lines, CF and FG, are medials commensurable in square only   But the rectangle contained by two medial lines commensurable in square is either rational or medial, as Euclid has proved (Book X, prop 25)   Therefore the rectangle contained by the two lines, CF and FG, since it is not rational, is medial   Therefore the line CG is a second bimedial (Book X prop 38). When therefore, the square upon a binomial or the square upon a major is applied to a medial line, it produces as breadth a first or a second bimedial[146].

§ 28   Again let the line AB be either a first bimedial or the side of a square equal to a rational plus a medial area, let the line CD be a medial and apply to it a rectangle (DG) equal to the square upon AB, and let the line LM be rational and the rectangle MP equal to the square upon AB   The line LP is, then, a second binomial, when the line AB is a first bimedial, and a fifth binomial, when the line AB is the side of a square equal to a rational plus a medial area   Divide LP into its two terms at the point O. Then in the case of both of these binomials (namely, the second and the fifth) the line OP is commensurable with the given rational line (i. e , LM), the rectangle NP is rational, and the rectangle MO is medial. Cut off [from DG] the rectangle DF equal to the rectangle MO   The remaining rectangle EG is, then, equal to the rectangle NP. The rectangle DF is, therefore, medial. But the rectangle EG is a rational rectangle applied to the medial line CD. Therefore the line FG is medial — And since the rectangle DF is a medial rectangle applied to the medial line CD, therefore the square upon CD can be either commensurable with the rectangle DF, or incom-

Page 60

Ms 40 x °

mensurable with it In the first place let it be commensurable with it. Then the line CD is commensurable with the line CF The line CF is, therefore, medial — And since the line FG is commensurable with the line CD in square [only], but the line CD commensurable with the line CF in length, therefore[117] the line FG is commensurable with the line CF in square [only] But since the line CD is commensurable with the line CF in length. and the ratio of the line CD to the line CF is that of the rectangle contained by CD and FG to that contained Page 61 by CF and FG, therefore these [rectangles] are also commensurable[148]. But the rectangle contained by CD and FG is rational, since it is the rectangle EG. Therefore the rectangle contained by CF and FG is rational Therefore the line CG is a first bimedial. — Let now the square upon CD be incommensurable with the rectangle DF The ratio, then, of the line CD to the line CF is that of a medial area to a medial area incommensurable with it The lines, CD and CF, are, therefore, commensurable in square But the square upon CD is medial Therefore the line CF is medial And in the same way as before it can be proved that the line CG is a second bimedial. — If, therefore, the square upon a first bimedial or the side of a square equal to a rational plus a medial area be applied to a medial line, it produces as breadth a first or a second bimedial.

§ 29 Again let the line AB be either of the two remaining lines of the irrationals that are formed by addition, i e , either a second bimedial or the side of a square equal to two medial areas Let the line CD be medial, and the line LM rational, and let the same construction be made as before The line LP, then, is either a third or a sixth binomial, since these are the [only] two that remain, neither of these is commensurable (i e., in their terms)[149] with the line LM in length, the two rectangles, MO and NP, are medial and incommensurable with one-another, and, therefore, the two rectangles, DF and EG, are also medials. But since the line CD and the two lines, CF and FG, are medial,

M. 41 r° it is also clear that one of them is commensurable with the line CD (i. e., in length), whenever[150] one of the two rectangles, DF or EG, is commensurable with the square upon CD The rectangle contained by CF and FG is [also], then, commensurable with one of them[151] Therefore the rectangle contained by CF and FG is medial The line CG, therefore, is a second bimedial — But if the square upon CD is not commensurable with either of them (i e, DF or EG), then neither CF nor FG is commensurable with the line CD Therefore the rectangle contained by CF and FG is not commensurable with either of them (i e, DF or EG), the two lines, CF and FG, are medial lines commensurable in square only and the rectangle contained by them therefore either rational or medial[152] If, therefore, the square upon a second bimedial or the side of a square equal to two medial areas be

Page 62 applied to a medial line, it produces as breadth either a first or a second bimedial which fact has already been proved in the case of the other lines[153] Therefore the square upon each of the [irrational] lines that are formed by addition, when applied to a medial line, produces as breadth a first or a second bimedial

§ 30 Having dealt with the irrational lines that are formed by addition, let us now consider the irrational lines that are formed by subtraction taken in pairs [as in the case of the former] Let the line AB be either an apotome or a minor, let the line CD be a medial, and let us describe upon it the rectangle DG equal to the square upon AB I maintain, then, that the line CG is either a first or a second apotome of a medial Let the line LM be rational· and let us describe upon it the rectangle MP equal to the square upon AB The line LP is then, a first apotome [if the line AB be an apotome], and a fourth apotome if the line AB be a minor Let the line PO be the annex of the line LP, and the rectangle EG equal to the rectangle NP[154] The ratio, then, of the rectangle MP to the rectangle NP is that of the rectangle DG to the rectangle EG so that the ratio of the line LP to the line PO is that of the line CG to the line FG

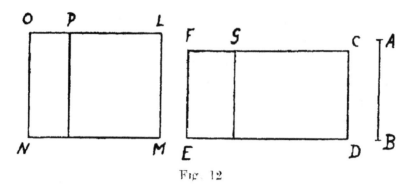

Fig. 12

But[155] the rectangle MO is rational, since we are dealing with a first or a fourth apotome, so that the line LO is commensurable [in length] with the given rational line LM[156], and the rectangle contained by them, therefore, rational, since they are commensurable in length. The rectangle DF is also, therefore, rational, since it is commensurable with the rectangle MO. But since the rectangle DF is a rational rectangle applied to the medial line CD, therefore the line FC is medial. And because the two lines, LM and PO are rational lines commensurable in square, since the line LP is either a first or a fourth apotome, therefore the rectangle contained by them NP, is medial. Therefore the rectangle EG is medial. But the square upon CD is also medial. Therefore they (i. e., EG and CD²) are either commensurable or incommensurable with one-another. — Let them be commensurable with one-another. The line FG is, then, commensurable with the line CD [in length] as we have shown before[157]. Therefore the two lines, FC and FG, are medials. But the three lines CD, FC and FG, are such that the ratio of the line CD to the line FG is that of the rectangle contained by CD and FC to that contained by FC and FG. These rectangles are, therefore, commensurable. But the rectangle DF is rational. Therefore the rectangle contained by FC and FG is rational. Therefore the line CG is a first apotome of a medial. — But if the square upon CD is incommensurable with the rectangle EG, then the line FG is not commensurable

Page 63

Ms. 41 v.º

with the line CD in length, but in square only, since the ratio
of CD to FG is that of the medial square upon CD to a medial
area incommensurable with it, namely, EG. The square upon
FG is, therefore, medial, and FG is, therefore, also medial. But
because the line FC is commensurable with the line CD in
square, and likewise FG, therefore FC and FG are commensurable with one-another in square. And because the line CD is
incommensurable with the line FG in length, and the ratio of
the line CD to the line FG is that of the rectangle DF to that
contained by FC and FG, therefore[158] these two rectangles are
also incommensurable. But the rectangle DF is rational
Therefore the rectangle contained by FC and FG is irrational
But the two lines FC and FG, are medial lines commensurable
in square only. Therefore the rectangle contained by them is
medial, since the rectangle contained by two medial lines commensurable in square is either rational or medial. Therefore the
line CG is a second apotome of a medial — If, then, the square
upon an apotome or the square upon a minor be applied to a
medial line, it produces as breadth a first or a second apotome
of a medial.

§ 31 Again let the line AB be either a first apotome of a
medial or that [line] which produces with a rational area a medial
whole, let the line CD be a medial, and let us describe upon it a
rectangle (DG) equal to the square upon AB I maintain, then,
that the line CG is either a first or a second apotome of a medial.
For[159] the line LM is rational, and there has been applied to it
the rectangle MP equal to the square upon AB Therefore the
line LP is a second or fifth apotome[160] Let the line OP be the
annex of LP, complete the rectangle MO, and let the rectangle
EG equal the rectangle NP Then because the line LP is
either a second or a fifth apotome, therefore the line OL is a
rational line commensurable in square with the given rational
line LM, and the line OP is [a rational line] commensurable in
length with it[161]. Therefore the rectangle NP is rational, and

the rectangle MO medial since the former is contained by two rational lines commensurable in length, whereas the latter is contained by two [rational] lines commensurable in square [only]. Therefore the rectangle EG is also rational, but the rectangle DF medial Because, then the rectangle EG is a rational rectangle applied to the medial line CD therefore its breadth FG is a medial line commensurable in square [only] with the line CD since a rational rectangle can be contained by medial lines, only if they are commensurable in square[162] But since the rectangle DF and the square upon CD are medial, they can be either commensurable or incommensurable with one-another Let them be commensurable with one another. Then the line CD is commensurable in length with the line FC Therefore the line FC is also medial But since the line FG is commensurable in square with the line CD therefore the lines, FC and FG, are commensurable with one-another in square But since the ratio of the line CD to the line FC is that of the rectangle contained by the two lines, CD and FG, to that contained by the two lines, FG and FC, if, then, you make the two lines, CD and FC then bases, and the line FG then height[163], it is clear that] the rectangle contained by the two lines, CD and FG, is commensurable with that contained by FG and FC But the rectangle contained by CD and FG is rational Therefore the rectangle contained by FG and FC is rational Therefore the line CG is a first apotome of a medial - But if the square upon CD is incommensurable with the rectangle DF then the ratio of the line CD to the line FC is that of a medial area to a medial area incommensurable with it They (i. e, CD and FC) are, therefore, commensurable with one-another in square [only] The line FC is therefore, medial Therefore the two lines, FC and FG, are commensurable with one-another in square [only], since each of them is commensurable with the line CD in square [only]. But because the line CD is incommensurable Ms. 42 r⁰ with the line FC in length, and the ratio of the line CD to the line FC is that of the rectangle contained by the two lines, CD and FG, to that contained by FG and FC, therefore these two rectangles are also incommensurable with one-another. But the rectangle EG is rational. Therefore the rectangle contained by FC and FG is not rational. But the two lines, FC and FG, are medial lines commensurable in square. Therefore the rectangle contained by them is medial. Therefore the line CG is a second apotome of a medial. If, then, the square upon a first apotome of a medial or the square upon that which produces with a rational area a medial whole, be applied to a medial line, it produces as breadth a first or a second apotome of a medial.

§ 32. Again let the line AB be one of the two remaining irrational lines, either a second apotome of a medial, or that which produces with a medial area a medial whole, let the line CD be a medial, and the rectangle DG equal to the square upon AB. and let the line LM be rational, and the rectangle, MP equal to the square upon AB. The line LP is, then either a third or a sixth apotome. according as the line AB is either the third or the sixth of the irrational lines that are formed by subtraction. Let OP be the annex of LP and the rectangle EG equal to the rectangle, NP. Then since the line LP is either a third or a sixth apotome, both of the lines, LO and OP, are incommensurable with the given rational line LM in length, but are rational and commensurable with it in square.[104] Both the rectangles, MO and NP, are, therefore, medial. Therefore both the rectangles, DF and EG, are medial. But since the square upon CD is medial. it is commensurable either with the rectangle DF or with the rectangle EG, or it is incommensurable with both of them. It cannot be commensurable with both of them. For, then, the rectangle DF would be commensurable with the rectangle EG, i e., the rectangle MO would be commensurable with [the rectangle] NP i e, the line LO would be commensurable with the line OP [in length]; but these were given incommensurable in length — Let the square upon CD be

commensurable with one of the rectangles DF or EG. Then
since both the rectangles, DF and EG, are medial but incommensurable with one-another, therefore the line FC is commensurable with the line FG in square [only]. But since the
square upon CD is commensurable with one of the rectangles,
DF or EG the line CD is commensurable with one of the lines,
FC or FG, in length. Therefore one of them is medial. But they
are commensurable in square. Therefore the other is medial,
since the area (i. e., square) that is commensurable with a medial
area is medial, and the side of a square equal to a medial area,
medial. The lines, FC and FG are, therefore, medial lines
commensurable in square [only]. But since the rectangle contained by CD and FC is medial, and likewise that contained by
CD and FG therefore the rectangle contained by FC and FG
is necessarily commensurable with one of them since the line
CD is commensurable with one of the lines FC or FG, in length.
Therefore the rectangle contained by FC and FG is medial.
Therefore the line CG is a second apotome of a medial — But
if the square upon CD is incommensurable with both of the
rectangles DF and EG[165] then the ratio of the line CD to each
of the two lines, FC and FG, is that of a medial area to a medial
area incommensurable with it. Therefore both the lines, FC
and FG, are commensurable with the line CD in square [only].
But because the rectangle DF is incommensurable with the
rectangle EG, and the line FC incommensurable with the line
FG in length, therefore the two lines, FC and FG, are medial
lines commensurable in square [only], and the rectangle contained by them either rational or medial. Therefore the line
CG is either a first or a second apotome of a medial. — Our
investigation, then, has shown that the squares upon everyone
of the irrational lines that are formed by subtraction produce,
when applied to medial lines, either a first or a second apotome
of a medial, just as the squares upon the irrational lines that are

Page 66

Ms 42 v°

11*

formed by addition, produce the two lines that are the contraries of these, namely, the first and second bimedial

§ 33 Various kinds of applications (i. e , of the squares upon irrational lines to a given irrational line) can, however, be made. If, for example, I apply the square upon a medial line to anyone of the lines that are formed by addition. the breadth is one of the lines that are formed by subtraction, the contrary, namely, of the line formed by addition, as we have shown above[166] And if I apply it to anyone of the lines that are formed by subtraction, the breadth is that line formed by addition which is the contrary of the one formed by subtraction. For if one of the two straight lines containing a medial area, in this case, namely, the [area of a] square upon a medial, be one of the irrational lines that are formed by addition, the other is its contrary of the lines that are formed by subtraction. and conversely, as we have demonstrated before[167] We can also determine the breadths, if we apply the squares upon the irrationals that are formed by addition to the lines that are formed by subtraction, and conversely, if we apply the squares upon the lines that are formed by subtraction to the lines that are formed by addition Whenever then, we make these applications [of squares] to a medial line, or to the lines formed by addition. [or to those formed by subtraction[168]], we find many of the definitions which govern these things (i e , ultimately, the irrational lines under discussion) and recognize various kinds of propositions[169]

§ 34. We will content ourselves at this point with our discussion, since it is [but] a concise[170] outline of the whole science of irrational lines For we now know the reason why these applications are necessary. [to show], namely the commensurabilities (i. e., of the irrationals)[171], and we are also well enough aware of the fact that the irrationals are not only many but infinite in number, the lines formed by addition and by subtraction as well as the medials, as Euclid proved [with respect to the last-mentioned][172], when he established that "from a medial [straight] line there arise irrational [straight] lines infinite [in number], and none of them is the same as any of the preceeding[173] But if from a medial line there can arise lines infinite in number, it is obvious to everyone what must be said concerning those that can arise from the rest of the irrationals. It can be affirmed, namely, that there arise from them infinite times a finite number[174]

§ 35 But we have discussed the irrationals sufficiently. We can investigate by means of the facts that have been presented, any problems that may be set, as, for example — If a rational and an irrational line be given, which line is the mean proportional[175] between them, and which line the third proportional to them, whether the rational line be taken as the first (i e , of the two lines) or the second ? Each of the irrationals is dealt with, in its turn, analogously For example, if a rational line and a binomial or an apotome be given, we can find which line is the mean proportional between them, and which is the third proportional to them and equally so with the rest of the lines. Also if a medial line is given, and then a rational or one of the irrational lines, we can find which line is the mean proportional between them, and which the third proportional to them For since the breadths produced by the application [of their squares] can be determined[176], and we know that the rectangle contained by the extremes is equal to the square upon the mean, it is easy for us to do this

The end of the second book and the end of the commentary Page 68 on the tenth book of the treatise of Euclid, translated by Abū 'Uthmān Al-Dimishqī. The praise is to God May he bless Muhammad and his family and keep them. Written by Ahmad Ibn Muhammad Ibn 'Abd Al-Jalīl in Shīrāz in the month, Jumādā 1 of the year 358 H (= March, 969).

NOTES.

[1] The phrase, "In the name of God, the Compassionate, the Merciful", given in the MS., is obviously an addition of the Muslim translator, or, perhaps, of the copyist

[2] WOEPCKE read *Mu'wwratun*, translating, *Corruptible* (Essai, p 44, 111, para 11). SUTER read, *Mu'auwwratun* or *Mu'auwaratun* (note 138), translating, *Corruptible* or *Corrupted* (Vergangliche, Verdorbene) But, in the first place, matter is not conceived of as corruptible or corrupted in Platonism, or Neoplatonism, or even in Neopythagoreanism generally (See the *Timaeus*, 52a) In the second place, *Mu'wwratun*, or *Mu'auwwratun*, or *Mu'auwaratun*, is applied in this sense only to men as *depraved*, so far as I can find, and even this is a late usuage On the other hand, matter is *Destitute of quality or form* (Cf Numenius, CCXCV, *Carentem qualitate* and Plato's *Timaeus* 50a—52a, esp. 50e and 51a πάντων ἐκτὸς εἰδῶν), and *Mu'wwzatun* means *Needy or Destitute* Cf Part I, para 2 (end) and para. 3 (W p 29, l 3)

[3] Cf Part I, para 9 (beginning)

[4] Cf J L HEIBERG, *Euclidis Elementa*, Vol V, p 415, ll. 2—6

[5] That is, the areas which constitute by addition or subtraction those areas to which the squares upon the irrationals are equal, as in propositions 71—72, 108—110 Literally translated the last clause would run — "On condition that (or provided that) these areas are parts". The syntax of the Arabic is simple, SUTER's note 140 notwithstanding.

[6] Cf the previous note The reference is to propositions 21—22, 54—59, 91—96, where the areas to which the squares upon the irrationals are equal, are not compound areas (W. p 30, l 7)

[7] Book X, props 22, 60—65, 97—102.

[8] Book X, props 71—72, cf. 108—110. I read *Ka-l-Mujidd* (like one who is zealous) instead of *Ka-l-Muhiddun*? (W p 30, l 12)

[9] a) *Compound lines* is acceptable, these are the lines that are formed by addition But *apotomes* is incorrect, for it is spoken about the lines that are formed by subtraction G. J See Bemerkungen, page 25

b) The MS, however, gives *Munfasilatun*, which is the regular word throughout for *apotomes* Either, then, we have an extension of the term, apotome, to include all the irrational lines that are formed by subtraction, or a false or dubious translation of the original Greek term, whatever it was, or an error of the copyist The term occurs with the same meaning in para 13 of this Part (beginning). Perhaps, as Dr JUNGE suggests, we should read *Mufassalatun* in both cases, which would, then, correspond to *Murakkabatun* (W p 30, ll 15—16)

[10] Book X, props 108—110

[11] Book X, prop 21

[12] In the *Lisān al-'arab* (Bulaq, 1299–1308H), Part I, p 191 (top) *Awta'u* is explained as *Overcoming by proof or evidence*, or as *Struggling with and throwing down or making fast*; in this context, therefore, *To establish*. (W p 30, l 19)

[13] Book X, prop 19

[14] Book X, prop. 21

[15] Book X, prop 24

[16] Book X, prop 25

[17] a) Book X, prop 34, cf prop 40
b) It is the line the square upon which is equal to a rational plus a medial area, la_5 See Bemerkungen, p 25. G J

[18] a) Book X, props 33 & 35; cf props 39 & 41
b) That is, the major, and the line the square upon which is equal to two medial areas, twice two lines See Bemerkungen, p 25 G J

[19] The last three clauses are somewhat tautological The commentator, however, wishes to explain the phrase, 'Wholly incommensurable"

[20] That is, the line. What SUTER is translating, I do not know This paragraph is really the conclusion of the previous one and should be included in it The MS has no punctuation points after *Aydan* (also), but has two dots (thus,) after *Al-asmi* (name). Cf. Book X, prop 21 (W p 32, l 2)

[21] See Bemerkungen, page 24 G J

[22] Cf Book X, props 71 & 72

[23] Cf. Part 1, paras 21 & 4 (W. p 20, last line ff and W p 5, l. 7) That is, the medials in this case

[24] In this case the irrationals formed by addition

[25] This is not wholly correct The lines that are formed by addition, are co-ordinate with those that are formed by subtraction G J

26 a) That is, all the possible cases are given. SUTER has misunderstood the Arabic and omitted the phrase, *commensurable in length*, accordingly (W. p. 32, ll. 9-11).

b) The following lines show that the text means *commensurable with one-another* and not *commensurable with the assumed line*. G. J.

27 The medial, that is, having already been discussed.

28 Book X, prop. 15.

29 Book X, Def. 3 and prop. 23.

30 According to *The Dictionary of Technical Terms* etc., A. SPRENGER, Vol. II, p. 1219 (foot), *Qismatun* has the same general meaning as *Nasibun* (Substitute etc.). *Istaʿmala* can mean *To feign a thing* (W. p. 32, ll. 18-19).

31 With modern signs this proposition is very simple. Let the sum of the squares $= a$, twice the rectangle, b, where a and b are rational in the antique (i.e., Euclidian) sense (as also in the modern). The whole line is then $= \sqrt{a - b}$, rational in the antique (Euclidian) sense. G. J.

32 a) Book X, prop. 71. See Bemerkungen, page 24.

b) Always taking what was stated at the beginning of para 7 (Part II), as granted, namely, that the lines are commensurable in square with the assumed line and therefore with one-another. G. J.

33 Book X, prop. 59, Lemma.

34 Book X, prop. 71. See Bemerkungen, page 24.

35 Book X, prop. 72. See Bemerkungen, page 24.

36 Using the same letters, but following the text and figure given both in the MS. and by WOEPCKE, this passage runs — "Then the sum of the squares upon LN and NM is commensurable with the rectangle contained by LN and NM", and so on throughout. SUTER's reconstruction simplifies the operation and probably represents the true text, since the following proposition in para 8 (W., p. 34, l. 15) uses the same figure, but gives the lines as LM and MN.

37 Book X, prop. 15.

38 Let the line LN $= x + y$, where x^2 has to y^2 the ratio of a number to a number, but x to y not so. Presupposed is $x^2 + y^2$ commensurable with xy. But because x^2 is comm. with y^2, therefore $x^2 + y^2$ is comm. with x^2, and therefore x^2 with xy, or x with y, -which was not granted. G. J.

39 Cf. Part II, para. 7 (beginning).

40 Cf. the foregoing figure. The explanation of the following in modern signs is the same as in Note 31 above (Part II). G. J.

41 Book X, prop. 19.

[42] a) Book X, prop. 39.

b) The explanation of the word *Major* in the text is hardly true $\sqrt{a} + \sqrt{b}$ is, indeed, *Major*, where $a > \sqrt{b}$. But $\sqrt{a} - \sqrt{b}$ is called *Minor*, and here the rational part, a, is also greater than the medial, $\sqrt{b}$ — Cf NESSELMANN, *Algebra der Griechen*, Berlin 1842, S. 176. G. J.

[43] Book X, prop. 40.

[44] Book X, prop. 41.

[45] Cf para 7, above, Part II, towards the end (W., p. 33, last line, to p. 34, l. 1)

[46] Cf Book X, props 36 to 38 and 39 to 41 respectively. The Arabic says simply, "The two additions of lines", i. e., the addition of lines commensurable in square and the addition of lines incommensurable in square, as in these propositions. The Arabic may be read as either *Tarkibāni hutūtin* or *Tarkibāni hutūtan* (Cf. de Sacy's Grammar, 2nd Ed., Vol. II, p. 183, and FLEISCHER's *Kl. Schr.* Vol. 1, Teil I, p. 637 on de Sacy). On the use of the dual of the infinitive, cf. FLEISCHER, ibid p 633 to de Sacy, II, 175. (W. p 35, l 16) (W. p. 35, ll 16—17)

[47] Cf. Book X, props 71 and 72 respectively, 1) the addition of a rational and a medial area, 2) the addition of two medial areas. Cf the previous note on the Arabic. (W., p 35, l 17).

[48] That is, in props 71 and 72. Therefore *Maqālatun* means here *Section* and not *treatise* (W. p 35, l 18)

[49] Cf Book X, props 36 to 38.

[50] Cf Book X, props 39 to 41.

[51] WOEPCKE's conjecture (p 36, note 3) is manifestly correct. Cf Book X, props 37 and 38.

[52] Cf Book X, props 39 to 41. SUTER's note (no. 164) is incorrect. The Arabic means *the sum of the squares upon them*, literally it runs — "The area composed of the sum of the squares upon them", out of which SUTER somehow or other gets *areas* (W. p 36, l 8)

[53] As in Book X, props 36 to 38.

[54] I read *) ahtajja(i)*, not *) ahtaj* (need) (W p 36, l 18)

[55] The whole argument of the paragraph shows that Pappus is here referring to the lines. SUTER in note 167 maintains that this is incorrect, and that the reference should be to the squares upon the separate lines. But if the squares upon the lines are rational or medial, so then are the lines; and Pappus may quite well have stated the problem in this way. — See also Bemerkungen p 30

⁵⁶ SUTER omits this last sentence without remark But the sense is obviously that given above. *Al-Murakkabu minhā* can mean *the compound line* made up of LM and MN as well as the sum of the squares upon them (W p 37, ll 16—17)

⁵⁷ See Bemerkungen, page 24.

⁵⁸ Which, as SUTER adds, is impossible

⁵⁹ That is, so as to curtail the construction, which is obvious from the immediately preceding proposition, viz - , let LM² and MN² be medial, and let there be applied to AB a rectangle = LM² + MN², and let there be cut off from it the rectangle AF = LM², so that EC = MN². Therefore AF and EC are medial

⁷⁰ Because, as SUTER says, two rational lines commensurable in square only form a medial rectangle

⁶¹ Cf SUTER, note 172, who supposes that in the propositions just given Pappus tries to set up another mode of division for the irrationals of the first hexad (as he puts it)

⁶² These propositions appear in Euclid implicitly but not explicitly. G. J.

⁶³ That is, without qualification by any such term as rational or medial.

⁶⁴ Cf Book X, Def. 2

⁶⁵ That is, the six irrationals formed by addition (Cf Book X, props 71 and 72

⁶⁶ Cf Book X, props 19 and 21 respectively

⁶⁷ See the whole discussion from para 4 to para 8 of Part II, where the order and number of these irrationals are discussed (W., p 30, foot, to p 35).

⁶⁸ That is, the six irrationals formed by addition

⁶⁹ a) That is, one of the six formed by subtraction.
b) If $x + y$ is an irrational formed by addition, then $x - y$ is an irrational formed by subtraction; granted $x > y$ G J

⁷⁰ That is, the greater and the less of the two terms (or lines) that added together produce one of the six irrationals formed by addition, considered as a whole line and as a part of it as above See Bemerkungen, page 24, for the various irrationals.

⁷¹ *Nazīr* may mean *like, equal, corresponding to, or contrary*. In the next paragraph (W p 40, l 19) the apotome and the binomial are said to be *contraries* of one-another (— *Wāḥiduhuma yukhāliju-l-ākhara* —), in paragraph 16 (W p 44, ll 13, 20, 21; p 45, l 1) the lines formed by addition and subtraction are said to be *contraries* respectively of one-another, and the like is asserted of them in paragraphs 19, 22, 23 (W. p 47, l. 14; p. 48, l 23; p. 53, ll. 11, 13), only here the word, *Muqā-*

balun (-opposite, contrary), replaces the *Yukhālifu* of paragraph 16. Contraries, moreover, may be homogeneous, belonging to the same genus at opposite poles of it (Cf Aristotle's *Metaph.*, 1055a. 3ff., esp. 23ff.). The meaning of *Nazir*, therefore, would seem to be *contrary*. I have used, however, *like (or contrary)*, throughout, inasmuch as Binomials etc and Apotomes etc are *likes*, since they are produced by the same terms or lines, but *contraries*, since they are produced by addition and subtraction respectively (W p. 39, l 19)

[72] Cf Part II, note 9

[73] AB and BC are, therefore, rational and commensurable in square only.

[74] a) Cf prop 7, Book II of Euclid, which gives the positions of AB and BC as in the figure above, which is given by SUTER, but not in the MS nor in WOEPCKE.

b) It is $AB^2 + BC^2 - 2AB \cdot BC = AC^2$, since $AC = (AB - BC)^2$ G. J.

[75] AB and BC being commensurable in square $(AB + BC$, a binomial)

[76] The clause, "Now the squares . . . . . medial *(Fa-Murabba'u . mawsitan)*, probably represents a Greek genitive absolute construction Pappus shows by Euclid's prop 7, Book II, that if $AB + BC$ is a binomial, then $AB - BC$ is an apotome For $AB^2 + BC^2 - 2AB \cdot BC + AC^2$ Therefore $AC^2 = AB^2 + BC^2 - 2AB \cdot BC$ But $AB^2 + BC^2$ is rational and $2AB \cdot BC$ is medial, and AB^2 is $> BC^2$ by the square upon a straight line commensurable with AB Therefore $\sqrt{AC^2}$ (i e, $AC = AB - BC$) is an apotome See prop 108 and compare it with prop 71 (W p. 40, ll 9 - 11)

[77] Cf note 71, Part II

[78] Note that $AB + BC$ is in this case a first bimedial Cf Book X, props. 109 and 71

[79] See note 76, Part II If $AB + BC$ is a first bimedial, $AB - BC$ is a first apotome of a medial

[80] Cf. the statement of the first of this series of propositions in para 13, Part II (W, p 40, ll 8—9)· 'Let AB produce with BC a binomial'' The text is quite sound as it stands, and does not need to be emended to, "Let AB and BC be commensurable in square", as SUTER erroneously suggests (note 183).

[81] WOEPCKE's suggestion (p 41, note 2) that this phrase be added to the text is sound, if not exactly necessary. In fact, since $AB + BC$ is given as a second bimedial, the previous phrase is also unnecessary. But both are perfectly sound consequences of the given fact, and if the first be given, so should the second.

[28] It does not seem necessary to insert the phrase, *Murabba'ai . . .*

. *min*, as WOEPCKE does (p 41, ll. 7—8, enclosed thus, (3) ...
.. (3)) The sense of the Arabic is quite plain without it It
says, ' The sum of the squares etc being greater than twice the rectangle,
it is, then, the square upon the line AC" That is, it is greater by the
square upon AC

[83] That is, the lines, AB and BC G. J.

[84] That is, if $AB + BC$ is a second bimedial, $AB - BC$ is a second
apotome of a medial Cf Book X, props. 110 and 72

[85] That is, if $AB + BC$ is a major, $AB - BC$ is a minor. Cf Book X,
props. 108 and 71 AB^2 is, in this case, greater than BC^2 by the square
upon a line incommensurable with AB

[86] AB and BC being incommensurable in square

[87] Cf. Book X, props 109 and 71 If $AB + BC$ is the side of a square $= a$
rational + a medial area, $AB - BC$ is the line which produces with
a rational area a medial whole

[88] Cf Book X, props 110 and 72 If $AB + BC$ is the side of a square $= 2$
medial areas, $AB - BC$ is the line which produces with a medial area
a medial whole

[89] SUTER translates as if the Arabic word were a singular, probably for the
sake of clarity.

[90] I accept WOEPCKE's substitution of the marginal reading and translate
accordingly, although the reading of the text could be considered satisfactory and rendered thus -- "That a rational area remains from a
rational area (i e, in this case) (W, p 42, l 13, note 4)

[91] a) Two lines, since as the following sentence informs us, there are two
cases of subtraction of a medial from a rational
b) The reason must be sought in the relation of the medial, $\sqrt{b}$, to the
rational, a. For $\sqrt{a} - \sqrt{b}$ produces the apotome, when $a^2 - b$ $a^2 = a$
square number a square number Otherwise the minor arises See
para 24 (Part II) and Bemerkungen, page 25 G J

[92] I have supplied the words within brackets for the sake of clarity.

[93] The words within brackets, from "*The line*" to "*Arises,*" have been suggested by WOEPCKE and incorporated in his text, except "*Area*," which is
obviously to be supplied The Arabic text is, as SUTER says (Note 186,
p 48), "stark verdorben" WOEPCKE's conjectures, however, are,
from the mathematical point of view, necessary and, from the linguistic
point of view, quite acceptable (W p 43, ll. 3—4, notes 3 & 4).

[94] Cf. Part II, para 9 (W pp 35—36) for this statement In that paragraph Pappus asserts that Euclid should have treated the *compound
lines* after this method; and here and in the next paragraph he points

out how clear then would be the homogeneity, with the opposition, of *compound lines* and *those formed by subtraction* "*Two*" must be supplied after "*In each case*" (*Fi kulli wāhidin*) in the Arabic (W., p 43, 1 6).

[95] Cf the previous note and Book X, props. 36 41. These last two sentences connect para 14 with para 9 and also refer to the beginning of para 14 itself.

[96] Cf Book X, props 36 and 73

[97] Cf Book X, props 37 and 74

[98] Cf Book X, props 38 and 75

[99] Cf Book X, props 33, 39, and 76 The sum of the squares is rational and equal to the greater area, as is stated under "Sixthly" (prop 35)

[100] Cf Book X, props 34, 40, and 77 The sum of the squares is medial and equal to the greater area

[101] Cf Book X, props 35, 41, and 78 The sum of the squares is *medial* and equal to the greater area

[102] Cf Part II, para. 7

[103] Cf Book X, props 71 and 108 The lines formed by addition are respectively the likes (or contraries) of those formed by subtraction, as Pappus says towards the end of the paragraph As SUTER says (note 190), Pappus means by, 'Are taken', the kind of relation which the areas have with one-another, whether they are to be added together or subtracted from one-another See Part II, note 71, for 'Contraries'

[104] Cf Book X, props 36—38 and 39—41, 73 75 and 76 78 As Pappus says immediately after, the first three of each kind are respectively the contraries of the last three

[105] Cf Book X, props 109, 108, and 71 (parts 1 and 3). In the one case the rational is the greater, the medial the less, in another the medial is the greater, the rational the less, and in the third case both the greater and the less are medials SUTER's notes 191 and 192 show that he did not understand the Arabic Pappus now goes on to state what lines are the likes (or contraries) of one-another in these different respects

[106] That is, the irrationals formed by addition and subtraction fall into groups of three according as the areas are, 1) rational and medial, 2) medial and rational, and 3) medial and medial. G J

[107] SUTER points out (note 193) that the arithmetical mean by means of which the binomial is produced, is not mentioned If this failure be due to the copyist, it means that he omitted a whole line, which probably began like the succeeding one with the Arabic words, *Wa-idha akhadha* (And if he took), whence his omission Perhaps, however, Pappus himself overlooked this case or the translator failed to

reproduce it. Part 1, para 1 (W., p. 2, ll 2—3) says that *Theaetetus* divided the irrational lines according to the different means ascribing the medial line to geometry, the binomial to arithmetic, and the apotome to harmony.

[108] Part I, para 19 (beginning) (W., p 19, l 7 ff) explains what Pappus means by this clause He says there — "He (i e, Euclid) always assigns the general term, 'medial, to a particular species (i e, of the medial line) For the medial line the square upon which is equal to the area contained by two rational lines commensurable in length, is necessarily a mean proportional to these two rationals etc, but he does not name either of those [lines] medial, but only the line the square upon which is equal to the given area" (i e, the one contained by two rationals commensurable in square only) (W. p 45, ll 7 –8)

[109] Cf Book X, prop 21.

[110] The Arabic has simply, "The remaining proportioning' (Infinitive) The infinitive gives the abstract idea. The context shows that we must interpret as above (W p 45, ll 13- 14)

[111] WOEPCKE (W. p 45, l 4, foot, note 3) substitutes *Wa-kāna* for the MS's *Li-anna*. The form of the argument demands *Fa-li-anna* I have supplied, '*And so commensurable with them*", after the analogy of the argument given in the second succeeding case (W., p 46, l 2) The Arabic would run: — "*Wa-mushārikan la-humā*' See J L HEIBERG, *Euclidis Elementa*, Vol. V, p 551, ll 2 –19.

[112] The same phrase is used here and in the following enunciations as in the first instance I adopt '*Arithmetical mean*" for the sake of brevity

[113] That is, common to all the arithmetical means taken above

[114] The text of the MS, given by WOEPCKE, is obviously corrupt. It says — "Therefore these (i e, the various means, or, perhaps, the required irrationals) are *incommensurable* with the irrationals of one order or another" The demonstrative pronoun, *Hadhihi* (W, p. 47, l 7), which is feminine, must refer back either to the required irrationals or to the "*Them*' of "*All of them*" (i. e, the various means), and the latter is, logically, the more probable The substitution of the text's "Incommensurable" *(Mubāyinatun)* for the logically required "Commensurable" *(Mushārikatun)* cannot easily be explained. Perhaps the thread of the argument was lost, the antecedent of *Hadhihi* not being clear Possibly the error occurred in the Greek text.

115 That is, if a and b are the extremes and c the mean, then $ac + bc = 2ab$, or $c = \dfrac{2ab}{a + b}$. — Cf Bemerkungen p. 30.

116 Cf. Part II, note 71.

117 Cf Part II, paras 21 and 22

118 The next case (W., p 48, l. 6) shows that WOEPCKE's conjecture here (W., p 47, l 22, note 5) is incorrect. We must read — 'Fa-in kāna khattā, AB, BC, mantaqam fi-l-quwwat mushtarikam etc'

119 Cf. Part II, para 17, beginning (W., p 45, l 3ff).

120 Here, then, is used the Euclidian proposition, X, 112 The further propositions which are presupposed, over the other five lines that are formed by addition and the corresponding ones formed by subtraction, are first proved in para 21 G J

121 That is, will meet DF within the points, D and F Both WOEPCKE and the MS have AF But what succeeds shows that SUTER is correct in reading DF

122 Cf the previous paragraph, first sentence

123 Cf Book X, prop 112, "The square upon a rational straight line applied etc"

124 SUTER's note, 208, pointing out that Euclid does not prove these propositions, nor Pappus, but that they assume them to be self-evident, is false Euclid, X, 112, proves the whole of this G J

125 That is, as in the previous paragraph with the same figure

126 SUTER quite correctly (note 210) supplies the words within brackets, which do not appear in WOEPCKE's text nor in the MS See 'Notes on the Text" (W p 51, l 15)

127 The figure is not given in the MS. or WOEPCKE I follow SUTER

128 That is, in Part II, para 22 (W, p 51, l 8ff)

129 At the beginning of this paragraph Therefore CD is one of the lines formed by subtraction and of the same order as FB

130 Cf Part II, note 71

131 A proposition is used here, which is correct, but which neither Euclid nor our commentator enunciates, namely, 'It a line is commensurable in square with an irrational line formed by addition (or subtraction), then it is also an irrational line formed by addition (or subtraction) of the same order, G J

132 Cf Part II, paras 19 and 20 (W, p 47, l 8ff)

133 We must either read, 'Al-Khutūti-llati min ismaini wa-l-munfaṣilati-l-muqābalati laha", and translate as above, or, "Al-Khutti-lladhi min ismaini wa-l-munfaṣil l-muqābali lahu", and translate, "Points of

difference between the binomial and the apotome, its contrary". The former gives a sense more in keeping with the contents of the paragraph than the latter. Read 'Yatl'u", not 'Nahnu'. The last letter is certainly a 'Ya" (W, p. 55, ll. 3—4).

134 For this and the following sentences cf. Euclid, Book X, Definitions 11, 1—6 (See HEIBERG, Vol. III, p. 136, HEATH, Vol. III, pp. 101—102)

135 Cf. Part II, para 12 (Beginning, W, p. 39, l. 9ff). If $AB + BC$ — B is a binomial, then $AB - BC$, i. e., AC, is an apotome. "Al-Muntasila" (W, p. 55, l. 17) is an absolute nominative, which receives its syntactical relation when it is caught up and repeated in the phrase, "Huwa munfasilun" (W, p. 55, l. 19)

136 Ma'na means definition, as may be seen from BESTHORN and HEIBERG. Euclidis Elementa. Al-Hajjaj, Vol I, pp. 40—41. Cf. also the present text (W, p. 6, l. 7, p. 10, l. 21, p. 11, l. 1, p. 27, l. 17). Al-Akwān according to M. HORTEN, Z. D. M. G., 1911, Vol. 65, p. 539, means die Formen des veranderlichen Seins, or Seinsformen (W, p. 56, l. 7). It might be rendered, however, by the form of their being or existence, i. e., in time and space

137 For this proposition as also for paragraphs 27—32 (Part II) see Bemerkungen, p. 31

138 Since LM is rational and $MP - AB^2$ (Cf. Euclid, Book X, prop. 60 G. J.)

139 Since LM is rational and $MP - AB^2$ (Cf. Euclid, Book X, prop. 63 G. J.)

140 That is, the squares upon a binomial and a major. Cf. Part II, para 25

141 Cf. Euclid, Book X, prop. 71.

142 The names of the two rectangles have been interchanged. EG should be the one mentioned first. Cf. the next paragraph, 28 (W., p. 60, l. 15)

143 In the previous paragraph. Cf. Euclid, Book X, prop. 25. CF is medial and commensurable with CD in square

144 One would expect this sentence to begin, 'Wa-dhalika innahu li-anna', as the corresponding sentence of the next part of the proof (14 lines later, W, p. 59, l. 19) has, "Wa-dhalika innahu lamma" "Wa-dhalika innahu" should, therefore, I think, be inserted in the text (W. p. 59, l. 7).

145 Cf. Euclid, Book X, prop. 37.

146 It is to be shown that CG is a first or a second bimedial, i. e., is of the form, $\sqrt[4]{b} (a + \sqrt{b})$ or $\sqrt[4]{c} (a + \sqrt{b})$. In the first case the rectangle contained by the two parts (terms) is rational, namely,

$\sqrt[4]{b} . a \sqrt[4]{b} \sqrt{b} = ab$; in the second case it is medial, namely, $\sqrt[4]{c} . a \sqrt[4]{c} \sqrt{b} = a . \sqrt{bc}$ — This rectangle is geometrically $CF . FG$. The rectangle $CF . CD$ is in any case rational. The two cases can also, therefore, be distinguished from one-another, according as FG is commensurable with CD in length or not, or, — and the commentator always begins with this —, according as the rectangle EG is commensurable with CD^2 or not (G J

147 SUTER translates correctly, but has failed to remark that his translation does not give the Arabic text as it stands. This last clause in the Arabic is conjunctive with the two previous and not the apodosis of a conditional sentence. We must read, therefore, '*Fa-Khattu* ' and not, '*Wa-Khattu* ", as in WOEPCKE and the MS. (W., p 60, l 20)

148 Cf the previous paragraph on this point at note 145. SUTER does not give the correct connection of the Arabic clauses

149 To make sense of this clause and to make it correspond with paras 27—32, the Arabic must mean that neither of the two terms of these binomials is commensurable with the line LM (G J

150 Dr JUNGE points out that we must translate thus in order to give a meaning to this clause. The Arabic reads, "*Wa-li-anna*", which would ordinarily be translated, "*But since* etc", the beginning of a new statement altogether. But the clause obviously qualifies the previous one, as WOEPCKE felt, when he suggested that we read '*Li-anna*', instead of "*Wa-li-anna*' This suggestion, however, does not remove the difficulty. It is probable that the Greek at this point had some particle such as ὅτε or ἐπειδή —, which the Arab translator understood in its causal instead of its temporal sense, thereby introducing confusion into the text (W p 61, l 15)

151 Namely, the one commensurable with CD^2.

152 Cf Book X, prop 25 CG, therefore, is either a first or a second bimedial (Cf props 37 and 38), and Pappus has demonstrated his proposition, SUTER notwithstanding (See his note 232)

153 That is, of those formed by addition

154 SUTER deems it necessary to give the construction of these rectangles, but the sense is quite clear, as the text stands

155 The reading of the MS. ("But because the rectangle is rational etc") is obviously incorrect. It assumes what is to be proved, namely, the rationality of the rectangle MO. We must read simply "*But*" ('*Wa-lakin*", or better, perhaps, just '*Wa*") and omit the "*Because*" ('*Li-anna*") SUTER did not understand the argument, as his translation of the next clause shows

¹⁵⁶ According to definition. See Euclid, Book X, Defs III, 1 & 4 (HEI-BERG, Vol V, p 255; HEATH, Vol III, p. 177) (W p. 62, l. 15).

¹⁵⁷ Cf Part II, para 27 (W, p 59, l 4ff)

¹⁵⁸ Better to read 'Fa-hadhāni' and not 'Wa-hadhāni' as in the MS. and in WOEPCKE, since this clause gives the result of the facts stated in the two former clauses (W p 63, l 13)

¹⁵⁹ So runs the Arabic text, referring evidently back to the last figure given. SUTER translates as if it were a part of the construction The sense is the same in both cases

¹⁶⁰ That is, according as AB is a first apotome or a medial or that which produces with a rational area a medial whole

¹⁶¹ According to definition (See Euclid, Book X, Defs III, 2 & 5, HEI-BERG, Vol V, p 255; HEATH, Vol III, p 177)

¹⁶² Cf Book X, props 24 and 25

¹⁶³ Cf Part II, para 27, second figure

¹⁶⁴ According to definition (See Euclid, Book X, Defs III, 3 & 6, HEIBERG, Vol V, p 255, HEATH, Vol III, p 177).

¹⁶⁵ SUTER's note, 237, that the text here is corrupt, is correct. We must read 'Li-kulli wahidin' (W p. 66, l 1)

¹⁶⁶ Cf Part II, para 21, first sentence (W, p 49 foot) and the whole of para 23 (W, p. 53, l. 12ff)

¹⁶⁷ Cf. the previous note

¹⁶⁸ SUTER quite rightly adds this phrase The copyist probably inadvertently omitted it by haplography See "Notes on the Text" (W p. 66, l 21).

¹⁶⁹ Cf, e g, Part II, para 26 etc I end paragraph 34 here instead of two sentences later, as WOEPCKE, by so doing, has separated two sentences which in the Arabic are dependent and conjunctive.

¹⁷⁰ Read 'Mūnzatun'', not 'Muwahhadhatun'' (W., p. 67, l. 1)

¹⁷¹ a) The MS reads "Quwan", apparently, written, however, with an Alif at the end instead of the usual Ya The marginal reading is 'Hiya'', which with WOEPCKE I have adopted The MS text could be translated, "And the possibilities of commensurability" (i e, which the irrationals show) (W p 67, l 2)

b) The allusion is, apparently, to the terms of an irrational line (formed by addition or subtraction), whether they are commensurable to one-another or to the given rational line G J

¹⁷² Cf. Book X, prop. 115.

¹⁷³ One has only to insert a negative into the Arabic of this clause in WOEPCKE's text to reproduce the Greek of the last clause of propo-

sition 115; and in the MS there stands before ' *Bi-Hasabi*", ' *Lahu*", scored out apparently by two almost perpendicular strokes, but with an asterisk above it calling attention to some fact or other. The asterisk does not refer to the elimination of the two words, *La* and *Hu* This is not the practice of the copyist It calls attention to the fact that the *Hu* is scored out by the left-hand stroke, and that the right-hand stroke is an *Alif*, making with the *Lam* the negative *La*. Read, therefore, "*La bi-Hasabi*" (W , p 67, l 6)

[174] a) SUTER rightly calls attention to the fact that the text given by WOEPCKE has a meaning that is not to be taken in a strict mathematical sense, namely, "Infinite times an infinite number", since the correct mathematical number is $12 . \iota = \infty$ (Not 13ι, as SUTER has it; only the lines formed by addition and subtraction are referred to in this clause) But the MS gives, as WOEPCKE shows (P 67, note 4), "*Ghairu Mutanāhiyatin mirāran mutanāhiyatin*", which may be rendered as above and satisfy the mathematical requirements

b) For Euclid the irrational lines were already infinite in number The binomials, for example, were $1 + \sqrt{2}, 1 + \sqrt{3}, 1 + \sqrt{5}, 1 + \sqrt{6}$ ad infinitum On the other hand the groups of irrationals were, for Euclid, 13. Our commentator, however, treats of the number of the groups The trinomial $(1 + \sqrt{2} + \sqrt{3})$, the quadrinomial $(1 + \sqrt{2} + \sqrt{3} + \sqrt{5})$, are ever new groups, the number of which is infinite (G J

[175] SUTER translates The geometric mean", but the Arabic, strictly speaking, has only "The mean proportional" without specifying which (W p 67, l 12).

[176] Or, 'Is definite (W p. 67, l 19)

12*

APPENDIX A.

Paragraphs 10 and 11 of Part I discuss the definition of lines commensurable in length and square found in Plato's *Theaetetus* (147 d.—148 a.) in respect of that of Euclid (Book X, prop 9). Unfortunately the Theaetetus passage affords little help for the interpretation of these two paragraphs, since commentators of the Theaetetus seem to be hopelessly at odds over the interpretation of this passage and, in especial, concerning the meaning of the two key-words, δύναμις and τετραγωνίζειν

Some commentators (e g , M WOHLRAB (1809), B GERTH, and OTTO APELT (1921)) hold that δύναμις in 147 d means *square*, and this is the only sense in which it is used as a mathematical term by Pappus Alexandrinus (Cf FR. HULTSCH, Vol. III, Index Graecitatis, p 30.) and by Euclid Others (e. g., L FR HEINDORF (1809), SCHLEIERMACHER, JOWETT, CAMPBELL (1883), PALEY (1875), and A. DIES (1924) contend that it must be taken in the sense of *square root*, or, in geometrical terms, *side of a square* Some commentators derive the meaning, *square root*, or *side of a square*, for the δύναμις of Theaetetus 147 d from a comparison of its use in 148 a. as a general term for all lines that are incommensurable in length but commensurable in square, but find, then, a difficulty in explaining what exactly 147 d ff means. CAMPBELL *(The Theaetetus of Plato* 2nd Ed , Oxford, 1883, p. 21, note 1.) supposes that δύναμις in 147 d is an abbreviation for ἡ δυναμένη γραμμὴ εὐθεῖα and bases this assumption on Euclid's use of δυναμένη in Book X, Definitions 3—11 etc The fact remains, however, that Euclid uses δύναμις in Book X in the sense of *square* only.

Another argument in support of the meaning *square root*, or *side of a square*, goes back to HEINDORF (1805), who says (*Platonis Dialogi Selecti*, Vol. II, p 300, § 14, Berlin 1805) — "Scilicet δύναμις τρίπους est εὐθεῖα δυνάμει τρίπους (velut Politic p 266 b. dicitur ἡ διάμετρος ἡ δυνάμει δίπους), seu latus quadrati trepedalis'. This suggestion is adopted by B H. KENNEDY (Cambridge University Press 1881) who omits, however, HEIN- DORF'S "scilicet" and says — 'τρίπους. as HEINDORF says, is εὐθεῖα δυνάμει τρίπους", and naturally δύναμις is *square root* or *side of a square*. But the analogy of HEINDORF's phrases is extremely doubtful, and the contraction finds no support in later mathematical usage

STALLBAUM (*Platonis Opera Omnia*, Vol VIII, sect I, 1839) and PALEY (*The Theaetetus of Plato*, London, 1875) also adopt HEINDORF's interpretation of δύναμις τρίπους. They contend, however, that Plato in 147 d is considering rectangles com- posed of a three foot and a five-foot line The relation then, of 147 d to the discussion in 148 a is somewhat obscure, to say the least.

The Arabic word for δύναμις is "*Quwwatun*", and it means as a mathematical term *square* and *square* only. *The Dictionary of Technical Terms* (Calcutta, A SPRENGER, Vol II, p 1230, top) defines it as "*Murabba'u-l-Khatti*", i e , "the square of the line", "the square which can be constructed upon the line", and goes on to say that the mathematicians treat the square of a line as a *power* of the line, as if it were potential in that line as a special attribute Al-Tūsī (Book X Introd, p 225, l 9) says — "The line is a length actually (reading "*bi-l-fi'li* 'tor" *bi-l-'aqli*) and a square (*murabba'un*) potentially (*bi-l-quwwati*) i e , it is possible for a square to be described upon it Lines commensurable in *power* ("*bi-l-quwwati*") are those whose squares ("*murabba'ātu-hā*") can be measured by the same area etc", and in Book X he uses "*Quwwatun*" in the sense of *square* only and only in the phrases, *lines commensurable (etc.) in* square and *the square on a straight line etc*, and in the latter phrase the word, *"Murabba'un"* (square) is sometimes used instead of *"Quwwatun"*.

An analysis of our two paragraphs (10 & 11) shows that *"Quwwatun"* (power) is used in two senses. It is used in paragraph 11 once (p 11, l 15) in the same sense as δύναμις in Theaetetus 148a, i e as *the side of a square which is commensurable in square but not in length*. In all other cases it means *square* and *square* only. Its use in the first sense is quite exceptional and is explained by its occurring in a direct citation of the Theaetetus passage where δύναμις is used in this sense and Pappus explains in paragraph 17 (p 17, ll 16—17) that the word δύναμις (*"Quwwatun"*) was used in this case, "because it (the line) is commensurable with the rational line in the area which is its square (literally, which it can produce)". The origin of this sense is, therefore, quite clear.

In paragraph 10 (p 10, ll 7, 8, 18) the phrase, *commensurable in square*, occurs. In paragraph 11 (p 11, l 22—p 12, l. 2) we find the significant statement that "It is difficult for those who seek to determine a recognized measure for the lines which have the power to form these *powers* i e, the lines upon which these *powers* can be formed —, to follow the investigation of this problem (i e of irrationals)", where the word, *powers*, must mean *squares*. Paragraph 11 (p 11, ll 17—18) is quite as significant, pointing out that 'The argument of Euclid, on the other hand, covers every *power* and is not relative only to some assumed rational *power* or *line*,' where the words, *"or line"* show that *power* is to be taken in the sense of square. Finally in paragraph 10 (p 10, l 17—p 11, l 8) *Quwwatun* (power) can signify *square* and *square* only. For in the first place, in Euclid's definition of lines commensurable in length and square as those whose *powers* (*quwāhum*) have to one-another the ratio of a square number to a square number (p 10, ll 17—18), *powers* must mean *squares* (cf. Bk X, prop. 9). It follows also that *powers* must mean *squares* when three lines later it is stated (p. 10, l 21—p 11 l 2) that the idea (found in the Theaetetus) of determining those *powers* by means of the square numbers is a different idea altogether from that (in Euclid) of their having to one-another the ratio of a square number to a square number" or what other basis for the comparison of the two definitions is there ' The two *powers* of p 11, ll. 2ff are also squares, for they have to one-another the ratio of a square number to a square number, as in Euclid's definition, and their sides also are commensurable according to the same authority

The fact that the two *powers* of p 11, ll 2—8 are squares, eliminates two difficulties that arise, namely the meaning of the Arabic word, *Rabba'a* and of the phrase, "The *power* whose measure is a foot or three feet or five feet etc " For it is evident that the phrase, ' A *power* whose measure is eighteen (or eight) feet", must mean, "A *power* (square) whose measure is eighteen (or eight) square feet", since power here means square (p 11, ll 2—3)¹ Accordingly the phrase ' A *power* whose measure is one foot", can and does mean, "A *power* (square) whose measure is one square foot ', and the same argument is valid in the case of the two phrases, "The *power* whose measure is three feet", and "The *power* whose measure is five feet" (p. 10, ll. 10—11; p 11, ll 11, 13, 16 20 p 11, l. 12)

The verb, *rabba'a*, occurs in two phrases, "The *powers* which *square* a number whose sides are equal", and "Those which *square* an oblong number" (p 10, ll 14 15 p 11, ll. 14, 15) The Greek word behind *rabba'a* here is evidently the τετραγωνίζω of Theaetetus 148a But neither *rabba'a* nor τετραγωνίζω means as CAMPBELL supposes in the latter case, *To form as their square*, i. e , *The square on which is*, but *To form into a square figure*, *Ad quadratam formam redigere*, as WOHLRAB puts it; and this is the only sense in which Pappus Alexandrinus uses the verb τετραγωνίζω (Cf FR HULTSCH, III. Index Graecitatis, p 111), and he employs its participle τετράγωνον and τετράγων in the same way with reference to the problem of *squaring* the circle

Accordingly the phrase, "The *powers* which *square* a number etc", means "The *powers* (squares) which form such a number into a square figure"[2]. WOHLRAB and APELT have interpretated the Theaetetus passage (148 a) in this way, the former translating it. "Alle Linien welche die gleichseitige Produktzahl als Quadrat darstellen", and the latter, "Alle Linien nun, die die Seiten eines nach Seiten und Fläche kommensurabeln Quadrates bilden"

To sum up. The Arabic word *Quwwatun*, means as a mathematical term *square* and *square* only. In our two paragraphs it signifies *square* save in one instance, where it is used to render the δύναμις of Theaetetus 148 a , which use of it is clearly exceptional. Such phrases, therefore, as "The *power* whose measure is a foot", must be interpretated as "The *power* (square) whose measure is a square foot", and the verb, *rabba'a*, must be rendered, *To form into a square figure.* Pappus, therefore, on this evidence, took the δύναμις of Theaetetus 147 d. in the sense of *square*, and the τετραγωνίζω of 148 a in the sense of *to form into a square figure*[2] That is, the phrase "All the lines which *square* a number whose sides are equal", in 148 a , meant for Pappus, "All the lines which are the sides of a square *squaring* such a number", as in the problem of *squaring* the circle: and what Theaetetus did, then, was to distinguish between squares commensurable in length and square, and squares commensurable in square only

NOTES.

[1] Cf. p. 15, ll 21 22, where similar phrases evidently denote the square measures

[2] That is, 4, which is a square number, has for its *sides* (factors), $\sqrt{4} = 2$ But 6, which is an oblong number, has for its *sides*, 3 and 2; and the side of the square formed from it would be $\sqrt{6}$, which is inexpressible, i e , in whole numbers

INDEX.

N. B. The numbers after those giving the Part of the Treatise refer to the paragraphs.

A

B.

C

D

E.

The Equal (of Parmenides)   Part I, 13
Euclid.   Part I, 1, 3, 6, 7, 10, 11, 16, 19, Part II, 1, 16, 22, 25, 27.
Euclid's Elements   Part I, 1, 3, 4, 11, 12, 16 etc.
Eudemus the Peripatetic.   Part I, 1
Extension   Part I, 13, Part II, 18, 19

F.

Figure   Part I, 13
The Finite.   Part I, 3, 6, 8
The First Cause   Part I, 13
Form   Part I, 13

G

The Greater (of Parmenides)   Part I, 13

I

Incommensurability   Part I, 1, 4, 9, 13, 14, 21, 24, 35, 36
Incommensurable (of lines and magnitudes)   Part I, 3, 7, 12, 13; Part II,
    11
Inconceivable (= Irrational)   Part I, 2
The Infinite   Part I, 3
Irrationality   Part I, 9, 13.
Irrationals   Part I, 1, 2, 3, 4, 5, 7, 11, 12, 14, 15, 18, Part II, 4, 34
Ordered irrationals   Part I, 1; Part II, 1, 2
Unordered irrationals   Part I, 1, Part II, 1, 2
Irrationals formed by addition.   Part I, 4, 21, 23, 26, 27, 29, 30, 31, 36;
    Part II, 2, 3, 12, 13, 14, 16, 17, 19, 25, 26, 32, 33, 33.
Irrationals formed by subtraction   Part I, 4, 21, 23, 32, 33, 34, 35, 36.
    Part II, 2, 6, 12, 13, 14, 16, 17, 19, 25, 26, 32, 33
Irrational magnitudes   Part I, 5

L

Length (= Rational)   Part I, 11
The Less (of Parmenides)   Part I, 13
Limit   Part I, 13
Line   Part I, 13
Compound lines (those formed by addition).   Part II, 3
The line the square upon which is equal to a rational plus a medial area.
    Part I, 22, 32; Part II, 4, 8, 12, 15, 17, 18, 19, 20, 22, 25, 28
The line the square upon which is equal to two medial areas.   Part I,
    22, 32. Part II, 4, 8, 12, 15, 17, 18, 19, 20, 22, 25, 29.

The line which produces with a rational area a medial whole. Part I,
    23, 32, Part II, 12, 13, 14, 15, 19, 20, 22, 31.
The line which produces with a medial area a medial whole   Part I,
    23, 32, Part II, 12, 13, 14, 15, 19, 20, 22, 32.

M

Magnitudes   Part I 5, 13, 14
The major   Part I, 22, 32, Part II, 4, 8, 12, 13, 15, 17, 18, 19, 20, 22,
    25, 27
Matter   Part I, 13
Matter intelligible and sensible   Part I, 13
Maximum   Part I, 3, 5
Means   Part I, 1, 9, 18, 19
Arithmetical mean   Part I, 1 9, 17   Part II, 17, 18, 20
Geometric mean   Part I, 1, 9, Part II, 17, 20
Harmonic mean   Part I, 1, 9, Part II, 17, 19, 20
Measure (unit of measurement)   Part I, 5, 13, 14
The medial   Part I, 1, 4, 6, 7, 9, 14, 15, 19, 20, 21, 25, 36, Part II, 4,
    5, 6, 17, 20, 26, 33
Medial area   Part I, 4, 19, 28, Part II, 4
Minimum   Part I, 3, 5, 6
The minor   Part I, 23, 32, Part II, 12, 13, 14, 15, 19, 20, 22, 30

N

Numbers   Part I, 3, 5, 8, 10, 11, 13

O

One   Part I, 3

P

Parts   Part I, 3, 13
Plane   Part I, 13
Plato   Part I, 1, 3, 10, 11, 12, 13 17
Plato's De Legibus   Part I, 12
Plato's Parmenides   Part I, 13.
Plato's Theaetetus   Part I, 1, 10, 11, 12, 17, 20.
Plurality.   Part I, 3, 8.
Potential   Part I, 13
Power (= square)   Part I, 1, 10, 11
Power (= surd)   Part I, 11 (once)
Proportion.   Part I, 6, 9, 24, Part II, 17, 19.

THE ARABIC TEXT.

بسم الله الرحمن الرحيم

المقالة الاولى

من كتاب ببس فى الاعظام المنطقة والصمّ

التى ذكرها فى

المقالة العاشرة من

كتاب اوقلدس

فى الاسطقسات

ترجمة ابى عثمن الدمشقى [1]

---

§ 1 ان القصد فى المقالة العاشرة من كتاب اوقلدس فى الاصول [2] هو

البحث عن الاعظام المشتركة والمتباينة والمنطقة والصمّ وذلك ان هذا العلم

ابتدأ به اولا شمعة بوناعورس وراد فيه زيادة كثيرة نااطيطس الاينى

الذى كان على حال من الفطنة فى هذه الاشياء وغيرها من اصناف التعاليم

يستحق بها التعجب منه وكان مع ذلك من اجود الناس جبلة [3] وتأتّى

لاستخراج [3] الحق الذى فى هذه العلوم كما يشهد له بذلك فلاطن فى الكتاب [4]

الذى سماه باسمه فاما تمييزها اليقنى وبراهينها التى لا يلحقها طعن فاطن

ان هذا الرجل حاصة احكمها وبعده ابلوبيوس الحلبل الذى هو فى عاية

ما يكون فى القوة فى التعاليم حرص وعنى الى ان | راد فيها اصنافا[5] عجيبة Pag 2

لان تاطيطس ميّز القوى المشتركة فى الطول من المتـاينة وقسّم المشهورة

جدّا من الخطوط الصمّ على الوسائط فجعل الخط الموسط للهندسة ودا

الاسمين للعدد والمنفصل للتالف كما اخبر[6] اوذيمس[7] المشّاء فاما اقلبدس

فانه قصد قصد قوانين لا يلحقها طعن فوضعها لكل اشتراك وتـان ووضع

حدودا وفصولا للمنطقة والصم ووضع ايضا مراتـا كثرة للصم ثم آخر

ذلك اوضح[8] جميع التنـاهى الذى فـها واما الموبيوس ففصّل انواع الصم

المنتظمة واستخرج علم التى تسمى عير منتظمة وولد منهـا جملة كثره

جدّا بالطرق اليقينة

§ 2 فاذ كان هذا هو العرض والقصد فى هذه المقالة فتثبتنا للمنفعة فيها

لـس هو من الفضل فان شيعة بوثاغورس بلع من اجلالهم[9] لهذه الاشـاء

ان كان غلب علـهم[10] قول من الاقاويل وهو ان اوّل من اخرج علم الصم

وعبر المنطقة واذاعه فى الجمهور لقد غرق وخلق انهم كانوا يعنون ذلك

على طريق اللعر ان كل ما كان فى الكل من اصم وعبر منطق وعير مصوّر

فالستر به اوْلى وان كل نعس تطهر وتكشف بالحيرة[11] والعمل ما كان فيها

او فى هذا العالـم مما هذه حاله[12] فانها تجول فى بحر عدم التشابه عرقة فى

مرور الكون[13] التى لا نظام لها فهذه ما[14] كانت تراه شيعة بوثاغورس

والغرب الانبى يسوق الى الحرص والعناية بهذ الامور ويوجب عانة[15]

الجهل على من بتوهم انها ئىء خسس

§ 3 فاذا الامر على هذا ثن اثر ممّا ان ننفى عن نفسه مثل هذا العار

فليعلم هذه الامور من فلاطن ميّر الاحداث[16] المستحقة للعار[17] وليهم

Pag. 3 | هذه الاقاويل التى قصدنا قصدها⁽¹⁸⁾ وليتامل الاستصفاء العجيب الذى
استقصاه اقليدس فى واحد واحد من معانى هذه المقالة لان هذه الاشياء
التى قصدنا⁽¹⁸⁾ فى هذا الموضع لتعليمه هى خاصّة المقومة لذات الهندسة
وذلك ان⁽¹⁹⁾ المتباين⁽²⁰⁾ والاصمّ امّا فى الاعداد فغير موجودة بل الاعداد
كلها منطقة ومشتركة فاما فى الاعظام التى اعنا النظر فيها للهندسة فقد
تتخيّل⁽²¹⁾ والعلة فى ذلك ان الاعداد تتدرج وتتريد من شىء هو اول
قليل وتمرّ الى غير نهاية فاما الاعظام فعكس ذلك اعنى انها تنتدى من
الجملة المتناهية وتمرّ فى القسمة الى غير نهاية فاذا⁽²²⁾ كان الشىء الذى هو
اقل قليل غير موجود فى الاعظام من البيّن انه ليس بوجد قدر ما مشترك
لجميعها كما بوجد الوحده للاعداد لكنه واجب ضروره الّا بوجد فيها
الشىء الذى هو اقل قليل وادا لم يوجد فغير ممكن ان يدخل الاشتراك
فى جميعها فان طلب احد من النـاس العلة التى لها بوجد اقل القليل فى
الكمية المنفصله ولا يوجد فيها اكثر الكثر وفى الكمية المتصلة بوجد
اكثر الكثر ولا يوجد اقل القلل فمنبغى ان نقول له ان امثال هذه
الاشياء اما تمرت محسب محانستها للنهاية وما لا نهاية وذلك ان فى كل
واحد من تقابل الموجودات اشياء هى دوات نهاية واشياء متوالدة عما لا
نهاية مثل تقابل الشبه وغير الشبه والمساوى⁽²³⁾ وغير المساوى⁽²⁴⁾ [والوقوف]
والحركة [فانّ الشبيه والمساوي] والوقوف يؤ[دّون] الى التناهى واما غير
الشبه وغير المساوى⁽²⁴⁾ والحركة هؤدية الى ما لا نهاية وكذلك الحال فى
سائر الاشياء الاحر وعلى هذا المثال يجرى الامر فى الوحده والكثرة
والجمله والاجزاء والواحد والجملة بين انها من حيّز التناهى والاجزاء

والكثرة من حيز ما لا نهاية فلذلك صار الواحد محصلا محدودا فى الاعداد Pag. 4

فان الوحدة هذه حالها والكثرة تمر بلا نهاية[25] وصار فى الاعظام الامر[25]

بالعكس اما الجملة فمحصلة واما الاجزاء فبين بالتقسيم[26] ما لا نهاية

وذلك ان فى الاعداد[27] الواحد يقابل للكثرة[27] لان العدد قد يحصل فى

الكثرة كتحصيل الشيء فى جنسه والوحدة التى هى مبدأ العدد اما ان

تكون هى الواحد واما ان تكون اولى الاشياء باسم الواحد واما فى الاعظام

فتقابل الجملة للجزء وذلك ان الجملة انما تليق بالاشياء المتصلة كما ان الكل

انما تليق بالاشياء المنفصلة فالحال فى هذه الاشياء على ما وصفنا

وقد يجب ان نتأمل ايضا نظم معانى اشكال اقليدس وكيف يبتدى 4 §

من الاشياء التى منها يجب الابتداء ثمّ يمر بالوسائط كلها على نظام

مستو[28] حتى ينتهى على الصواب الى نهاية الطريق اليقينى وذلك ان[29]

بين باول اشكال هذه المقالة خصوصية الاشياء المتصلة خاصة وعلة التباين

وذلك ان الشيء المقوم[30] خاصة للاشياء المتصلة هو ان الجزء الاقل منها

نظهر له ابدا جزء هو اقل منه وان تنقصها لا يقف التة وذلك انهم

يحدّون المتصل بانه المنقسم الى ما لا نهاية ويفيدا ايضا فى هذا الشكل اول

علل التباين[31] كما قلنا ومن هذا الموضع ابتدأ يبحث بحثا كليّا عن الاشتراك

والتباين ويميز ببراهين عجيبة ما منها مشتركا على الاطلاق وما منها مشتركا

فى القوة والطول معا وما منها متباينا فى كل واحد منها وما منها متباينا

فى الطول مشتركا فى القوة ويبين كيف نستخرج خطين متباينين لخط معلوم

احدهما فى الطول فقط[32] والاخر فى الطول[33] والقوة ثم ياخذ فى صفة Pag. 5

الاشتراك والتباين[34] فى النسبة وكذلك الاشتراك والتباين[34] فى التركيب

والتقسيم فانه قد استقصى الكلام فى هذه كلها ووفاه حقّه على النام ثم انه
يَعقب الاقاويل المشتركة فى الاعظام المشتركة والمتباينة ننطر فى امر
المنطقات والصم وبين ما منها منطقة [35] فى الامرين جميعا اعنى فى الطول
والقوة وهى التى لا يتخيّل [36] فيها شىء من الصم وما [37] منها منطقة فى
القوة وهى المحدثة لاول الخطوط الصم الذى [38] نسميه الموسط وذلك ان
هذا الحط اكثر الخطوط مجانسة للخطوط المنطقة ولذلك صارت الخطوط
الموسطة منها ما هى موسطة فى الطول [39] والقوة على مثال [40] ما يوجد عليه
المنطقة ومنها موسطة [41] فى القوة فقط والشىء الذى يتبين به حاصة
محاستها هو هذا ان المنطقة فى القوة تحيط بسطح موسط والموسطة
فى القوة ربما تحيط بمنطق وربما تحيط بموسط وتولد [42] من هذه خطوطا
احر [43] صما كثيرة الاصناف فنها ما تولده بالتركيب ومنها ما تولده
بالتقسيم ويتبين اختلافها من مواضع كثيرة وخاصة من السطوح التى تقوى
عليها ومن اضافة هذه السطوح الى الحط المنطق وبالجملة لما افادنا العلم
باشتراكها واختلافها انتهى الى اظهار عدم تناهى الصم وتميزها ودلك انه
بين انه انه من حط واحد اصم وهو الموسط تحدث صم بلا نهاية مختلفة فى
النوع وجعل انقضاء المقالة من هذا الموضع وترك النطر فى الصم لخروجها
الى ما لا نهاية فهذا مقدار ما كان يجب ان نقدم من القول فى عرض
هذا الكتاب ومنفعته وقسمة حمله

Pag. 6
§ 5

|وينبغى ايضا ان سحث من الراس لنعلم الى اى شىء ذهبوا عند ما
ميزوا المقادير فقالوا ان بعضها مشترك وبعضها متباين اذ كان لا يوجد فى
الاعظام قدر هو اقل القليل لكن الامر فيها على حسب ما بين فى الشكل

الاول انه قد يمكن ان يوجد لكل قدر مفروض ⁽⁴¹⁾ اصغر من قدر

قدر احر اصغر ⁽⁴⁵⁾ منه وبالجملة كيف يمكن ان يوجد اصناف المقادير الصم

اد كانت الاعظام المتناهية كلها لبعضها عند بعض نسبة وذلك اه قد يمكن

ادا ضوعفت ان يفضل بعضها على بعض لا محالة وهذا هو معنى ان يكون

لشيء نسة عند شيء كما تعلمنا فى المقالة الخامسة فنقول اه متى دهب

احد الى هذا المذهب لم يسلم له اه بوجد قدر اصم او عر منطق ولكن

نبغى ان نعلم من هذا الامر ما هذا مَلَعه ⁽⁴⁶⁾ وهو ان القدر اما فى

الاعداد فوجود بالطبع واما فى الاعظام فليس هو ⁽⁴⁷⁾ موجود بالطبع لسبب

القسمة التى تقدّمنا ⁽⁴⁸⁾ وقلنا مرارا انها تمر بلا نهاية لكنه قد ⁽⁴⁹⁾ بوجد فيها

بالوضع وتحصل التوهّم ⁽⁵⁰⁾ وذلك اما فرض قدرا ما محدودا ونسمه ⁽⁵¹⁾

دراعا او شبرا او شيئا ⁽⁵²⁾ احر شبها بدلك ثم نظر الى ذلك العدد ⁽⁵³⁾

المحدود المعلوم عندنا فما امكنا ان نقدره به من الاعظام سميناه منطقا وما

لم يقدره هذا القدر جعلناه فى مرتبة الاعظام الصم فيكون المنطق على هذا

الوجه ليس هو شيئا اخذناه عن الطبيعة لكنه مستخرج من خيلة الفكر

الدى حصل القدر المفروض ولذلك وجب ان لا يكون الاعظام كلها منطقة

بحسب قدر واحد مشترك لان القدر المفروض ليس هو قدرا لها كلها ولا

هو فعل من افعال الطبيعة لكنه من افعال الفكر ولا الاعظام ايضا ^(53a)

كلها صم لانا قد نسب مساحة اقدار ما الى حد معلوم عندنا منتظم

واما ينبغى ⁽⁵⁴⁾ ان نقول ان التناسب بسه ⁽⁵⁵⁾ فى الاعظام المطلقة

اعى المتناهية ⁽⁵⁵⁾ المتجانسة يكون ⁽⁵⁶⁾ على وجه ويقال فى الاعظام المشتركة

على وجه اخر وفى الاعظام التى تسمى المنطقة على وجه اخر وذلك ان

النسبة فيها فى بعض المواضع اما [57] تعلم على هذا المعنى فقط وهو انها
اصاقة اعظام متناهية بعضها الى بعض فى باب العظم والصغير وفى بعض
المواضع على انها موجودة باصافة من الاضافات الحاصلة [58] فى الاعداد
ولذلك تبين ان الاعظام المشتركة كلها نسبة بعضها الى بعض كنسبة عدد
الى عدد وفى بعض المواضع اذا جعلنا النسبة بحسب القدر المفروض المحدود
وقفنا على الفرق بين المنطقة والصم [59] لان الاشتراك ايضا قد وجد فى
الصم [59] وقد علمنا ذلك من اوقلدس نفسه اذ يقول ان بعض الموسطات
مشتركة فى الطول وبعضها مشتركة فى القوة فقط والامر بين ايضا ان
المشتركة هى الصم نسبة بعضها الى بعض كنسبة عدد الى عدد الا انه ليس على
ان النسبة تكون [60] بحسب ذلك القدر [61] المفروض وذلك انه ليس يمنع مانع
من ان تكون فى الموسطة نسبة الضعيفين والثلثه الاضعاف ومقدار الثلث
والنصف ليس يعلم كم هو وهذا المعنى ليس يعرض فى المنطقة اصلا لانا
نعلم [62] لا محالة ان الاقل فى تيك معروف [63] اما ان تكون مقدار ذراع او
ذراعين او محصل محدد ما اخر حاله هذه الحال فاد الامر على هذا فالمتناهية
كلها حالها فى النسبة بعضها الى بعض على وجه ما وحال المشتركة على وجه
اخر وحال المنطقة كلها على وجه اخر غير ذنك الوجهين وذلك ان نسبة
المنطقه هى نسبة المشتركة ايضا وهى نسبة المتناهية ونسبة المتناهية ليس هى
لا محالة نسبة المشتركة لان هذه | النسبة ليست من الاضطرار كنسبة عدد Pag 8
الى عدد ونسبة المشتركة ليس هى ضرورة نسبة المنطقة وذلك ان كل منطق
مشترك وليس كل مشترك منطقا

§ 7 ولذلك متى فرض خطان مشتركان وجب ضروره ان نقول انها اما

منطقان جميعا واما اصمان ولا نقول ان احدهما منطق والاخر اصم لان المنطق لا يكون[64] فى حال من الاحوال مشاركا للاصم فاما اذا اخذ خطان مستقيمان غير مشتركين فلَنْ يخلُوا ضرورة من احد امرين اما ان تكون احدهما اصم[65] والاخر منطقا واما ان يكون كلاهما اصمين وذلك ان الخطوط المنطقة انما يوجد فيها الاشتراك فقط فاما الصم فقد يوجد فيها الاشتراك من جهة والتباين من اخرى فان المختلفة فى النوع من الصم متباينة لا محالة وذلك انها اذا كانت مشتركة فهى لا محالة[66] متّفقة فى النوع اذا كان الخط المشارك للموسط موسطا والمشارك للمنفصل منفصلا وكذلك الامر فى الخطوط الاخر كما يقول المهندس

§ 8 فليس كل نسبة اذًا توجد فى العدد وليس كل ما له نسبة فنسبته كعدد الى عدد لان ذلك لو كان لكانت كلها مشاركة بعضها لبعض وخليق ان يكون لما[67] كل عدد مجانس للنهاية فان العدد ليس هو كثرة كيف ما اتفقت لكنه الكثرة المتناهية[68] وكانت النهاية[69] محاوزة لطبيعة[69] العدد صارت النسبة التى من النهاية توجد فى الاعظام من جهة والنسبة التى من العدد اذ هو متناه من جهة اخرى غيرها ونسبة المتناهية نفرزها من الاشياء التى لا تتناهى فقط ونسبة المشتركة نفرزها من المتباينة وذلك ان تيك النسبة تحصّل اصغر[70] الاجزاء ولذلك تجعل كل ما حصلت فيه مشتركا وهذه تحصّل مرة اعظم الاجزاء ومرة اصغرها وذلك ان كل متنـاه انما تناهى بسب النهاية التى هى اول النهايات ونعطى[71] ابصا لبعض المقادير النهاية بصورة ونعطيها لبعضها[72] صورة اخرى فهذا ما ينبغى ان نحتجّ به فى هذه الاشياء

Pag 9

§ 9   ولما كان عدم المنطق يحدث على ثلث جهات اما على جهة التناسب

واما على جهة التركيب واما على جهة القسمة فانا ارى اولا ان هذا امر

يستحق ان تعجب منه وهو ان قوة الثلثة [73] الضابطة للكل [74] كيف

تميز وتحدد [75] الطبيعة الصماء فضلا عن غيرها وتبلغ [76] الى الاواخر

وتشرق [77] الحد الماخوذ منها على [78] جميع الاشياء ثم بعد ذلك ان كل واحد

من هذه الثلثة الاصناف [79] يميزه لا محالة احد [80] التوسطات فاحدها يميزه

التوسط الهندسى والاخر [80] التوسط العددى والثالث التوسط التاليفى

ويشبه [81] ان يكون جوهر النفس اذا حال فى طبيعة الاعظام من قرب على

حسب ما بوجه ما فيها من معانى التوسطات وميز وحصل [82] كل ما كان

فى الاعظام غير محدود ولا محصّل وصورها من جميع الجهات ضبط عدم

تناهى الصم فهذه الثلثة رباطات لئلا يغلب [83] شىء من الاواخر فضلا عن

غيرها من النسب [84] الموجودة فيه [85] لكنه متى بعد عن واحد منها [85] من

تلقاء طبيعة عاد [86] من الراس الى غيره وصار الى تشابه النسب النفسانية

فيها [87] كان فى الكل من قوة غير منطقة او اجتماع ملتأم من اشياء كثرة

Pag. 10   اجتمعت غير تحديد [88] او عدم | ما غير مصور بالطريق الذى يقسم الصور

فاها كلها تضبط بالنسب الحاصلة فى النفس فيتصل ويأتلف التباين اذا ظهر

فى الكل عن قسمة الصور بالتوسط التاليفى ويتميز عدم تحديد التركيب

بحدود الاعداد الميزة بالتوسط العددى ويستوى جميع اصناف الصم المتوسطة

الحادثة فى القوى الصم بالتوسط الهندسى ففيما ذكرنا من هذا كفاية

§ 10   ولان المؤثرين للنظر فى علم فلاطن يظنون ان التحديد الذى ذكره فى

كتابه المسمى ثاطيطس فى الخطوط المستقيمة المشتركة فى الطول والقوة

والمشتركة فى القوة فقط عبر موافق ⁽⁸⁹⁾ اصلا لما رهنه اقليدس فيها راينا ان

نقول فى ذلك بعض القول وهو ان تاطيطس لما حادثه ⁽⁹⁰⁾ تاودورس فى

راهين القوى المشتركة والمتباينة فى الطول بقياسها الى القوة التى مقدارها

مقدار قدم التجأ الى حد مشترك لهذه كالمنته على العلم اليقيى بالطبع

فقسم العدد كله قسمين ووجد احد القسمين متساويا مرارا متساوية والاخر

يحيط به ابدا صلع اطول وصلع اقصر وشبه الاول بالشكل المربع والثانى

بالمستطيل وحكم على القوى التى تربع العدد المتساوى الاضلاع انها مشتركة

فى القوة والطول وان التى تربع العدد المستطل ماينة للاول بهذه الجهة

الا ان بعضها على حال مشارك لبعض بجهة من الجهات واما اقليدس فلما

امعن قللا فى المقالة وحصل الخطوط المشتركة فى الطول والقوة وهى التى

نسبة قواها بعضها بعضها الى بعض كنسبة عدد مربع الى عدد مربع بين ان كل

ما كانت هذه حاله من الخطوط مشتركة فى الطول ابدا ⁽⁹¹⁾ وليس يخفى

علىك الفرق بين هذا من قول اقليدس وبين القول الذى تقدم من قول

تاطيطس وذلك ان ليس المعنى فى تحصيل القوى | بالاعداد المربعة والمعى _{Pag 11}

فى ان تكون لها نسبة كنسبة مربع الى مربع معى واحدا لانه ⁽⁹²⁾ ان كانت

مثلا قوه مقدارها ثمنية عشر قدما واخرى ثمنية اقدام هن البين ان نسبة

الواحدة ⁽⁹³⁾ الى الاخرى كنسبة عدد مربع الى عدد مربع وهما العددان

اللذان هذاى ضعفاها وقد تحصلان ⁽⁹⁴⁾ بعددين مستطيلين واصلاعهما على مذهب

اقليدس مشتركة فاما على مذهب ⁽⁹⁵⁾ تاطيطس فبعدان ⁽⁹⁶⁾ من هذه الحال

لايهم ليستا ربعان العدد المتساوى الاصلاع بل انما ربعان العدد المستطيل ⁽⁹⁷⁾

وهذا فيما يحتاج الانسان ⁽⁹⁷⁾ ان نقف عليه من هذه الاشياء

§ 11   وينبغى ان نقول ان كلام ثاﺍطيطس لم يكن فى جميع القوى المشتركة فى الطول والمتباينة لكن فى القوى التى اما النسب لها بالقياس الى قوة ما منطقة اعى القوة التى مقدارها قدم وذلك انه ابتدا ثاودورس بالبحث عن القوة التى مقدارها ثلثة اقدام والقوة التى مقدارها حمسة اقدام من هذا الموضع فقال اﺍﻬا عبر مشاركتين[98] للقوة التى مقدارها قدم ولخص ذلك بان قال ان التى تربع العدد المتساوى الاصلاع قد حددنا اﺍﻬا طول والتى تربع المستطيل حددنا اﺍﻬا قوى من قبل اﺍﻬا فى الطول عبر مشاركة لتلك اعى للقوة التى مقدارها قدم والقوى المشاركة لهده القوة فى الطول ومشاركة للسطوح التى تقوى عليها فاما اقلدس فان كلامه فى جميع القوى وليس اﺍﻤا كلامه بالقياس الى قوة ما معروصة منطقة والى خط ما وليس يمكن ان نكون قد بين نقول من الاقاويل ان القوى التى وصفنا مشتركة فى الطول وان لم تكن مشاركة المقوة التى مقدارها قدم ولم يكن اﺍصا العدد المقدر المحطوط اعى[99] عنها تصوّرت[100] هده القوى منطقا فلذلك

Pag 12   صار البحث عن ذلك معتاصا عند الدين يطلبون ان يحدّدوا للخطوط[101] التى تقوى على هده القوى قدرا معلوما على اﺍه قد يتهيا للاسان ادا ازم برهان اقلدس ان يجدها مشتركة لا محاله لاﺍه قد يتبين ان لها سبة كعدد الى عدد فهذا ملع ما نقوله فى ثك فلاطن

§ 12   ومن الاشياء التى اثبتها الفلسوف ان هاهنا مقادير متباينة واﺍه ليس ينبغى ان نقبل ان الاشتراك موجود فى جميع المقادير كما هو فى الاعداد واﺍه متى لم يتفقد هذا[102] لرمه جهل كثير منكر من ذلك ما قاله الاﺍبى العرس فى المقالة السابعة من كتاب النواميس وبعد هذه الاشياء

قد يوجد فى جميع الناس جهل قبيح بالطبع يضحك منه بجميع [103] الاشياء
التى لها اطوال وعروض واعماق عند المساحة ومن البين انه قد يخلصهم
من هذا الجهل التعاليم قال وذلك انى ارى ان هذا امر بهيمى لا انسانى
وانى لاستحى لا لنفسى فقط لكن لجميع اليونانيين من طرن من يُقدّم من
الناس الظن الذى يظنه فى هذا الوقت الجمهور من ان الاشتراك لازم لجميع
المقادير فانهم كلهم يقولون انا قد نعقل اشياء واحدة بعينها يمكن فيه
بجهة من الجهات ان يكون بعضها يقدر بعصا وانما الحق فيها ان بعضها يقدر
ياقدار مشتركة وبعضها لا يقدر اصلا وقد تبين بالقول الذى فى الكتاب
المعروف بثااطيطس بيانا كافيا كيف ينبغى ان تميز الخطوط المشتركة فى
الطول والقوة بالقياس الى الخط المنطق المفروض اعنى [104] الذى مقداره
قدم من الخطوط المشتركة فى القوة فقط ووصفنا ذلك فيما تقدم وقد يسهل
علينا مما قبل فى الكتاب المعروف ثتتا ان نعلم انه قد وصف لنا ايضا الاختلاف
الذى فى تركيب الخطوط المنطقة وذلك انه يقول اذا كان الخطان كلاهما
منطقين | فقد يمكن ان يكون الكل مرة منطق [105] ومرة غير منطق فان
الخط المركب من خطين منطقين فى الطول والقوة منطق لا محالة والخط
المركب من خطين منطقين فى القوة فقط غير منطق

Pag 13

وان كان ينبغى ان لا يجحده ما ذكره فى الكتاب المنسوب الى 13 §
برمايدس فقد بين [106] العلة الاولى فى قسمة الخطوط المشتركة والمتباينة
وذلك انه وصف المساوى والاعظم والاصغر معا على الوضع الاول واحد
المشترك والمتباين فى هذا الموضع على انها قائمتان فى الوهم مع المقدار ومن
البين ان هذه تمسك طبيعة الاشياء التى من شانها ان تقسم وتضبط الاجتماع

والافتراق (107) التى وبها يقوى الله المطيفة بالعالم وذلك ان العدد (108)
الالاهى من طريق ما يتقدم وجود قوام هذه الاشياء فهى كلها مشتركة
بحسب تلك العلة لان الله بقدر الاشياء كلها اكثر مما يقدر الواحد (109)
للعدد ومن طريق ان تباين الهيولى يلزم ان يكون هذه الاشياء وجدت
فيها قوة التباين ونشته ان يكون الحد اولى ان يستولى فى المشتركة لانه
متولد عن القوة الالاهية وان يكون الهيولى تفضل (110) فى المقادير التى يقال
لها المتباينة لانك ان اردت ان تعلم من اين دخل على المقادير التباين لم
يجد (111) ذلك من شىء من الاشياء الا ما تتحمله من قسمة الاجراء بالقوة
الى ما لا نهاية والاجراء لا محالة انما هى من الهيولى كما ان الكل من
الصورة وما (112) بالقوة انما يوجد لجميع الاشياء من الهيولى كما ان ما بالفعل
من المبدا الاحر فلم يوجد التباين اذًا للاعظام التى فى الهندسة من قبل
الهيولى وعلى اى جهة يوجد الا لان الهيولى كما يقول | ارسطوطالس صنفان
احداهما (113) معقولة والاخرى محسوسة وذلك ان نحل الحجم وبالجملة
تخبل (114) العدد انما هو فى الصور الهندسية من قبل الهيولى المعقولة لان
الموضع الذى يوجد فيه الصورة والحد فقط فهناك الاشياء كلها بلا ابعاد
ولا اجراء وهذه الصورة (115) كلها طبيعة غير محسمة والرسم والشكل
والحجم وجميع ما للقوة المصورة التى فينا قد تشارك بضرب من الضروب
الخاصة الهيولانية ولذلك صارت طبيعة الاعداد بسيطة ورئة من هذا
التباين من عير ان تتقدم الحيوة التى ليست هيولانية واما الحدود التى
جرت من هناك الى التخييل والحدوث (116) الى هذا الفعل المصور فقد
امتلات من عدم النطق وشاركت التباين وشانها بالجملة العوارض الهيولانية

§ 14 وينبغي ان نعود الى الشيء الذي قصدنا له وننظر [117] هل يمكن ان يكون خطوط ما منطقة مبابنة للخطوط المفروضة [118] من اول الامر منطقا وننظر بالجملة هل يمكن ان تكون قدر واحد بعينه منطقا واصم [119] فنقول ان المقادير انما هي بالوضع لا بالطبع كما قلنا مرارا كثيرا ولذلك وجب ضرورة ان ننتقل المنطق والاصم على حسب وضع العدد المفروض وليس كما ان المتباين لا يجوز ان يكون مشتركا بوجه من الوجوه كذلك المنطق لا يجوز ان يوجد اصم [120] اد كانت المقادير قد تنتقل ولكن لما كان ينبغي ان تكون خواص المنطقة وخواص الصم محدودة مجملة [121] وصنف قدرا واحدا وبينا بالقياس اله خواص الاعظام المنطقة والصم لانا لو لم نجعل تمييزنا لها بالقياس الى شيء واحد لكن سمينا العظم الذي لا يقدره المقدار المفروض منطقا لما كانت حدود هذا العالم [122] محفوظة عندنا مميزة عبر مضطربة بل كان الخط الذي سبين انه نحي انه موسط يحكم علمه عيرنا انه لس بان يكون موسطا اولى منه بان نكون منطقا ادا ما هو عبر العدد وهذا ليس هو طريقا علمنا لكن ينبغى ان يكون خط واحد منطقا كما يقول اقليدس

§ 15 فلندع الخط المفروص منطقا وذلك انه ينبغى ان ناخذ خطا واحدا منطقا ونسمى كل مشارك له فى الطول كان او فى القوة منطقا ويعكس احدهما على الاحر وبصع ان المشارك للخط المنطق مطق والمنطق مشارك للخط المنطق وذلك ان المباين لهذا الخط قد حده اقليدس بانه اصم فى هاهنا لا يجب ان نسب حمع الخطوط المشتركة فى الطول وان كانت تسمى منطقة الى الخط المفروص ولا يجب ان تسمى مشتركة على ان هذا الخط

بقدرها لكن متى كانت لها نسبة الى الخط المفروض اما فى القوة واما فى
الطول سميت لا محالة منطقة ودلك اى كل واحد من الخطوط المشاركة
للخط المفروض فى القوة او فى الطول منطق فاما كوى هده الخطوط
مشركة فى الطول او فى القوه فقط فصاف اليها من خارج وليس هو
بحسب نسبتها الى الخط المفروض ودلك ان الخطوط الموسطة ربما
كانت ⁽¹²³⁾ مشاركة فى الطول وربما كانت ⁽¹²³⁾ مشرككه فى القوة فقط فلم
يصب اذا ⁽¹²⁴⁾ من قال ان جميع الخطوط المنطقة المشركة فى الطول فانما ⁽¹²⁵⁾
هى منطقة من قبل الطول ولدلك ليس بقدر جميع الخطوط المنطقة بالخط
المفروض لا محالة فان الخطوط المشاركة فى القوة للخط المنطق المفروض
قد تسمى على الاطلاق منطقه من دالك ان لو احدى موضعين مربعين
مساحة احدهما حمسون قدما والاحر ثمنية عشر قدما لكان الموضعان
مشتركين ⁽¹²⁶⁾ للمربع الدى من الخط المفروض منطق ومقداره قدم وكان
الخطان اللدان بقويان عليهما احدهما مشارك للاحر وهما مبابنان
‖ Pag. 16 للخط المفروض ولن يمنع مانع اى سمى هدان الخطان منطقين مشركين
فى الطول اما منطقين فلان المربعين اللدين منها مشاركتان للمربع الذى
من المفروض واما مشركين فى الطول فانه وان لم يكن العدد المشترك ⁽¹²⁷⁾
لهما هو الخط المفروض منطقا فقد بقدرهما قدر اخر ⁽¹²⁸⁾ فليس شىء من
الاشياء اذا يجعل منطقا غير مشاركة الخط المنطق المفروض ⁽¹²⁹⁾ فاما الاعطام
المشركة فى الطول وفى القوه فقط فقد نجعلها كدلك القدر المشترك
كائنا ما كان

§ 16   فاد تبرهن ان الموصع الدى يحيط به خطان منطقان مشركان فى الطول

منطق فليس بمنع مانع ان يكون الخطوط التي تحيط بالموضع (130) اما
منطقة من قبل مجانستها للخط المنطق كيف كانت حالها عنده فى الطول او
فى القوة فقط واما مشتركة فى الطول فمن قبل ان لها لا محالة قدرا مشتركا
وذلك انه ينبغى ان نزل ان هاهنا خطين بهذه الصفة محيطان بالسطح
المفروض بسمان منطقين وهما مشتركان فى الطول الا انه ليس يقدرهما الخط
المفروض منطقا لكن المربعين اللذين منها مشاركين (130b) للمربع الذى من ذلك
الخط فهذا الموضع (131) قد تبرهن انه منطق لانه مشارك لكل واحد من
مربعى الخطين اللذين محيطان به وقدكان ذلك مشاركين للمربع الذى من
الخط المفروض فيجب ان يكون هذا السطح ايضا مشاركا له فهذا الموضع (132)
اذا منطق فان نحن اخذنا الخطين المفروضين مشتركين فى الطول على انها
غير مشاركين للخط المنطق من اول الامر لا فى الطول ولا فى القوة لم نتبين
من وجه من الوجوه ان السطح الذى محيطان به منطق ولكن ان انت
جعلت الطول على العرض فوجدت عدد الموضع لم يكن بعد يثبت انه منطق مثال
ذلك ان تكون نسبة الخطين اللذين محيطان به نسبة الثلثة الى الاثنين

Pag. 17

وذلك ان الموضع تكون مساحته (131) لا محالة ستة اشياء الا ان هذه الستة
الاشياء ليس يعلم ما هى لان النصف والثلث فى الخطين انفسها (134) قد
كانا اصمين ولا ينبغى لاحد ان يقول ان الخطوط المنطقة صنفان منها ما
يقدره الخط المنطق من اول الامر ومنها ما يقدره خط اخر ليس هو
مشاركا لهذا الخط ولكن الخطوط المشتركة فى الطول صنفان منها ما يقدره
الخط المنطق من اول الامر ومنها ما هى مشتركة وان كان يقدرها خط
اخر غير مشارك لذلك الخط ولسنا نجد اقليدس فى موضع من المواضع

سمى الخطوط المباينة فى كل واحدة من الجهتين للخط المفروض منطقا
منطقة وما الذى كان يمنعه من ذلك اذ كان حكمه على الخطوط المنطقة
ليس انما هو بالقياس الى ذلك الخط فقط لكنه قد كان يحكم عليها ايضا
بان ياخذ قدرا ما اخر من الخطوط التى يقال لها المنطقة فينسبها [135] اليه

§ 17 واما فلاطن فقد يجعل للخطوط المنطقة انفسها [136] اسماء مختلفة ونرى
ان يسمى الخط المشارك فى الطول للمفروض منطقا طولا ويسمى المشارك
له فى القوة فقط واصاف الى ما قاله من ذلك السبب فقال لانه
مشارك للخط المنطق بالسطح الذى يقوى علمه فاما اقليدس فيسمى الخط
المشارك للمنطق كيف ما كانت مشاركته له منطقا من غير ان يشترط فى
ذلك شيئا ولذلك صار سبب [137] حيرة للذين يجدون عنده خطوطا ما
يقال لها منطقة وبعضها مع ذلك مشاركا لبعض فى الطول وهى مباينة
للخط المفروض منطقا واعله ليس يرى ان [138] يقدر جميع الخطوط المنطقة
بالخط المفروض من اول الامر لكنه يرى ان يترك ذلك القدر وان

| Pag. 18 كان فى الحدود قد يرى ان يجعل سبة المنطقة اليه ويتقل الى قدر اخر
مباين للاول وقد يسمى امثال هذه الخطوط وَهوَ لا يشعر [139] منطقة لانها
مشاركة للخط المفروض منطقا بوجه من الوجوه اعنى بالقوة فقط وينسب
اشتراكها فى الطول الى قدر اخر بدهب فى ذلك الى ان [140] الاشتراك لها
فى كل واحدة [141] من الجهتين والنطق ليس فى كل واحدة منها

§ 18 وذلك ان [142] نقول ان من الخطوط المستقيمة خطوطا عير منطقة اصلا
ومنها منطقة فغير المنطقة هى التى ليس اطوالها مشاركة لطول الخط المنطق
ولا قواها مشاركة لقوته والمنطقة هى المشاركة للخط المنطق بوجه من

الوجوه وهذه المنطقة ايضا فنها ما بعضها مشارك لبعض فى الطول ومنها ما
هى مشاركة [143] فى القوة فقط والتى بعضها مشارك لبعض فى الطول منها ما
هى مشاركة للخط المنطق فى الطول ومنه غير مشاركة له وبالجملة فكل
خطوط منطقة مشاركـة فى الطول للخط المنطق فبعضها مشارك لبعض
ولبس [111] كل منطقة فبعضها مشارك لبعض فى الطول فهى مشاركة للخط [111]
المنطق والخطوط المشاركة للمنطق فى القوة ولذلك ما تسمى هى ايضا منطقة
فنها ما بعضها مشارك لبعض فى الطول لا بالقياس الى ذلك الخط ومنها
ما هى مشتركه فى القوة فقط ودلك بين من اما ان ازلنا موضعا بحيط به
خطـان منطقـان فى القوة مشاركـان للخط المفروض واحدهما مشارك للاخر
فى الطول صار هدا الموضع منطقا وان كان الموضع بحط به خطان مشتركان
ومشاركان للخط المنطق فى القوه فقط صار متوسطا وهدا مبلغ ما نقوله فى
هده الاشياء ومن البين ان الموضع الدى بحط به خطان منطقان فى القوة
مشركان فان خطيه المنطقين مشركان ومشاركان للمفروض منطقا فى
القوة [111] فقط فاما الموضع الدى بحط به خطان منطقان |فى الطول مشتركان Pag ١٩
فان خطيه المنطقين مرة نكونان مشركين ومشاركين للخط المنطق فى الطول
ومره نكونان مشاركين للمنطق فى القوه فقط ومشتركين بجهة اخرى

§ ١٩ والواجب ان يتامل هدا المعنى ايضا وهو اه لما وحد بالنسبة الهندسية
الخط الموسط متوسطا بين خطين منطقين فى القوة فقط مشتركين ولذلك
ما صار يقوى على الموضع الدى بحيطان به فان المربع الدى من الخط
الموسط مساو للموضع الذى بحيط به الخطان الموضوعان عن جنتيه وضع
فى كل موضع الاسم العام للموسط على طبيعة جزءية لان الخط الموسط الدى

يقوى على الموضع الذى يحيط به خطان منطقان فى الطول مشتركان متوسط لا محالة لذينك[146] المنطقين والخط الذى يقوى على الموضع الذى يحيط به خط منطق وخط اصم على ذلك المثال ايضا ولكنه لا يسمى ولا واحد من هذين موسطا بل انما يسمى موسط الخط الذى يقوى على الموضع المفروض وايضا فانه قد يشتق فى كل موضع اسم القوى من التى تقوى عليها فيسمى الموضع الذى من الخط المنطق منطقا والذى من الموسط موسطا

§ 20 وايضا فانه يشبه النظر فى الموسطات بالخطوط المنطقة وذلك انه يقول ان هذه الخطوط مثل تيك اما ان تكون مشتركة فى الطول او مشتركة فى القوة فقط وان الموضع الذى يحيط به موسطان مشتركان فى الطول موسط اصطرارا كما ان الموضع هناك الذى يحيط به منطقان مشتركان فى الطول منطق والموضع ايضا الذى يحيط به موسطان مشتركان فى القوة فقط يكون منطقا ومرة موسطا وذلك انه كما ان الخط الموسط يقوى على الموضع الذى يحيط به منطقان فى القوة مشتركان كذلك الخط المنطق ربما قوى

Pag 20 | على السطح الذى يحيط به خطان موسطان فى القوة مشتركان فيصير الموضع الموسط على ثلثة أنحاء اما ان يحيط به خطان[117] منطقان فى القوة مشتركان او موسطان فى الطول مشتركان او موسطان فى القوة مشتركان ويصير المنطق على جهتين اما ان يحيط به خطان[148] منطقان فى الطول مشتركان او خطان موسطان فى القوة مشتركان ويشبه ان يكون الخط المأخوذ فى النسبة فيما بين موسطين مشتركين فى الطول موسطا والمأخوذ فيما بين منطقين فى القوة مشتركين من جميع الجهات موسطا والخط المأخوذ فيما بين خطين[149] موسطين فى القوة[149] مشتركين ربما كان منطقا وربما كان

موسطا ولذلك صارت القوه التى منه [150] ربما كانت منطقة وربما كانت
موسطة وذلك اه قد يمكن ان يوجد خطان موسطان فى القوة مشتركين
كما انه يمكن ان يكون خطان منطقان فى القوة فقط مشتركين فنبغى ان
يكون السبب فى اختلاط المواضع التى يحيط بها الخطان الخط المناسب
الذى فيما بين الطرفين الذى هو اما موسط فيما بين منطقين او موسط فيما
بين موسطين او منطق فيما بين موسطين وبالجملة فربما شبه الرباط بالطرفين
وربما جعله غير مشبه لهما ولكن فيما قلناه من هذه الاشياء كفاية

§ 21 وبعد نظره فى الخط الموسط واستخراجه اتاه اخذ فى البحث لما امعن
عن الخطوط الصم فى التركيب والقسمة على حسب ما استعمل من البحث
عن الاشتراك والتباين [151] وذلك ان الاشتراك والتباين [151] قد تجدهما
فى الخطوط المركبة والمنفصلة وذو الاسمين يتقدم الخطوط التى بالتركب

لاه ايضا اكثر الخطوط محانسة للخط المنطق وذلك اه مركب من خطين | Pag 21
منطقين فى القوه مشتركين والمنفصل تقدم الخطوط التى بالتفصيل وذلك
ان حدوث المنفصل ايضا انما يكون بان يفصل من خط منطق خط
منطق [152] مشارك للكل فى القوة وذلك ان نستخرج الخط الموسط بان
نضع ضلعا منطقا وقطرا معروصا وماخد خطا متوسطا فى النسبة بين هذين
الخطين وذلك ان نستخرج ذا الاسمين بان نزكب الضلع والقطر وذلك ان
نستخرج المنفصل بان نفصل الضلع من القطر وقد ينبغى ان نعلم ايضا اه
ليس متى يركب خطان فقط منطقان فى القوة مشتركان اخدا الذى من
اسمين لكن قد يحدث ذلك ايضا ثلثة خطوط واربعة على ذلك المثال اما
اولا فقد يحدث الذى من ثلثه اسماء اذا كان الخط كله اصم [153] وثانيا

يحدث الذى⁽¹⁵⁴⁾ من اربعة اسماء ويمر ذلك بلا نهاية والبرهان على ان الذى

من ثلثة خطوط منطقة فى القوة مشتركة⁽¹⁵⁵⁾ اصم هو بعينه البرهان الذى

تبرهن به على الحطين المركبين

§ 22 وقد⁽¹⁵⁶⁾ يسعى ان نقول من الراس هكذا انه لبس انما يمكنا ان ناخد

خطا واحدا فقط متوسط بين خطين فى القوة مشتركين بل قد يمكنا ان

ناخد ثلثة واربعة ويمر ذلك الى غير نهاية ادكان قد يمكنا ان ناخد فيما

بين كل خطين مستقيمين مفروصين خطوطا كم شئنا على نسبة وفى⁽¹⁵⁷⁾ التى

بالتركيب ايضا فلس انما يمكنا ان نعمل⁽¹⁵⁸⁾ حطا من اسمين فقط بل قد

يمكنا ايضا ان نعمل الذى من ثلثة اسماء والذى من ثلثة موسطات الاول

والثانى والذى من ثلثة خطوط مستقيمه متباينة فى القوة بصر احدها⁽¹⁵⁹⁾

مع كل واحد من الاتنين محموع المربع الكائن منها منطقا والقائم الروايا

Pag 22 الذى منها موسط حتى يصير الاعظم مركبا من ثلثة خطوط | وسبر على

ذلك المثال الخط الذى يقوى على منطق وموسط من ثلثة خطوط وكدلك

الذى⁽¹⁶⁰⁾ يقوى على موسطين ودلك انا نزل ثلثة خطوط منطقة فى القوة

فقط مشتركة والحط اذا المركب من الاتنين اصم وهو الذى من اسمين

فالموصع اذا الذى من هدا الحط ومن الحط الباقى اصم والموضع ايصا الذى

من هدين الخطين مرتين اصم ثمربع الحط كله المركب⁽¹⁶¹⁾ من الثلثة الحطوط

اصم فالحط اذا اصم وسمى من ثلثة اسماء واذا كانت اربعة خطوط كما

قلنا مشتركة فى القوة جرى الامر فيها هذا المحرى بعينه وما يتلوا⁽¹⁶²⁾

ذلك فعلى هذا المثال فليكن ثلثة خطوط موسطة مشتركة فى القوة احدها

مع كل واحد من الباقيين يحيطان بمطق فالمركب⁽¹⁶³⁾ الذى منها اذا⁽¹⁶⁴⁾

14*

اسم [165] يسمى من موسطين الاول والخط الباق موسط والموضع الذى منها

اسم [165] فريع الكل اذًا اصم والحال فى سائر الاخر حال واحدة فالخطوط

المركبة [166] اذًا فى جميع التى تكون بالتركيب تمر بلا نهاية

§ 23 وكذلك ليس ينبغى ان نقتصر فى الخطوط الصم التى بالتفصيل على ان

فصلها [167] انفصالا واحدا فقط حتى نجد الخط المنفصل او منفصل الموسط

الاول او منفصل الموسط الثانى او الاصغر او الذى يجعل الكل موسطا

مع منطق او الدى يجعل الكل موسطا مع الموسط لكنا فصلها فصلين

وثلثة واربعة فانا اذا فعلنا ذلك بنينا على ذلك المثال ان الخطوط التى

تبقى صم [168] وان كل واحد منها واحد من الخطوط التى بالتفصيل اعنى

انا ادا فصلنا من خط منطق خطا منطقا مشاركا للكل فى القوة كان لنا

الخط الباق منفصلا وان فصلنا من ذلك الخط المفصول المنطق الدى سماه

اقليدس اللفق |خطا اخر منطقا مشاركا له فى القوة كان لنا [169] الجزء الباق

Pag 23 منه منفصلا كما انا [169] ايضا ان فصلنا من الخط المنطق المفصول من ذلك

الخط خطا اخر مشاركا له فى القوة صار الباق منفصلا وكذلك الحال فى

تفصيل سائر الخطوط فليس يمكن ادا الوقوف لا فى التى بالتركيب [170] ولا

فى التى بالتفصيل لكنه يمر بلا نهاية اما فى تيك فالزياده واما فى هده

فتنقيص الخط المفصول ونشبه ان يكون عدم نهاية الصم يظهر بامثال هذه

الطرق من عبر ان نقف التناسب فى كثرة محدودة للوسائط ولا ينتهى [171]

التركيب بالمركبات ولا يتحصل الانفصال عند حد ما وقد ينبغى ان نكتفى

بهدا [172] فى العلم بالمنطقة

§ 24 ونعود من الراس فنصف [173] جملها فنقول ان الجملة الاولى فى الاعظام

المشتركة والمتباينة وقد يتبين فيها ان هاهنا تباينا واى الاعظام هى المتباينة وكيف ينبغى ان نمير وما الاشتراك والتباين فى التناسب وانه ممكن ان ناخذ التباين على وجهين احدهما فى الطول والقوه والاخر فى الطول فقط وكيف حال كل واحد منها فى التركيب والتقسيم وكيف حالها فى الزيادة والنقصان وذلك ان بهذه الاشكال كلها وهى خمسة عشر شكلا افادنا العلم بالاعظام المشتركة والمتباينة

§ 25   والجملة الثانية ذكر فيها الخطوط المنطقة والموسطات المشارك بعضها لبعض فى القوه والطول وذكر المواضع التى نحيط بها هذه الخطوط وذكر [174] مجانسة الخط الاوسط للمنطق والفرق بينهما واستخراجه وما اشبه ذلك وذلك ان الامر فى انه ليس انما يمكننا فقط ان نجد خطين منطقيين فى الطول مشتركين [175] بل وفى القوة ايضا بين انه قد يمكنا ان ناخذ |Pag 24 خطين متباينين للخط المعلوم احدهما فى القوه والاخر فى الطول فقط فانا ان احدنا لخط مفروض منطقا خطا مباينا فى الطول كان لنا خطان منطقان مشتركان فى القوة فقط واذا اخذنا لهذين متوسطا فى النسبة كان لنا الخط الاصم الاول

§ 26   والجملة الثالثة يجعلها علة لاستخراج الصم التى تكون بالتركيب ان نقدم لاستخراجها خطين موسطين مشتركين فى القوة [176] فقط يحيطان عذ[طق] وخطين ايضا موسطين فى القوة مشتركين [176] يحيطان عوسط وخطين ايضا مستقيمين غير موسطين ولا منطقين متباينين فى القوة يجعلان المربع الذى منها معا منطقا والسطح الذى يحيطان به موسطا وعكس ذلك يجعلان المربع الذى منها معا موسطا والسطح الذى يحيطان به

منطقا او يجعلان كل واحد من المربع والسطح موسطا ويكونان متباينين
وذلك ان هذه الاشكال وجميع ما حصل فى الجملة الثالثة اعا اخذ من اجل
استخراج الخطوط الصم التى تكون بالتركيب لانه اذا ركب الخطوط
المستخرجة فاحدث منها تلك الخطوط الصم

§ 27 والجملة الرابعة يفيدنا فيها الستة الخطوط الصم بالتركيب والتركيب ربما
كان من خطين منطقين فى القوة مشتركين وذلك ان الخطين المشتركين فى
الطول اذا ركبا جعلا الخط كله منطقا وربما كان من خطين موسطين
مشتركين فى القوة وذلك ان الموسطين ايضا المشتركين فى الطول تكون
جملتها خطا موسطا وربما كان من خطين على الاطلاق⁽¹⁷⁷⁾ ومتباينين فى
القوة⁽¹⁷⁷⁾ وثلثة من هذه صم للسبب الذى ذكرنا واثنان من الموسطين
المشتركين فى القوة وواحد من منطقين مشتركين فى القوة فمجمع ذلك
ستة وبسبب هذه التى ثبتت فى الجملة الرابعة احدثت الجملة الثالثة | فهذه
Pag 25
الجملة الرابعة افادنا فيها تركيب الخطوط الستة الصم بان جعل بعضها من
خطوط مشتركة فى القوة وهى الثلثة الاولى⁽¹⁷⁸⁾ وبعضها من متباينة فى
القوة وهى الثلثة الثانية وفى كل واحد من هذه اما ان ياخذ المربع المركب
من مربعيهما منطقا والسطح الذى يحيطان به موسطا او عكس ذلك ياخذ
المربع الذى من مربعيهما موسطا والسطح الذى يحيطان به⁽¹⁷⁹⁾ منطقا او ياخذ
المربع الذى منها موسطا والسطح الذى يحيطان به⁽¹⁷⁹⁾ موسطا ويكونان
متباينين لانها ان كانا مشتركين صار الخطان المركبان فى الطول
مشتركين وبين ايضا عكس تيك الاشكال بضرب من الضروب وهو ان
كل واحد من هذه الستة الصم اما ينقسم على نقطه واحدة فقط وذلك

انه يبين ان الخطين ان كانا منطقين فى القوة مشتركين فان الخط المركب
منها من اسمين وان كان هذا الخط من اسمين فانه مركب من هذين
فقط لا من غيرهما وكذلك يجرى القياس فى الخطوط الباقية وهى هذه الجملة
ستتان من الاشكال الستة الاولى تركب الستة الخطوط الصم والثانية
تبين انعكاسها

§ 28 والجملة الخامسة مع هذه الجمل يستخرج فيها الخط الذى من اسمين وهو
اول الخطوط التى بالتركيب وهو مصرف على ستة انحاء وهذا امر لست
اطن به [180] انه فعله باطلا بل انما استعده للعلم باختلاف الستة الخطوط الصم
التى بالتركيب الذى يمكن ان يوقف عليه حاصة من المواضع التى تقوى عليها

§ 29 وكذلك تتبع هذه الجملة بالجملة السادسة التى يبحث فيها عن هذه
المواضع وبين ان الذى من اسمين يقوى على موضع يحيط به خط منطق
والخط الذى من اسمين الاول وان الخط الذى من موسطين الاول يقوى
Pag 20. على موضع يحيط به خط منطق والذى من اسمين الثانى وما يتلوا | ذلك
على هذا المثال وهذه الخطوط اذا تحدث ستة مواضع يحيط بها خط منطق
وواحد من الستة التى من اسمين

§ 30 وللجملة السابعة يذكر فيها امر الاشتراك الذى [181] بين الستة الخطوط
الصم التى بالتركيب ويتبين ان الخط المشارك لكل واحد من هذه الخطوط
فهو من نوعه ولما اصاف ايضا قواها الى الخطوط المنطقة بحث عن عروض
مواضعها واستخرج ستة اخرى بعكس الستة التى ذكرها فى الجملة السادسة

§ 31 والجملة الثامنة استخرج فيها اختلاف الستة الصم التى بالتركيب من
المواضع التى تقوى عليها وبين مع ذلك تبسنا واصحا من تركب السطح

المنطق والموسط او من الموضعين الموسطين تميز الحطوط الصم التى
بالتركيب[182] التى لبعضها عند بعض[182]

§ 32 وبعد هذه الاشياء وصف فى الجملة التاسعة الستة الخطوط الصم التى
تكون بالتفصل على مثال ما وصف الستة التى بالتركيب فجعل المنفصل نظير
الدى من اسمين وذلك ان الحطين اللذين ركب منهما الدى من اسمين بها
نظير المنفصل تفصيل الاصغر من الاعظم وجعل منفصل الموسط الاول نظير
الدى من موسطى الاول ومنفصل[183] الموسط الثانى نظير الدى من موسطى
الثانى والاصغر للاعظم والدى يجعل الكل مع منطق موسطا[184] للذى
يقوى على منطق وموسط والدى يجعل الكل مع موسط موسطا للذى
يقوى على موسطين والسبب فى وضع اسمائها بين وكما بين فى التى[185] بالتركيب
ان كل واحد منها هو منقسم على نقطة احدة كذلك بين يعقب هذه فى[186]
التى بالتفصل ان لفق كل واحد منها واحد

§ 33 وبين فى الجملة العاشرة خطوطا منفصلة مستخرجة على مثال ما استخرج[Pag. 27]
الذى من اسمين حتى يحد فصول هذه الستة الحطوط الصم

§ 34 وذلك انه يتبع هذا ما بين فى الجملة الحادية عشرة[187] الستة
الخطوط[188] الصم التى بالتفصل التى تقوى على موضع يحيط به خط منطق
وواحد من الحطوط[188] المنفصلة التى هى ايضا ستة على ترتيبها

§ 35 ولما بحث عن هذا فى الجمله الحادية عشرة[189] وصف فى الجملة الثانية
عشرة[190] امر الاشتراك الدى فيما بين هذه الستة الصم وبين ان المشارك
لكل واحد منها فهو مشاركه فى النوع لا محالة ووصف ايضا الاختلاف

الذى لبعضها عند بعض وهو الاختلاف الذى يبين من⁽¹⁹¹⁾ المواضع التى
ادا اصيفت⁽¹⁹²⁾ الى المنطق جعلت العروض مختلفة

§ 36 ولما صار الى الجملة الثالثة⁽¹⁹³⁾ عشره بين ان الخطوط الستة⁽¹⁹⁴⁾ الصم
التى بالتركيب مخالفة للخطوط التى بالتفصيل وان هذه التى بالتفصيل بعضها
مخالف لبعض وميزها ايضا من تفصيل المواضع كما ميز الخطوط التى
بالتركيب من تركيب وذلك انه لما فصل سطحا موسطا من سطح منطق
او سطحا منطقا من سطح موسط او سطحا موسطا من سطح موسط
وجد الخطوط التى تقوى على هذه السطوح وهى الصم التى⁽¹⁹⁵⁾ بالتفصيل
واحر ذلك لما اراد ان يظهر عدم التناهى الذى فى الصم وحد خطوطا
بلا نهاية مختلفة فى النوع حادثة عن الخط الموسط وجعل هذا المعى
اقصاء هذه المقالة وترك الصمم يمر بلا نهاية

تمت المقالة الاولى

من تفسير المقالة العاشرة

بسم الله الرحمن الرحيم

المقالة الثانية

من

تفسير المقالة العاشرة

من كتاب اوقلبدس

فى الاصول

- - - •••

§ 1 الذى ينعى ان علمه فى نطام الصم بايجـاز هو هذا امـا اولا فان اقلبدس افادنا المنتطمة منها والمجانسة للمنطقة وذلك ان الصم منها ما هى غير منتطمة وهى من حيز الهـولى التى يقال لها المَعورة وتخرج بلا نهاية ومنها ما هى منتطمة ويحيط بها علم ونستها الى تلك نسبة المنطقة [196] اليها واوقلبدس اما عى [107] بالمنتطمة المجانسة للمنطقة التى ليس خروجها عنها خروجا كثيرا فاما الموبيوس يعى غير المنتطمة التى البعد بنها وبين المنطقة بعد كثير

§ 2 ثم بعد ذلك ينعى ان نعلم ان الصم وجدت على ثلث جهـات اما بالتناسب واما بالتركيب واما بالتفصيل ولم توجد على جهة اخرى غير

هذه الثلث جهات اصلا وذلك ان غير المنتظمة انما اخذت من المنتظمة [Pag 30]

باحدى [198] هذه الجهات واوقليدس انما وجد خطا واحدا امم [199]

بالتناسب وستة بالتركيب وستة بالتفصيل وعند ذلك تتمّ [200] جميع عدد

الصم المنتظمة

§ 3 وثالثا بعد هذين ينبغى ان ننظر فى جميع الصم من المواضع التى تقوى

عليها وجميع الاختلافات التى لبعضها عند بعض من هذه ننعى ان يوجد

وان ننظر اى المواضع التى تقوى عليها واحد واحد منها على انها اجزاء

وانما هى التى تقوى عليها على انها كليات وذلك انا نجد الموسط على هذه

الجهة تقوى على موضع يحيط به خطان منطقان فى القوة مشتركان وكذلك

نجد كل واحد من الاخر ولذلك يصف اضافات القوى ايضا فى واحد

واحد [201] منها ولستخرج [202] عروص المواضع واخر ذلك يرك كالمحد [203]

فى اطهار عرصه المواضع اسهل فتقوم الصم التى بالركب فانه اذا رك

منطق [204] وموسط حدث اربعة خطوط صم وادا رُكب موسطان حدث

الخطان الباقيان وذلك ان هذه الخطوط ايضا قد تسمى مركبة من قبل

تركيب المواضع وكذلك تسمى التى بالتفصيل منفصلة [205] من قبل تفصل

المواضع التى تقوى عليها والموسط ايضا انما سمى موسطا لان المربع الذى

منه مساو للموضع الذى يحط به خطان منطقان فى القوة مشتركان

§ 4 فاد قد قدمنا واوطانا هذه الاشياء وينبعى ان نقول ان كل موضع [206]

قائم الزوايا فانه اما ان يكون يحط به خطان منطقان او خطان اصمان

او خط منطق وخط اصم واله ان كان الخطان اللذان يحيطان به منطقين

وهما اما مشتركان فى الطول او مشتركان فى القوة فقط [207] وان كان كلاهما [Pag 31]

اصمين فهما اما ان يكونا مشتركين فى الطول او مشتركين فى القوة فقط [207]
او متباينين فى الطول والقوة وان كان احدهما منطقا والاخر اصم فهما
لا محالة متباينين فان كان يحيط بالموضع المفروض خطان منطقان فان
المنطقين ان كانا فى الطول مشتركين فالموضع منطق كما بين المهندس
ان الموضع يحيط به منطقان مشتركان فى الطول منطق وان كانا فى القوة
فقط مشتركين فان الموضع اصم وسمى موسطا والخط الذى يقوى عليه
موسط وهدا ايضا قد بينه المهندس اعنى ان القائم الزوايا الذى يحيط به
منطقان فى القوة مشتركان اصم والخط الذى يقوى عليه اصم وليدع موسطا
وان كان الخطان المحيطان بالموضع اصمين فقد يجوز ان يكون الموضع
محال من الاحوال منطقا ويجوز ان يكون اصم وذلك ان الخطين ان كانا
فى الطول مشتركين فالموضع لا محالة اصم كما بين فى الموسطة وهذه الجهة
من البرهان توجد فى جميع الاصم وان كانا مشتركين فى القوة فقد يمكن
ان يكون منطقا ويمكن ان يكون اصم فانه قد تبين ان الموضع الذى يحيط
به خطان موسطان فى القوة مشتركان اما ان يكون منطقا واما اصم واذا
كانا متباينين من جميع الوجوه فقد نكون الموضع [208] الذى يحيطان به
منطقا ويكون اصم ودلك انه قد وجد خطين مستقيمين متباينين فى القوة
يحيطان بمنطق ووجد اخرين على دلك المثال [209] يحيطان بموسط وهما ايضا
متباينين فى القوة وهدا هو المعنى فى ان يكون الخطوط متباينة من جميع
الوجوه لان المتباينة فى القوة هى لا محالة متباينة فى الطول ايضا

فالخط الموسط وجده بالتناسب الهندسى يقوى على موضع موسط وهدا ٥ ﷺ

Pag 52 | ‖الموضع[210] مساو للموضع الذى يحيط به خطان منطقان فى القوة مشتركان ولذلك ما سماه بهذا الاسم

§ 6 واما الستة الصم التى بالتركيب التى بينها فينها من تركيب المواضع التى تقوى عليها وهذه المواضع منطقة وموسطة وذلك انه كما نجد الحط الموسط بالمنطقة وحدها كذلك نجد الخطوط الصم التى بالتركيب بكلى هذين الامرين اعنى بالمنطقة والموسطة لانه يبنغى دائما ان يكون الصم التى هى اقرب الى المنطقة تعدنا مبادى علم[211] التى هى اعد منها لانا ايضا انما نجد الخطوط التى بالتفصيل بالخطوط التى بالتركيب ولكن هذه سنصفها[212] باحره ولكن نجد الخطوط التى بالتركيب باخذ حطين مستقيمين فلس يخلوا من ان يكونا اما مشتركين فى الطول او مشتركين فى القوة فقط او متباينين فى القوة والطول وليس يمكن اذا كانا مشتركين فى الطول ان يستعملا فى وجود سائر الصم الساقية لان جملة الحط المركب من حطين مشتركين فى الطول مساوية فى النوع للخطين المركبين وان كانا منطقين جحملتها ايضا منطقة وان كانا موسطين فهى موسطة وذلك انه متى ترك عطين مشتركان فان جملتها مشاركة لكل واحد منها والمشارك للمنطق منطق والمشارك للموسط موسط

§ 7 فواجب ضرورة ان يكون الحطان المركبان اما مشتركين فى القوة او متباينين فى القوة والطول فلكونا اولا مشتركين فى القوة ثم نستعمل القسمة من الراس فنقول اما ان يكون المجتمع من مربعيها منطقا والموضع الذى يحطان به موسطا او يكون كل واحد منها موسطا او يكون المجتمع من مربعيها موسطا والموضع الذى يحطان به منطقا او يكون كل واحد

منها منطقا ولكن ان كان كل واحد منها منطقا فالخط باسره منطق
وليكن كل واحد منها منطق ولنضف الى خط منطق وهو اب
موضع ⁽²¹³⁾ ال مساويا لمربع خط هز باسره ولنفرر منه موضع اط مساويا
للموضع المركب من مربعى هد حر فموضع طى الباقى اذا مساو للموضع
الذى يحط به هد جر مرتين فلان كل واحد من الموضعين المضافين الى

Pag. 33

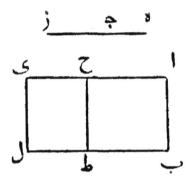

خط اب المنطق منطق فكل واحد من خطى اح حى منطق ومشارك
لخط اب فى الطول فكل واحد منها مشارك للاحر فاى باسره مشارك
لها ولخط اب فموضع ال اذا منطق ⁽²¹⁴⁾ فنجب ان نكون المربع الذى من
هر ايضا منطقا لحط هر اذا منطق ⁽²¹⁴⁾ فليس ينبغى اذا ان ناخد كل واحد
منها منطقا اعى المركب من مربعى هج جر والموضع الذى يحطان به
فقى اذا ان يكون المركب من مربعيها منطقا والذى يحيطان ⁽²¹⁵⁾ به موسطا
او بعكس ذلك او ان ⁽²¹⁶⁾ يكونا جميعا موسطين فان كان المركب الذى من
مربعيها منطقا والذى يحيطان به موسطا فالخط باسره من اسمين يقوى على
موضعى منطق وموسط والمنطق اعظم من الموسط لانه قد تبين انه متى
قسم خط بقسمين مختلفين فان القائم الزوايا الذى يحيط به القسمان المختلفان

مرتبى اقل من الموضع المركب من مربعيها وان كان الامر بالعكس اعنى
اى يكون الموضع الذى يحيط به الخطان المفروصان المشتركان فى القوة
فقط منطقا والمركب من مربعيها موسطا والخط باسره اصم وهو الذى من
موسطين الاول وهو يقوى على موضعين منطق وموسط والموسط اعظم
من المنطق وان كان كل واحد منهما موسطا فان هذا هو الذى نقى اعنى
المركب من مربعيها والذى يحيطان به فان الخط باسره اصم وهو الذى من
موسطين الثانى وهو يقوى على سطحين موسطين اقول ان هذين الموسطين

Pag 34 | متباينان فان لم يكونا كذلك فليكونا مشتركين فان كان [217] المجتمع من مربعى
اب بج [218] مشاركا للذى يحيط به اب بج لكن المركب من مربعى اب بج
مشارك لمربع اب وقد كان مربع اب مشاركا لمربع بج لانه قد وضع خطا
اب بج بالقوة مشتركين ومتى تركب خطان مشتركان فان مجموعهما
مشارك لكل واحد منهما هو مربع اب اذا مشارك للذى يحيط به اب بج
ونسبة مربع اب الى الموضع الذى يحيط به اب بج كنسبة خط اب الى
خط بج اذا مشارك فى الطول لخط بج وذلك ما لم نفرض لانها
مشتركين فى القوة فقط فالمركب اذا من مربعى اب بج باضطرار مباين
للقائم الزوايا الذى يحيطان به وهذه اذا ثلثة خطوط صم تحدث اذا كان
الخطان المفروصان مشتركين فى القوة

٨ ‏*‏ وقد تحدث ثلثة احر اذا كانا متباينين فى القوة وليكن اب بح متباينين
فى القوة فاما ان يكون المركب من مربعيها منطقا والقائم الزوايا الذى
يحيطان به منطقا او يكونا كلاهما موسطين او يكون احدهما منطقا والاخر
موسطا وهذا على جهتين كالحال فى الخطان المشتركين فى القوة ولكن ان

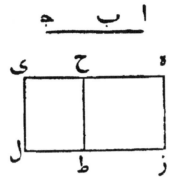

كان المركب من مربعى اب بج منطقا والذى يحيطان به منطقا والحط باسره

منطق وليفرض ايضا حط منطق وليصف اليه موضع مساو لمربع اج وليمرر

من هذا الموضع موضع مساو للمركب من مربعى اب بج وهو موضع هط

محل الباقى اذا مساو للقائم الزوايا الذى يحيط به اب بج (219) مرتين فهط حل

اذًا منطقان وقد اضيما الى خط هز المنطق وكل واحد منها اذًا يحدث

عرصا منطقا مشاركا لخط هز فهج وحى اذًا مشتركان فهى مشارك لكل

واحد منها فهو اذًا منطق ومشارك فى الطول لخط هز والقائم الزوايا

الذى يحيط به خطان منطقان فى الطول مشركان منطق فموضع هل اذًا

منطق فمربع اج منطق فاج منطق وذلك ان الحط الذى يقوى على منطق

منطق فلانا نلتمس ان نبرهن ان الحط باسره اصم فلس ينبعى لنا ان

ناخذكل واحد من الموضعين منطقا لكنه ينبعى ان ناحدهما اما موسطين

كليها (220) او احدهما منطقا والاخر موسطا ويكون هذا على جهتين وذلك

انه اما ان يكون الاعظم هو المنطق او الموسط اذ لبس بتهـا ان بكونا

متساويين لثلا يكونا مشتركين ويكون المنطق موسطا والموسط منطقا فان

كان المركب من مربعى اب بج منطقا وكان القائم الروايا الذى من اب بج

موسطا فليدع اج الاعظم لان المنطق هو الاعظم وان كان الامر بالعكس
فكان المركب من مربعى اب بج موسطا والقائم الروايا الذى يحيط به (221)
اب بج منطقا فليدع اج اصم يقوى على منطق وموسط وذلك انه ينبغى
ان يسمى من كل واحد من الموضعين اما من المنطق فلانه افضل بالطبع
واما من الموسط فلانه فى هذا الموضع الاعظم وان كان الموضعان كلاهما
موسطين فليدع الخط باسره اصم يقوى على موسطين وفى هذا الموضع ايضا
يريد اقليدس فى قوله ان الموسطين متباينان

§ 9   وان الصم بالتركيب ليس ينبغى لنا ان نظن ايها تركيبان خطوط بل
تركيبان المواضع التى تقوى عليها وهذا شىء قد صرح به (222) اقليدس
الا قليل (223) فى اخر المقالة حيث بين انه اذا ترك موضع منطق وموسط
حدث عنها اربعة خطوط (224) صم واذا تركك موسطان حدث الاثنان
الباقيان فهو بين عندنا ان الخطين اذا كانا مشتركين فى القوة حدث ثلثة
خطوط ضروره واذا كانا متباينين فى القوه حدث ثلثة وذلك انه ليس
يمكن ان يكونا مشتركين فى الطول ولكنه واجب ان نطلب لم لما (225)

وصف المشتركة (226) فى القوه ذكر نوعها ايضا فقال منطقين فى القوة
مشتركين او موسطين والمتباينة فى القوة لما وضعها لم يسمها (227) منطقة او
موسطة وقد كان ينبغى ان نقول فى ذلك ايضا على مثال ما قال فى هذه
متى ترك خطان مستقيمان فى القوة مشتركان جعلا المركب من موضعيها (228)
موسطا والذى يحيطان به منطقا (228) فالخط باسره اصم ويدعى من موسطين
الاول وكذلك فى الذى من موسطين الثانى وذلك انه هكذا قال فى المتباينة
فى القوة ايضا من غير ان يسميها موسطة او منطقة لكنه انما نطق فى

المواضع فقط اعى المركب من مربعيها والدى يحيطان به واخذهما اما

موسطين جميعا واما احدهما منطقا والاخر موسطا والاعظم منها اما المنطق

واما الموسط فاقول احسب بان اقليدس يرى ان الخطين متى كانا فى القوة

مشتركين وكان الموضع المركب من موضعيها منطقا فان مربع كل واحد

منها منطق وان كان المركب من مربعيها [229] موسطا فان مربع كل واحد

منها موسط وان كانا فى القوة متباينين وكان المركب من مربعيها [229] منطقا

لم يكن مربع كل واحد منها منطقا وان كان المركب من مربعيها موسطا

لم يكن مربع كل واحد منها موسطا ولدلك لما اخد المشتركة فى القوة سماها

منطقة او موسطة لان الخطوط التى تقوى على المواضع المنطقة منطقة والتى

تقوى على الموسطة موسطة ولما اخد المتباينة فى القوة لم يَحْتَجّ ان يسميها

منطقة او موسطة لانه انما ينبغى ان سمى منطقين الخطين اللذين كل

واحد منها يقوى على منطق لا اللدين [230] المركب من مربعيها منطق

ومربعاهما [231] ليسا منطقين لان الموضع المنطق ليس ينقسم لا محالة الى

موضعين منطقين وسمى موسطين الخطين اللدين كل واحد منها يقوى على

موسط لا اللذين المركب | من مربعيهما موسط ومربعاهما [232] ليسا موسطين   Pag 37

لان الموضع الموسط لس ينقسم لا محالة الى موضعين موسطين

اما المعنى الذى اراده فهنا ولكنه يحتاج الى برهان اه متى كان خطان § 10

مشتركان فى القوة وكان المركب من مربعيهما منطقا او موسطا فانهما يكونان

منطقين او موسطين فان كانا متباينين فى القوة لم يكن هدا القول فيهما

صادقا وليكن خطا اب بج فى القوه مشتركين [233] ولبكن المركب من

مربعيهما منطقا فاقول ان هذين منطقان [234] فلان خط اب فى القوة مشارك

لخط بج فمربع اب مشارك لمربع بج فالمركب من الاثنين مشارك لكل واحد

منهما والمركب من الاثنين منطق فكل واحد منهما منطق فخط

اب بج [235] اذًا منطقان مشتركان فى القوة وليكن ايضا المركب موسطا اقول

ان هذين الخطين موسطان فلان اب بج فى القوه مشتركان فمربعاهما

مشتركان فالمركب من هذين مشارك لكل واحد منهما والمركب من المربعين

موسط فمربعا [236] اب بج اذًا موسطان فهما ايضا موسطان لان المشارك

للمنطق منطق والمشارك للموسط موسط والخط الذى يقوى على المنطق

منطق [237] والذى يقوى على الموسط موسط فان كان مربعا اب بج موسطين

فان المركب منهما موسط وان كان المركب منهما موسطا فهما موسطان

اذكان اب بج فى القوة مشتركين [238] ولكن فليكونا متباينين فى القوه

اقول انه ليس ان كان المركب من مربعيهما منطقا فهما منطقان ولا ان

كان موسطا فهما موسطان فان كان ذلك ممكنا فلنكن مربعا اب بج

Pag 38 منطقين وليصف [239] الى خط منطق وهو هز | موضع مساو للمركب من

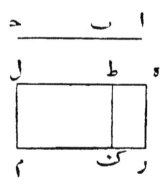

مربعى اب بج وهو هم وليفصل منه موضع مساو لمربع اب وهو هك

فالباقى اذًا وهو طم مساو لمربع [240] بج فلان مربع اب مباين لمربع بج

15*

لأهما فى القوة متباينان فبين ان هك مباين لطم مخط هط اذًا مباين فى
الطول لخط طل ولان مربعى اب بج منطقان فموضعا هك طم منطقان
وقد اضيفا الى خط هز المنطق مخطا هط[241] طل اذًا منطقان فى القوة
فقط مشتركان لان موضع هك مباين لموضع طم مخط هط مباين فى الطول
لخط طل[212] مخط هل اذًا من اسمين فهو اذًا اصم ولكن موضع هم منطق
لانه مساو للمركب من مربعى اب بج وهو منطق وقد اصيف الى حط
هز المنطق مخط هل اذًا منطق فهو اذًا بعينه منطق واصم فلبس اذًا مربعا
اب بج منطقين ولكن ايضا المركب من مربعى اب بج المتباينين فى القوة
موسطا اقول ان مربعى اب بج لبسا موسطين فان كان ذلك ممكنا فنفرص
هز منطقا ولكن الموصعان بعينها موسطين[213] فكل واحد من خطى
هط طل منطق[214] وهما فى القوة مشتركان هل اذًا مخط هل اذًا من اسمين وهو اذًا
اصم لكنه منطق وذلك ان المركب من مربعى اب بج موسط وقد اضف
الى هر المنطق فاحدث عرصا منطقا فليس اذًا مربعا اب بج موسطين فقد
تبين اذًا ان الخطين المتباينين فى القوة لبس اذا كان المركب من مربعبها
منطقا او موسطا فهما ايضا منطقان او موسطان فلما بين اوقليدس ان ذلك
فى المشتركة فى القوة حق وفى المتباينة فى القوة بحق ليس بحق سمى تلك
المشتركة فى القوة منطقة وموسطة ولم يسم هذه لكنه سماها متباينة فى
القوة على الاطلاق

§ 11 فلان القسمة التى من اول الامر انما يأحد الخطوط المشتركة فى القوة
Pag 39 والمتباينة فى القوة ستخرج بها الخطوط الصم تركيب المواضع اما المنطقة
والموسطة[215] واما الموسطة المتباينة لانه قد ينبغى بهذين الموصعين من

قبل انها يتولدان من المنطقة فمتى كان الخطان اللذان يحيطان بالموضع
منطقين واما ان يكونا كذلك فى الطول فيكون الموضع الذى يحيطان به [216]
منطقا واما ان يكونا كذلك فى القوة فيكون الذى يحيطان به [246] موسطا
فلذلك استخرج [247] الستة الصم التى بالتركيب من احاطة الخطوط [247]
المنطقة احد هذين الموضعين فليكف [218] عما وصفناه فى الصم التى بالتركيب
اذ قد بينا ترتيبها وعددها من القسمة

§ 12 وقد نجد الستة التى بالتفصل من التى بالتركيب لانا اذا نظرنا الى
كل واحد من الخطوط الصم التى وصفنا فجعلنا حال احد الخطين اللذين
ركب منها الى الاخر كحال خط ما باسره الى جزء منه فان الفضل الباقى
منه يحدث واحدة من هذه الستة الصم فمتى احدث الخط المستقيم باسره
مع جزء منه الخط الذى من اسمين حدث المنفصل ومتى احدث الذى من
موسطين الاول حدث [219] منفصل الموسط الاول ومتى احدث الذى من
موسطين الثانى حدث منفصل الموسط الثانى ومتى احدث الاعظم حدث
الاصغر ومتى احدث الذى يقوى على منطق وموسط حدث الذى يصر [250]
الكل مع منطق موسطا ومتى احدث الذى يقوى على موسطين حدث
الذى يصر الكل مع موسط موسطا وعلى هذا الوجه تبين ان تولد هذه
من تلك الستة وانها نظائر لها وان التى بالتفصل محانسة للتى بالتركب
Pag. 40 فالمنفصل [251] محانس للذى من اسمين ومنفصل | الموسط الاول محانس للذى
من موسطين يحيطان بمنطق ومنفصل الموسط الثانى محانس للذى من موسطين
يحيطان بموسط والباقية من هذه نظيرة للباقية من تيك على هذا المثال

§ 13 وليس ينبغى ان نظن فى الصم التى بالتفصيل [252] انا انما نسميها

منفصلة (253) من قبل انفصال جزء من الخط من جملته كما انا لم نسم الستة
التى بالمركب مركبة من قبل تركيب الخطوط لكنا انما نسميها من قبل
المواضع المنفصلة المنقوصة كما اما اما سمينا تلك الصم التى بالتركيب
مركبة من قبل المواضع المركبة التى تقوى عليها ولنضع خط اب وليحدث
مع بج الذى من اسمين مربعا اب بج مساويان للقائم الروايا الذى يحيط
به اب بج مرتين ومربع جا ولكن قد صار الذى من مربعى اب بج
منطقا والذى يحيطان به موسطا فان ات اذا نقصت من موضع منطق
موضعا موسطا فان الخط الذى يقوى على الباقى المنفصل فكما انه اذا
تركب موسط ومنطق وكان المنطق هو الاعظم امكن ان يحدث الذى من
اسمين كذلك (254) ادا نقص من منطق موسط فان الخط الذى يقوى على
المنفصل ولذلك سمينا الذى من اسمين بالتركيب والمنفصل بالتفصيل
وذلك انا هناك ركبنا موسطا اصغر مع (255) منطق اعظم وهاهنا فصلنا من
المنطق بعينه الموسط بعينه هناك وجدنا الذى يقوى على الكل وهاهنا
وجدنا الذى يقوى على الساق فنفصل اذا والذى من اسمين متجانسان (255b)
واحدهما يخالف الاخر واصا اذاكان خطا اب بج فى القوة مشتركين
وكان مجموع اللذين منها موسطا والذى يحيطان به منطقا صار الموسط
مساويا للمنطق مرتين (256) والذى من خط اج الباقى فبعكس ذلك فى هذا
الخط ان نقص من موسط منطق فان |الذى يقوى على الباقى منفصل الموسط
الاول لان المنطق اصغر (257) من الموسط فكما انا صيّرنا الذى من موسطين
الاول بتركب الموسط والمنطق على ان المنطق الاصغر والموسط الاعظم
كذلك نقول ان منفصل الموسط الاول هو الذى يقوى على الموضع الباق

Pag. 41

بعد انفصال المنطق من الموسط وايضا اذا احدث اب بج الذى من موسطين
الثانى وكان مجموع اللدين يكونان منها موسطا [258] وكان مجموع الذى من
اب بج اعظم من الذى يحيطان به مرتين والذى من [259] خط اج فان انت
فصلت من موسط موسطا وكان الحطان اللدان يحطان بالموسط المفصول
مشتركين فى القوة فان الحط الدى يقوى على الباقى منفصل الموسط الثانى
وذلك انه كما ان الخط الدى يقوى على هدين الموصعين الموسطين اذا احذنا
بالتركيب كان يسمى الذى من موسطين الثانى كذلك الخط الذى يقوى على
الباقى من انفصال الاصغر من الموسطين من الاكبر سمى منفصل الموسط
الثانى وايضا متى كان خطا اب بج بالقوة متباينين وكان المركب من مربعيها
منطقا والذى يحطان به موسطا فان الموسط مرتين اذا فصل من المنطق
بقى مربع اج فهو يسمى الاصغر كما ان ذلك يسمى الاعظم لان ذلك كان
يقوى على موصعين [260] وهدا يقوى على الباقى بعد التفصيل فلدلك سمى
هذا الاصغر لمقابلته لدلك الذى يسمى الاعظم وايضا ان كان المركب
من مربعى اب بج موسطا والذى يحيطان به منطقا وانزعت المنطق
مرتين من الموسط الذى من مربعيها فان الدى يقوى على الباقى بعد
الانفصال هو خط اج [261] ويسمى الذى يبصر الكل مع منطق موسطا
لان مربعه ادا ركب مع القائم الزوايا الذى يحط به خطا اب بج مرتين
وهو منطق فن البين انه مساو للمركب من مربعى اب بج وايضا اذاكان | Pag. 42
خطا اب بج فى القوة متباينين وكان الدى من مربعيها موسطا والدى
يحيطان به موسطا [262] وكان الموصعان متباينين ثم فصلنا الذى يحيطان
به مرتين من الموسط الاعظم المركب من مربعيها فان الخط الذى يقوى على

الباقى هو خط آج ⁽²⁶³⁾ ويسمى الذى يعمل الكل مع موسط موسطا وذلك

ان مربعه والذى يحيط به آب بج مرتين اذا اخذا معا كانا مساويين

للمركب من مربعى آب بج الذى هو موسط

§ 14 فاذا ركبت المواضع المنطقة مع الموسطة او الموسطة مع الموسطة فقد

تبين ان الخطوط الصم التى تقوى على المركب منها هى التى تسمى بالتركيب

واذا فصلت مواضع موسطة من منطقة ومنطقة من موسطة وموسطة

من موسطة فقد تبين لنا الخطوط الصم التى بالتفصيل وذلك انا فى هذه

المواضع لسنا نفصل ⁽²⁶⁴⁾ منطقة من منطقة لئلا يكون الباقى منطقا لانه

قد نبين ان المنطق ⁽²⁶⁵⁾ يفصل المنطق بمنطق ⁽²⁶⁵⁾ وان الخط الذى يقوى

على المنطق منطق فان كان ينبغى ان يكون الخط الذى يقوى على الباقى

من الانفصال اصم ويقوى على موضع اخر اصم هذه الصفة فليس ينبغى

ان يكون الموضع المنفصل من المنطق منطقا فبقى ان ننزع ⁽²⁶⁶⁾ اما منطق

من موسط او موسط من منطق واما موسط من موسط ولكنا اذا فصلنا

موسطا من منطق جعلنا الخطين اللذين يقويان على الباقيين اصمين فان

كان المحيطان ⁽²⁶⁷⁾ بالموسط بالقوة مشتركين حدث المنفصل وان كانا فى

القوة متباينين حدث الاصغر واذا نحن فصلنا منطقا من موسط ⁽²⁶⁸⁾ عملنا

خطين اخرين ايضا فان كان الخطان اللذان ⁽²⁶⁹⁾ يحيطان بالمنطق والمفصول

فى القوة مشتركين حدث منفصل الموسط الاول وان كانا فى القوة متباينين

حدث الذى يجعل الكل مع منطق موسطا واذا ما فصلنا من الموسط ⁽²⁷⁰⁾

موسطا فكان الخطان اللذان يحيطان بالموسط ⁽²⁷¹⁾ فى القوة مشتركين وان

الخط ⁽²⁷²⁾ الذى يقوى على ⁽²⁷²⁾ الباقى ⁽²⁷³⁾ هو منفصل الموسط الثانى وان

كما في القوة متباينين حدث⁽²⁷³⁾ الذى يجعل الكل مع موسط موسطا لانا لما الفنا⁽²⁷⁴⁾ فى التركب المواضع الموسطة مع المنطقة او المنطقة مع الموسطة او الموسطة مع الموسطة احدثنا الخطوط الستة الصم فقط فى كل واحد اثنان⁽²⁷⁵⁾ فضرب الاخذ بالمركب التى تحط بالمواضع الصغرى وتقوى على المواضع العظمى واخذناها مرة فى القوة مشتركة ومرة فى القوة متباينة

§ 15 ونحن نقول جملة ان الموسط اذا ركب مع منطق جعل الذى يقوى على الكل من اسمين واذا نقص منه جعل الذى يقوى على الباقى منفصلا متى كان يحيط به خطان فى القوة مشتركان ومنطق اذا ركب مع موسط جعل الذى يقوى على الكل من موسطين الاول واذا نقص من موسط جعل الذى يقوى على الباقى منفصل موسط⁽²⁷⁶⁾ الاول متى كان يحيط به خطان فى القوة مشتركان وموسط اذا ركب معه موسط جعل الذى يقوى على الكل من موسطين الثانى واذا نقص من موسط جعل الذى يقوى على الباقى منفصل موسط الثانى متى كان الخطان اللذان يحيطان به فى القوة مشتركين⁽²⁷⁷⁾ وايضا اذا ركب موسط مع منطق جعل الذى يقوى على الكل الاعظم واذا نقص من منطق جعل الذى يقوى على الباقى الاصغر متى كان الخطان اللذان يحيطان به ويقويان على منطق فى القوة متباينين واذا ركب منطق مع موسط جعل الذى يقوى على الكل⁽²⁷⁵⁾

Pag 44 القوى على منطق وموسط واذا نقص من موسط جعل الذى يقوى على الباقى الذى يجعل الكل مع منطق موسطا متى كان الخطان اللذان يحيطان به ويقويان على موسط فى القوه متباينين واذا ركب موسط مع موسط جعل الحط القوى على الكل الذى يقوى على موسطين واذا نقص

موسط من موسط جعل الخط القوى على الباقى الدى يجعل الكل مع
موسطا موسطا متى كان الحطان اللذان يحيطان بالاصغر نسبه وتقويان
على الاعظم فى القوة متباينين فاخذ المواضع اذًا يكون على ثلثة جهات
موسط مضاف الى منطق او منطق مضاف الى موسط او موسط مضاف الى
موسط ودلك ان احذ منطق مضاف الى منطق لس يوجد كما تبين
وحدوث الحطوط التى تحط بها يكون على جهتين اما فى القوة مشتركة
واما فى القوة متباينة لانه ليس يمكن ان تكون مشتركة فى الطول [279]
واصناف اخذها انصا صنفان اما بالتركيب واما بالتفصيل

§ 16 فالحطوط الصم اذا اثنى عشر يخالف بعضها بعضا اما بجهة اخد
المواضع فادا ركبنا مرة موسطا [280] مع منطق وفصلنا مرة موسطا [281] من
منطق واما بحسب الحطوط التى [282] تحط بالاصاغر [283] فتقوى على
العظمى مثال ذلك اذا كانت فى القوه مشتركة واذا كانت فى القوة متباينة
واما بحسب اختلاف المواضع مثال ذلك اذا قصنا مرة منطقا من
موسط ومره موسطا من منطق ومرة يكون المركب مع الموسط منطقا
ويكون الاصغر ومرة يكون المركب مع المنطق موسطا ويكون الاصغر جميع
الحطوط التى بالتركيب يخالف التى بالتفصيل بجهة الاخذ فاما بحسب
الحطوط التى تحط بالمواضع فقد يخالف الثلثة المتقدمة ومن التى بالتركيب
والتى بالتفصيل للتالية واما بحسب اختلاف المواضع فان | الصم المنتطمة
Pag 45
فى ثلثة ثلثة منها يخالف بعضها بعضا فهذه حال قسمة الصم وترتيبها على
راى اقليدس

§ 17 ولان القوم الذن اقتصوا هذه الاشياء زعموا ان ثاطيطس الاثنى اخد

خطين فى القوة مشتركين فبرهن انه اذا اخذ فيما بينهما خط على نسبة فى
التناسب الهندسى حدث الخط الذى يسمى الموسط واذا اخذ فى
التناسب التاليفى حدث المنفصل فنحن نقبل هذه الاشياء اذكان ثااطيطس
يقولها ونضيف اليها ان التوسط الهندسى هو الخط الموسط بين خطين منطقين
فى القوة مشتركين والتوسط العددى هو كل واحد من الخطوط التى
بالتركب [281] والتوسط التالمى هو كل واحد من الخطوط التى بالتفصيل
وان اصناف التناسب الثلثة تحدث جميع الخطوط الصم وقد برهن اقلدس
برهانا واضحا انه متى كان خطان منطقين فى القوة مشتركين وواحد خط [285]

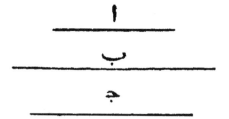

فيما بينهما مناسب لهما مناسبة هندسية فان الخط الماخوذ اصم ويسمى
الموسط واما الصم الباقية فسنبين فيها التناسب الباقى فلنضع خطين
مستقيمين وهما خطا آ ب وخط ما موسط فيما بينهما على التناسب
العددى وهو خط جـ اذًا اذا ركبا كانا ضعف خط جـ لان هذه
خاصة التناسب العددى فان كان خطا آ ب منطقين فى القوة مشتركين
خط جـ من اسمين لانهما اذا ركبا صارا ضعف جـ ولكنهما اذا ركبا
احدثنا الذى من اسمين فلان [286] خط جـ نصفهما فهدا [287] الخط من
اسمين ايضا واذا كان خطا آ ب موسطين فى القوة مشتركين يحيطان
بمنطق فان المركب منهما وهو ضعف خط جـ يصير من موسطين الاول

Pag. 46 فخط جـ اذا حاله هذه الحال لانه نصف المركب من الطرفين فان كانا

موسطين فى القوة مشتركين يحيطان بموسط فان المركب منهما يصير من

موسطين الثانى ومشاركا لخط جـ لانه ضعمه فخط جـ اذا من موسطين

الثانى ايضا وان كان خطا آ ب فى القوة متباينين وكان الذى من مربعيهما

منطقا والذى بنهما اصم فان خط جـ يصير الاعظم لان المركب من خطى

آ ب هو الاعظم وهو صعف خط جـ فخط جـ اذا الاعظم وان كان الامر

بالعكس اعى ان كان خطا آ ب فى القوة متباينين وكان الذى من

مربعيهما موسطا والذى بينهما منطقا صار خط جـ القوى على منطق وموسط

لانه مشارك للمركب من خطى آ ب وقد كان المركب منهما القوى على

منطق وموسط وان كان خطا آ ب فى القوه متباينين وكان الذى من

مربعيهما والذى بينهما موسطين فان خط جـ يكون القوى على موسطين

اد كان المركب من خطى آ ب ضعف جـ وهو القوى على موسطين فخط

جـ قوى على موسطين فخط جـ اذا لما كان توسطا عدديا احدث جميع الخطوط

الصم التى بالتركيب

§ 18 وليكن المقدمات على هده الصفة الاولى [288] اذا اخذ خط موسط فيما

بين خطين منطقين فى القوة مشتركين على التناسب العددى فان الخط

الماخوذ يكون من اسمين والثانة اذا اخذ خط متوسط بين خطين موسطين

فى القوه مشتركين وكان الموضع الدى يحيطان به منطقا [289] على التناسب

العددى فان الخط الماخوذ يصر من موسطين الاول والثالثة اذا اخذ

خط متوسط بين خطين متوسطين فى القوة مشتركين يحيطان بموسط على

التناسب العددى صار الخط الماخوذ من موسطين الثانى والرابعة [290] اذا

اخد حط موسط بين خطين مستقيمين فى القوة متباينين فى التناسب
العددى الذى من مربعيهما منطق والذى فيا بينهما موسط صار الحط
الماخوذ اصم [291] وبسمى الاعظم والخامسة اذا اخذ حط متوسط من خطين
مستقيمين فى القوة متباينين الدى من مربعيهما موسط والدى بينهما | Pag 47
منطق على التناسب العددى صار الحط الماخود الذى يقوى على منطق
وموسط والسادسة اذا اخذ خط متوسط بين خطين مستقيمين فى القوة
متباينين الذى من مربعيهما موسط والدى يحيطان به موسط على التناسب
العددى صار الحط الماخوذ الدى يقوى على موسطين والبرهان العام
لجميعها هو ان الطرفين ادا تركبا صارا صعف الاوسط وهما محدثان الصم
المطلوبة فهده ادا تكوں مشاركة [292] للصم التى تحت نوع واحد

§ 19 | وينبغى اں ننطر بعد هذه فى الحطوط الصم التى بالتفصيل كف تظهر
بالتوسط التالفى ونقدم قبل دلك اں حاصة التناسب التالفى [293] اه
يجعل الدى يحيط به كل واحد من الطرفين مع المتوسط ضعف الدى يحيط
به الطرفان ومع هذا ايصا انه اذا كان خطان مستقيمان [294] يحيطان
بموضع منطق او موسط وكان احدهما واحدا [295] من الحطوط الصم التى
بالركيب فان الاخر واحد من الخطوط التى بالتفصيل وهو الدى على
مقابلته مثال ذلك انه ان كان احد الحطين المحيطين بالموضع من اسمين
فان الباقى المنفصل وان كان من موسطين الاول فان الاخر منفصل موسط
الاول وان كان من موسطين الثانى فان الاخر منفصل موسط الثانى وان
كان الاعظم فان الاخر الاصغر وان كان القوى على منطق وموسط فالاخر
الدى يجعل الكل موسطا مع منطق وان كان القوى على موسطين فاـ

الاخر الذى يجعل الكل مع موسط موسطا فاذ قد قدمنا واحدا هذه
الاشياء فلنضع خطين وهما خطا اب بج والمتوسط بينهما فى النسبة على
التناسب التالفى [296] خط بد [297] فان كان خطا اب بج منطقين فى القوة
مشركين [297] فان الذى بينهما موسط فان الذى بينهما مرتين |موسط Pag. 48

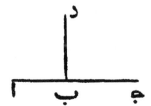

لكن الذى بينها مرتين مساو للموضع [298] الذى يحيط به خطا اب بد
وللذى يحيط به حطا بج بد فالذى يحيط به اذا اب بج بد بد موسط
ايضا لكن الذى يحيط به كل واحد من اب بج مع بد مساو للذى
يحيط به جميع حط اج وحط بد فالذى يحيط به اذا حطا اج بد موسط
ويحيط به خطان مستقيمان احدهما وهو خط اج من اسمين محط بد اذا
المنفصل وان كان خطا اب بج موسطين فى القوة مشتركين يحيطان منطق
فانا اذا عملنا ذلك العمل بعينه كان الذى يحيط به خطا اج بد منطقا وكان
خط اج من الموسطين الاول محط بد اذا منفصل الموسط الاول وان كان
خطا اب بج موسطين فى القوة مشتركين يحيطان بموسط يكون لتلك
الاسباب باعيانها الذى يحيط به اج بد موسط [299] وخط اج من موسطين
الثانى محط بد اذا منفصل موسط الثانى وان كان خطا اب بج فى القوة
متباينين والذى من مربعيها منطق والذى يحيطان به موسط فان الذى
يحيطان به مرتين يصير موسطا فالذى يحيط به اذا اج بد موسط وخط اج

الاعظم لخط بد الاصغر وان كان خطا اب بج فى القوة متباينين والذى من
مربعيهما موسط والذى يحيطان به منطق فان الذى يحيط به خطا اج بد
يصير منطقا وخط اج يقوى على منطق وموسط لخط بد اذا الذى يجعل
الكل مع منطق موسطا وان كان خطا اب بج فى القوة متباينين والمركب
من مربعيهما موسط والذى يحيطان به موسط ايضا صار الذى يحيط به
خطا اج بد موسطا وحط اج يقوى على موسطين لخط بد اذا الذى
يجعل الكل مع موسط موسطا فالمتوسط اذا العددى اذا اخذ من الخطوط
المركبة احدث واحدا من الخطوط الصم التى بالتركب والتوسط التاليفى
واحدا من الخطوط التى بالتفصيل وهو المقابل للمركب من الخطوط المفروصة

§ 20   وليكن مقدمات هذه ايضا بهده الصفة الاولى اذا اخد توسط تاليفى من

Pag 49 | الخطين اللذين منهما كان الذى من اسمين فان الخط الماخوذ هو المنفصل
والثالثة اذا اخذ توسط تاليمى بين الخطين اللذين منهما من الموسطين
الاول فان الماخوذ هو منفصل موسط الاول والثالثة ادا اخذ توسط
تاليمى بين الخطين اللذين منهما يكون الذى من موسطين الثانى فان
الماخوذ منفصل موسط الثانى والرابعة اذا اخذ موسط تالمى بين الخطين
اللذين يكون منهما الاعظم فان الماخوذ هو الاصغر والخامسة اذا احذ
توسط تاليفى بين الخطين اللذين يكون منهما القوى على منطق وموسط
صار الماخوذ هو الذى يجعل الكل مع منطق موسطا والسادسة اذا اخذ
توسط تالبفى بين الخطين اللذين يكون منهما القوى على موسطين فان
الماخوذ يصر الذى يجعل الكل مع موسط موسطا فالتوسط اذا الهندسى
تبين لنا اول الخطوط [300] الصم وهو الموسط والتوسط العددى تبين لنا

جميع الخطوط (300) التى بالتركيب والتوسط التاليفى تبين لنا جميع الخطوط التى بالتفصيل ويبيّن (301) لنا مع ذلك من هذه الاشياء ان قول نااطيطس حق فان التوسط الهندسى بين خطين منطقين فى القوة مشتركين هو الخط الموسط والتوسط العددى بينهما هو الخط الذى من اسمين والتوسط التاليفى بينهما هو المنفصل فهذا مبلغ ماكان عندنا فى الخطوط الصم الثلثة عشر من ثنتنا لقسمتها و ترتيبها ومجانستها لاصناف التناسب الثلثة التى تمدحها القدماء

§ 21 واما الامر فانه (302) انا كان احد الخطين بمحطان بمنطق او موسط واحدا (303) من الخطوط الصم التى بالتركب فان الخط الباقى يكون الخط المقابل له من الخطوط التى بالتفصيل فينبغى ان نبينه على هذا الوجه بعد

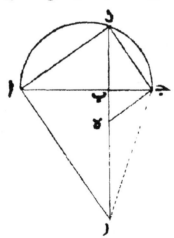

ان نقدم قبله هذا الشكل ليكن حطا اب بج بمحيطان بمنطق وليكن اب 50 'ag اعظم من بج ولنكن على خط اج نصف دائرة وهى ادج ولنخرج خط دب على زوايا قائمة فخط بد منطق ايضا لانه قد تبين انه متوسط فى النسبة بين خطى اب بج وادا (304) وصلنا بين دا و دج بخطين مستقيمين وذلك

ان زاوية د قائمة لانها فى نصف دائرة ولنخرج على خط دا خط از على

زوايا قائمة ولنخرج خط دب وللق حط از (305) على نقطة ز ولنخرج

حطا من دج على روايا قائمة اقول انه لا يلقى خط دز على نقطة ز ولا يمر

خارجا من از بل قد يقع داخله فان امكن فليلقه على ز فسطح دازج

ادا متوازى الاضلاع لان زواياه كلها قائمة وخط دا اكبر من خط دج

حط جز ادا اعظم من خط از لان الخطين المتقابلين متساويان فمربع (306)

جب ز اذا اعظم من مربعى اب ر حط بج اذا اكبر من خط با هذا

خلف لانه قد كان اصغر منه ومن الاجود ان نبينه على هذا الوجه لان

الزاويتين اللتين عند نقطى ا ج قائمتان وخطى اب بج عمودان فان

القائم الروايا الذى من دب بز مساو لمربع بج وهو بعينه مساو لمربع اب

مربع اب اذا مساو لمربع جب وقد وصفنا ان خط اب اعظم من خط

بج وعلى ذلك المثال بين انه لا يلقاه خارجا عن نقطة ز فليلقه اذا داخلها

على نقطة ه فاقول ايضا ان القائم الزوايا الذى من رب به مساو لمربع دب

وهو منطبق لان مثلث دجه قائم الراوية وخط جب عمود فان المثلثين

متشابهان فزاوية ه ادا مساوية لزاوية دجب (307) ولهذا بعينه راوية

دجب (308) مساوية لراوية بدا (309) ولهذا بعينه ايضا زاوية بدا (310) مساوية

لزاوية بار لان زاوية ج وزاوية د وزاوية ا جميعا قائمة وراوية ه ادا

مساوية لزاوية بار ولكن (311) الزاويتين اللتين عند ب قائمتان فزاوية بجه

الباقية اذا مساوية لزاوية ز مثلث بجه اذا مساوية زواياه لزوايا مثلث

باز فنسبة خط بر ادا الى خط با كنسبة خط بج الى خط به لانها توتر

زوايا متساوية فالقائم الروايا الذى يحيط (312) به زب به مساو للقائم الزوايا

Pag 51

الذى يحيط به اب بج لكن القائم الزوايا الذى يحيط به اب [313] بج مساو

لمربع دب فالقائم الزوايا اذاً الذى يحط به رب به منطق

§ 22 واذ قد تقدمنا وبينا هذه الاشياء فنحن مبينون الاشياء التى قصدنا

قصدها فليكن • خطا اب بج محيطان منطق وقد بين اوقليدس انه اذا

اصيف منطق [314] الى الذى من اسمين فان عرصه يكون منفصلا ومرتبته

مرتبته فان كان حط اب من اسمين فحط بج منفصل فان ذلك الذى

من اسمين الاول فهدا المنفصل الاول فان كان ذلك الذى من اسمين الثانى

فهدا المنفصل الثانى وان كان الثالث فهو الثالث وعلى هذا المثال يجرى الامر

فى الباقية وليكن ايضا خط اب من موسطين الاول فانا اذا عملنا ذلك

العمل تبين ان [315] حط بج منفصل موسط الاول فان [315] خط نز الذى

من اسمين الثانى لان ما نكون من الذى من موسطين الاول اذا اصيف الى

منطق فان عرصه نكون الذى من اسمين الثانى ولان القائم الزوايا الذى

يحيط به رب به منطق نكون حط به المنفصل الثانى وذلك ان منطقا

اذا اصيف الى الذى من اسمين الثانى كان عرصه منفصل [316] الثانى فحط

بج اداً منفصل موسط الاول وذلك انه اذا كان موضع يحيط به منطق

ومنفصل الثانى فان القوى على ذلك الموضع منفصل موسط الاول وايصا

فليكن خط اب من موسطين الثانى ولنحط مع خط بج بمنطق اقول ان

Pag. 52 حط بج منفصل موسط الثانى لانا اذا عملنا ذلك العمل بعينه فلان خط

اب من موسطين الثانى وحط دب منطق فحط نز من اسمين الثالث وذلك

ان ما يكون من [317] موسطين الثانى اذا اصيف الى منطق كان عرصه

الذى من اسمين الثالث ولان القائم الزوايا الذى يحيط به رب به منطق

يكون خط به المنفصل الثالث لانه اذا كان خطان بخطان بمنطق وكان

احدهما من اسمين فان الباق يكون المنفصل ومرتبته مرتبته وحط بز الدى

من اسمين الثالث فه اذًا منفصل الثالث وخط بد منطق وماكان بخط

به منطق والمنفصل الثالث فان الدى يقوى علٮه(318) منفصل الموسط الثانى

فخط بج اذًا منفصل الموسط الثانى لان القائم الروايا الدى بحط به

هـ بد مساو للمربع الدى من حط بج وذلك ان الزاوية التى عند ج قائمة

ولكـں حط اٮ الاعظم اقول اٮ خط بج الاصغر لانا اذا عملنا دلك

العمل بعينه فلان خط اٮ الاعظم وخط بد منطق فخط بز من اسمين

الرابع لان ما يكون من الاعظم اذا اصيف الى منطق فان عرضه يكون الذى

من اسمين الرابع لكن القائم الروايا الدى بحط به ربه منطق فحط به

اذًا منفصل الرابع ودلك ان مرتبة خط بز هى مرتبة حط ٮه بعٮنها لان

القائم الروايا الذى منهما منطق فلان حط بد منطق وخط ٮه منفصل

الرابع يكوں خط بج الاصغر لان القائم الروايا الذى بحط به منطق

ومنفصل الرابع فاں القوى علٮه هو الاصغر وايصا فلكن حط اٮ القوى

على منطق وموسط اقول ان خط بج هو الدى يصير الكل مع منطق موسطا

لانا اذا عملنا دلك العمل بعٮنه فلاں خط اٮ هو القوى على منطق وموسط

وحط بد منطق فحط بز من اسمين الحامس لان الدى يكون من القوى

على منطق وموسط اذا اصيف الى منطق نكون عرصه الذى من اسمين

الحامس ولاٮ |القائم الروايا الذى بحط به ربه منطق فخط به المنفصل

الحامس فلاٮ حط بد منطق فخط بج الذى يصير الكل مع منطق موسطا

لان الحط الذى يقوى على موضع مساو للموضع الذى بحط به منطق والمنفصل

16*

الخامس هو هذا الخط وايضا فليكن خط اب القوى على موسطين اقول

ان خط بج الذى يصبر الكل مع موسط موسطا لانا اذا عملنا ذلك العمل

بعينه فلان خط بد منطق وخط اب القوى على موسطين فخط بر من

اسمين السادس والقائم الروايا الذى يحيط به زبه منطق فخط به اذا المنفصل

السادس وخط بد منطق فربيع بج ادا يقوى عليه الحط الذى يصر الكل

مع موسط موسطا فخط بج اذا الذى يجعل الكل مع موسط موسطا فادا

كان اذا موضع منطق يحبط به خطان مستقيمان[319] احدهما اصم من

الخطوط التى بالتركيب فان الباق يكون المقابل له من[320] التى بالتفصيل[321]

ولكن هذا امر بين مما وصفنا

§ 23 فاما انه اذا كان خطان يحبطان بوسط وكان احدهما واحدا من

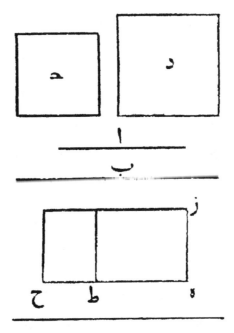

الخطوط الصم التى بالتركيب فان الباق بكون المقابل له من التى بالتفصيل[321]

فهو بين من هذه الاشياء ولنقدم انه اذا كان خطان مستقيمان نسبة احدهما

الى الاخر كنسبة موضع منطق الى موضع موسط او كنسبة موسط الى

موسط وكانت المواضع متباينة فان الخطين فى القوة مشتركان⁽³²²⁾ فلنضع

ان نسبة خط آ⁽*⁾ الى خط ب كنسبة موضع ج الى موضع د كان احدهما

منطقا والاخر موسطا او كانا كلاهما موسطين الا انهما متباينان ولنضع

خط هز منطقا وضف اليه موضعا مساويا لموضع ج وهو زط ونضيف

اليه ايضا موضعا مساويا لموضع د وهو زح فخطا طه هج اذا منطقان

فى القوة مشتركان⁽³²³⁾ كان الموضعان المضافان الى الخط المنطق منطقا

Pag 54 | وموسطا او موسطين بعدان يكونا متباينين فلان نسبة خط طه الى خط

حه كنسبة موضع زط الى موضع رح اعى كنسبة موضع ج الى موضع د

ونسبة موضع ج الى موضع د كنسبة خط آ الى خط ب فنسبة خط طه

اذا الى خط هج كنسبة خط آ الى خط ب وخطا طه هج فى القوة

مشتركان وخط آ اذا فى القوة مشارك لخط ب فاد قد تبين دلك فلناخد

فى برهان ما قصدنا له اذا كان خطان⁽³²⁴⁾ مستقيمان يحيطان بموسط وكان

احدهما من الخطوط الصم التى بالتركيب فان الباقى يكون المقابل له من

الخطوط التى بالتفصيل فليكن خطا اب جد ولكن الموضع الذى يحيطان

به موسطا واحدهما وهو خط اب واحد من الخطوط التى بالتركب اقول

ان حط جد الاخر وهو⁽³²⁵⁾ واحد من الخطوط التى بالتفصيل وهو المقابل له

فلنصف الى خط اب موضعا منطقا وهو الذى يحيط به ابح فخط بح اذا لما

تقدم من البيان واحد من الخطوط الصم⁽³²⁶⁾ التى بالتفصيل وهو المقابل لحط

اب وذلك ان الذى يحيطان به منطق فلان الموضع الذى يحيط به خطا

اب جد موسط والذى يحط به ابح منطق فنسبة خط حب الى جد [327]

كنسبة موضع منطق الى موضع موسط واذا كان هذا هكذا فهما فى القوة

مشتركان كما قد تبين واذا كان هذا هكذا ايضا فمن اى الخطوط الصم التى

بالتفصيل كان خط جد [328] نطهر الخط اب فان خط بح [329] مثله بعينه

وذلك ان الموضعين اللذين نقويان عليهما مشتركان [330] فتى كان اذا خطان

مستقيمان يحيطان اما بمنطق واما بموسط فانه اذا كان احدهما واحدا

من الخطوط التى بالتركسب فان الاحر الخط الذى هو نطره من التى

بالتفصيل فاذ قد تبينت هذه الاشياء فظاهر ان بالتناسب التاليفى يظهر

جمع الخطوط الصم [331] التى بالتفصيل من الخطوط [331] الى بالتركيب على

الجهة التى تقدم وصفها وليس شىء مما احدناه غير مبرهن

Pag 55

وتبع ما قلناه صمه ما يجىء [332] من اختلاف الخطوط التى من اسمين § 24

والمنفصلة المقابلة لها [333] وذلك انه جعل الذى من اسمين ستة اصناف

وكذلك المنفصل والحال التى بها جعل كل واحد منها ستة بين وذلك انه

اخذ القسم الاعظم والاصغر من الذى من اسمين وميز قواها لانه واجب

ضرورة ان يكون الخط الاعظم اعظم قوة من الاصغر اما بما يكون من مشارك

له واما بما يكون من مساين له فان كان اعظم قوة [334] منه بما يكون من

مشارك له فاما ان يكون هو مشاركا [335] للمعروض منطقا واما ان يكون

الاصغر واما الا يكون واحد منهما لانه ليس يمكن ان يكونا كلاهما مشاركين

له وذلك انه يكونا عند ذلك مشركين وهذا ممتنع فيهما وان كان الاعظم

اعظم قوة من الاصغر بما يكون من مباين له لزم مثل ذلك ايضا اما ان

يكون هو مشاركا [336] للمعروض منطقا واما ان يكون الاصغر واما الا يكون

واحد منهما لانه لا يمكن ان يكونا كلاهما (347) مشاركين له لذلك السبب بعينه فصير اذا نلثة خطوط من اسمين ان كان الخط الاعظم اعظم قوة من الاصغر بما يكون من مشارك له ونلثة ان كان اعظم قوة منه بما يكون من مباين له وايضا لانا قلنا ان المنفصل يكون اذا كانت نسة الخط باسره الى احد جزئية نسة الخط الذى من اسمين اذا كان القسم الاخر من اقسام الخط باسره هو المنفصل وكان واجب ضرورة ان يكون الخط باسره اعظم قوه من جزئه الاخر اما بما يكون من مشارك له واما بما يكون من مباين له وفى كل واحد من هدين اما ان يكون الخط باسره مشاركا للمفروض منطقا واما ان يكون جزؤه الذى نسته اله هى نسة الدى من اسمين واما الّا يكون | واحد منهما مشاركا (348) له لانه لدس يمكن ان يكونا كلاهما مشاركين Pag. 56 له كالحال فى الدى من اسمين وجب ضرورة ان يكون المنفصل ستة اصناف وان تسمى المنفصل الاول والثانى والثالث الى المنفصل السادس

§ 25 ⁣ فمن احل ما ذكر هذه الستة الخطوط المنفصلة والستة التى من اسمين الا لبين من الراس الحواس المختلفة للخطوط الصم التى بالتركب والتى بالتفصل ودلك انه ستخرج تدلها على ضربين اما على حسب معى كونها واما على حسب عروض المواصع التى تقوى عليها من دلك ان الذى من اسمين يخالف الذى من موسطين الاول فى الكون هسه لان الاول من منطقين فى القوه مشتركين والثانى من موسطين فى القوة مشتركين يحيطان عنطق ويختلفان ايصا فى العرض الذى يحدث من اصافة الموضعين اللذين منهما الى المنطق ودلك ان دالك جعل عرصه الدى من اسمين الاول وهدا بجعله الثانى كما ان الذى من موسطين الثانى بجعل عرصه الدى من اسمين

الثالث والاعظم يجعل عرضه الذى من اسمين الرابع والقوى على منطق
وموسط يجعله الخامس والقوى على موسطين يجعله السادس وذلك ان عدة
الخطوط التى من اسمين بعدة الخطوط الصم التى بالتركيب لان كل واحد
من الفريقين ستة ويصير (339) الخطوط التى من اسمين ستة عروصا عن اصافة
مواصع تبك الى خط منطق بحسب مراتبها الاول من الاول والثانى من
الثانى وما يتلوا ذلك على هذا المثال حتى يكون الذى من اسمين السادس
عرض الموصع الدى من القوى على موسطين المضاف الى منطق وعلى مثل
ذلك بعينه أضاف الخطوط المنفصلة الستة لبين بها اختلاف الصم التى
بالتفصل وليس انما يختلف فى كوبها فقط فان المنفصل ليس انما يخالف
منفصل الموسط الاول فقط فى أنه هو حدث عن انفصال خط | نسبته الى   P.19: 57
الخط الذى انفصل منه باسره لسبة الذى من اسمين وذاك حدوثه بانفصال
خط نسبته الى الخط الذى افصل منه باسره لسبة الدى من موسطين الاول
لكن قد يخالفه ايصا فى ان (440) الدى من المنفصل اذا اصيف الى منطق
تكون عرصه المنفصل الاول والذى من منفصل الموسط الاول يكون عرضه
المنفصل الثانى وكذلك الحال فى الباقية وذلك ان عدة الخطوط المنفصلة
كعده الخطوط الصم التى بالتفصيل وقوى هذه اذا اصفت (341) الى منطق
تكون عروصها الستة الخطوط المنفصلة على مراتبها فالقوة التى من الاول
يكون عرصها المنفصل الاول والتى من الثانى تكون الثانى والتى من الثالث
يكون الثالث والتى من الرابع يكون الرابع والتى من الخامس يكون الخامس
والتى من السادس يكون السادس وذلك ان هذا مبلغ كل واحد من
الصنيين اعنى الخطوط المنفصلة والخطوط الصم التى بالتفصيل وهى بطائر

فى المرتبة الاوائل عند الاوائل والمتوسطة عند المتوسطة والاواخر

عند الاواخر

§ 26 وينبغى ان نكون ذاكرين لهذه الاشياء انه اذا اصيف الذى يكون من

واحد من الخطوط الصم التى بالتركيب الى المنطق يكون عرضه واحدا [342]

من التى من اسمين وايضا اذا اصيف الذى يكون من واحد من الخطوط

التى بالتفصيل الى منطق بكون عرضه واحدا من الخطوط المنفصلة فاما

ان لم نصف المريعات انفسها الى منطق لكن اضيفت [313] الى خط موسط

فقد تبين ان العروص تكون اما فى التركب فالتى من موسطين الاوائل

والثوانى واما فى التى بالتفصيل فتنفصل الموسطات الاوائل والثوانى

Pag. 58 وواجب ضروره ان ناخد فى البرهان عليها انه اذا اصيف | منطق الى

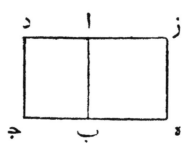

موسط كان عرصه موسطا فلكن موضع اج منطقا [344] مصافا الى خط

موسط وهو اب اقول ان خط اد موسط فلنرسم مربع اب فهو اذا موسط

ونسبته الى موضع اج كنسبة موسط الى منطق فنسبة را ايضا الى اد

هذه النسبة فخطا [345] زا اد ادا فى القوة مشتركان والذى من زا موسط

لان الذى من اب موسط فالذى من اد اذا موسط فخط اد ادا موسط

§ 27 واذ قد تقدمنا واخذنا هذا اقول انه اذا اضيف الذى [346] يكون من

الدى ⁽³⁴⁶⁾ من اسمين او الذى من الاعظم الى موسط يكون عرضه الدى من
موسطين الاول والدى من موسطين الثانى فليكن خط اب من اسمين

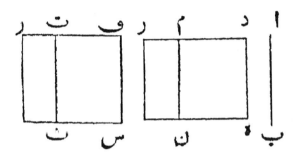

الاعظم ⁽³⁴⁷⁾ وحط ده موسط وموضع هز مساويا للدى من اب
ولنفرض حط فس منطقا وموضع سر مساويا للدى من اب فان
كان خط اب من اسمين فبس ان خط فر من اسمين الاول وان كان
اب اعظم فمر من اسمين الرابع فان هدا قد تبين فى اصافة المواضع
الموصوفة الى الخط المنطق ولنقسم ر والى الاسمين على نقطة ت فمى
كل واحد من اللدين من اسمين يكون خط فت مشاركا لخط فس
المفروض منطقا وموضع ست منطقا وموضع رث موسط وذلك ان خطى
فس فت فى الطول مشتركان فخطا ⁽⁴⁴⁸⁾ نت تر فى القوه مشتركان ومنطلقان
ولنفصل موضع هم مساويا لموضع ست فموضع ثر اذا الساق مساويا
لموضع نز وذلك انه قد كان موضع هر مساويا لموضع رس فموضع ر ادا
موسط وموضع هم منطق مصاف الى حط هد ⁽³⁴⁹⁾ الموسط فحط دم اذا موسط
كما تبين افا مربع ده ادا اذ هو موسط لانه من حط هد ⁽³⁵⁰⁾ الموسط
رس ⁽³⁵¹⁾ اما ان يكون مشاركا لموضع ر او مباينا له وليكن اولا مشاركا له
ولكن نسة الذى من هد ⁽³⁵²⁾ الى موضع ر ⁽³⁵³⁾ كنسبة خط هد ⁽³⁵⁴⁾ الى

Pag 59

حط مز لان ارتفاعهما جميعا واحد بعينه فخط هد [(355)] اذًا فى الطول مشارك
لحط مز فخط مر اذًا موسط دم خطا فخطا دم مر موسطان اقول ان الموضع الدى
يحطان به منطق ايضا ولان خط هد مشارك لحط مر ونسبة خط هد
الى خط مز كنسبة القائم الزوايا الدى يحط به ده دم الى الدى يحيط
به دم مز ان ات وضعت خطى هد دم مز متصلين على استقامة وصرت
حط دم الارتفاع فموضع هم اذًا مشارك للدى يحط به دم مر وموضع
هم منطق والذى يحط به اذا دم مر منطق ايضا فخط در اذًا من
موسطين الاول وليكن مربع هد غير مشارك لموضع ر فنسبة خط هد اذا
الى خط مز هى نسبة موضع موسط الى موضع موسط مباين له وقد تبين
هذا اذا نحى رسمنا الدى من هد لان [(356)] المرسوم وموضع [(356)] ر تحت
ارتفاع واحد بعينه فقاعدتاهما اذًا فى نسبة واحده بعينها اعى حط
مر [(357)] وخط هد لان هذا الحط مساو لقاعده الموصع الدى منه فخط هد
اذا فى القوه مشارك لحط مز وقد كان تبين هذا انفا فالذى من مز
اذًا موسط فخط مر اذًا نفسه موسط [(358)] فخطا دم مز اذا موسطان اقول ان
الدى يحطان به موسط ودلك انه لما كان موضع هم منطقا [(359)] وموضع ر
موسطا [(360)] فنسبة حط دم الى حط مز كنسبة موضع منطق الى موضع موسط
فخطا دم مر اذًا مشتركان فى القوة فان هذا قد تبين فيما قد تبين فلان حط
هد فى الطول مباين لحط مر وموضع هم مباين للذى يحط به دم مر
وموضع هم منطق فالدى يحط به اذا دم مز لس عنطق وخطا دم مز
موسطان فى القوة مشتركان والقائم الزوايا الذى يحط به حطان موسطان
فى القوه مشتركان اما ان يكون منطقا او موسطا كما بين اوقليدس

فالذى يحيط به اذا حطا دم مز اذ لبس هو منطقا فهو اذًا موسط فخط

دز اذًا من موسطين الثانى فاذا اضيف اذًا مربع الذى من اسمين او

مربع الاعظم الى موسط يكون عرضه الدى من موسطين الاول والذى من

موسطن الثانى

§ 28 وايضا فليكن خط اب اما الذى من موسطين الاول واما القوى على

منطق وموسط وخط ده موسطا وليصف [361] الى خط ده موضع مساو لمربع حط

با ولكن حط فس منطقا وموضع سر مساويا لمربع [362] اب فخط فر اذًا

من اسمين اما الثانى ان كان حط اب من موسطين الاول واما الخامس ان

كان خط اب القوى على منطق وموسط وليقسم على اسميه نقطة ت [363]

فخط تر [364] على كل واحدة من جهات اللدين من اسمين مشارك للخط المفروض

منطقا وموضع تر [365] منطق وموضع ست موسط ولنفصل موضع هم مساويا

لموضع ست فموضع تر [366] اذًا الباقى مساو لموضع تر [367] فموضع هم موسط

وموضع نز منطق وقد اضيف الى موسط وهو خط هد فخط مر اذًا موسط

فلان موضع هم موسط وقد اصيف الى خط موسط وهو خط هد فالذى من

هد [368] اما ان يكون مشاركا لموضع هم واما مباينا له وليكن اولا مشاركا له

فخط هد [369] مشارك لخط دم فخط دم اذًا موسط ايضا ولان خط مز مشارك

لخط هد فى القوة وحط هد مشارك فى الطول لخط مد فخط [370] مر فى القوة

مشارك لخط مد فلان خط هد مشارك فى الطول لخط دم ونسبة خط هد

الى خط مد كنسبة الدى يحيط به حطا هد [371] مر الى الدى يحيط به دم مز

Pag 61 فهذان ايضا مشتركان والذى يحيط به هد مز منطق لانه موضع نز والذى

يحيط به هد مز منطق فخط دز اذًا من موسطين الاول ولكن مربع

هد ماباينا لموضع هم فنسبة اذن خط هد الى خط مد النسبة التى لموسط
الى موسط مباين له فخطا هد دم فى القوة مشتركان ومربع دم موسط فخط
دم اذًا موسط وعلى مثال ما تقدم بعينه تبين ان خط دز من موسطين
الثانى فاد اضيف اذا مربع الذى من موسطن الاول او القوى على منطق
وموسط الى موسط يكون عرضه الذى من موسطين الاول والذى من
موسطين الثانى

§ 29   وايضا فلبكن خط اب [372] الخطين الباقيين من التى بالتركيب اعى
الذى من موسطين الثانى والقوى على موسطين وليكن خط هد موسطا
وخط فس منطقا وليكن تبك الاشباء بعينها فحط فر اذا من اسمس اما
الثالك واما السادس لان هدين هما اللدان بقيا وليس واحد منهما مشاركا
فى الطول لحط فس وموضعا ست ثر موسطان متباينان فموصعا هم نز
ايضا موسطان ولان خط هد [373] موسط وخطا مد مز موسطان فبين
ايضا ان احدهما مشارك لخط هد ولان [374] احد موضعى هم نز [375] مشارك
لمربع هد والذى يحيط به اذا دمر مشارك لاحدهما فالذى يحيط به دمز
اذا موسط [376] فحط در اذا من موسطى الثانى [376] واذكان مربع هد
عر مشارك لواحد منهما فلين واحد من دم مر مشاركا فى الطول [377]
لحط هد فليس الذى يحيط به دمز اذا مشاركا لكل واحد منهما وخطا
مد مز [378] موسطان فى القوة مشتركان والذى منهما [379] اذا اما ان يكون
منطقا او موسطا فاذا اصف اذا مربع الذى من موسطن الثانى والقوى
على موسطين الى خط موسط يكون العرض اما الذى من موسطين الاول
واما الذى من موسطبن الثانى وهذا شىء قد تسن فى الحطوط الصم الباقية

فمرع اذا كل خط من الخطوط التى بالتركب اذا اضيف الى خط موسط
يكون عرضه الذى من موسطبن الاول والذى من موسطس الثانى

ولنباخد بعد هذه الخطوط الصم التى بالتفصيل اثنين اثنين وليكن خط § 30
اب ايضا اما المنفصل واما الاصغر وليكن خط هد موسطا ولنصف اله

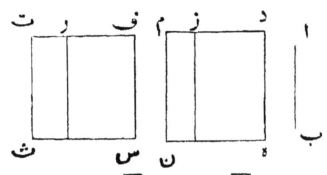

موضع هز مساويا لمربع اب اقول ان خط دز اما ان نكون منفصل الموسط
الاول واما ان نكون منفصل الموسط الثانى وليكن خط فس منطقا
ونضف اله موضع سر مساويا لمربع خط اب فخط فر اذاً اما المنفصل
الاول (380) واما المنفصل الرابع ان كان خط اب الاصغر ولكن خط رت لفق
حط قر (381) وموضع رن مساويا لموضع ثر فنسبة موضع سر الى موضع ثر
كنسبة موضع هز الى موضع نز فنسبة خط فر الى خط تر كنسبة
خط در الى خط مز ولكن (382) موضع ست منطق ودلك اه على المنفصل
الاول وعلى الرابع فخط فت مشارك للمفروض منطقا وهو خط فس والذى
يحيطان به اد هما فى الطول مشتركان منطق وموضع هم منطق لانه مشارك
لموضع ست ولان موضع هم منطق مصاف الى هد الموسط فخط هد موسط
ولان خطى (383) سف رت منطقان فى القوة مشتركان ودلك ان خط فر
اما المنفصل الاول والرابع (384) فالذى يحيطان به وهو ثر موسط فوضع

نر اذًا موسط لكن مربع هد ايضا موسط فهذان اذًا اما مشتركات واما

متباينان ولكونا مشتركين فحط زم اذا مشارك لحط هد كما بينا فى الاشياء

التى تقدمت فحطا مد مر موسطان ولان هاهنا ثلثة خطوط وهى هد دم مز

فنسبة حط هد الى خط مز كنسبة الذى يحبط به هد الى الذى يحط

به مد مر فهدان اذا مشتركان وموضع هم منطق فالذى يحيط به دمر اذ

منطق فحط در اذا منفصل الموسط الاول وان كان مربع هد مباينا لموصع

نز ولـس خط مز فى الطول بمشارك لحط هد ولكن فى القوة لان نسبته

اله كنسبة مربع هد الموسط الى موسط ماين له وهو موضع نز فريع مر

اذا موسط وهو اذا موسط ايضا ولان خط مد فى القوة مشارك لحط هد

وحط مر فى القوة مشارك له ايضا بعنه فهما ايضا فى القوة مشتركان فلان

حط هد ماين لحط مر فى الطول ونسة خط هد الى حط مز كنسبة

موضع هم الى الذى يحبط به دمر فهدان [385] ايضا متباينان وموضع هم

منطق فالذى يحط به اذا دمز عير منطق وخطا مد مر موسطان فى القوة

مشركان فالذى يحيطان [386] به اذًا موسط وذلك ان القائم الروايا الذى

يحيط به خطان موسطان [387] فى القوه مشركان اما منطق واما موسط

فحط دز اذا منفصل الموسط [388] الثانى فاذا اصف اذا مربع المنفصل او

مربع الاصعر الى حط موسط تكون عرصه [389] منفصل الموسط [389] الاول

او الثانى

§ 31 وليكن ايضا حط أب منفصل الموسط الاول او الذى بصير الكل مع

منطق موسطا ولكى خط هد موسطا ولنضف الى خط هد موصعا مساويا

لمربع أب اقول ان حط دز منفصل الموسط اما الاول واما الثانى وذلك ان

خط فس منطق وقد اضيف اليه موضع سر مساو لمربع اب فخط فر اذا اما
المنفصل الثانى واما الخامس وليكن خط تر لفقا له ولنتمم موضع ست
وليكن موضع زن مساويا لموضع تر فلان خط فر المنفصل اما الثانى واما
الخامس فخط فت اذا منطق فى القوة مشارك لخط فس فالمفروض منطقا
وخط تر فى الطول مشارك له فوضع تر منطق وموضع ست موسط لان
ذاك يحيط به منطقان فى الطول مشتركان وهذا يحيط به خطان فى القوة
مشتركان وموضع نز اذا منطق وموضع هم موسط فلان موضع نز منطق
مصاف الى خط هد الموسط فعرضه وهو خط من موسط فى القوة مشارك
لخط هد لان المنطق انما يحيط به من الموسطات المشتركات فى القوة ولان
موضع هم ومربع ده موسطان فهما اما مشتركان او متباينان [390] فلكونا
مشتركين فخط ده اذا مشارك فى الطول لخط دم فهو اذا موسط اصما
فلان خط زم فى القوة مشارك لخط ده فخطا دم من فى القوة مشتركان فلان
نسة خط ده الى خط دم كنسبة الذى يحيط به خطا ده زم الى الذى يحيط
به خطا زم مد ان انت جعلت قاعدتيها خطى ده دم وارتفاعها حط زم
والدى [391] يحيط به خطا ده رم مشارك للذى يحيط به زم مد والدى يحيط
به ده زم منطق والدى يحيط به رم مد اذا منطق فخط زد اذا منفصل
موسط الاول وان كان مربع ده مباينا لموضع هم فنسبة خط ده الى خط
دم كنسبة موسط الى موسط مباين له فهما اذا فى القوة مشتركان فخط دم
اذا موسط فخطا دم من فى القوة مشتركان وذلك ان كل واحد منها فى
القوة مشارك لخط هد فلان خط هد فى الطول مباين لخط دم ونسبة خط
هد الى خط دم كنسبة الذى يحيط به خطا ده زم الى الذى يحيط به

زم مد فهذان⁽³⁹²⁾ ايضا متباينان وموضع زن منطق فليس الذى يحيط به

دمز اذا بمنطق⁽³⁹³⁾ وخطا دم مز موسطان فى القوة مشتركان فالذى

يحيطان⁽³⁹⁴⁾ به اذا موسط فحط دز اذا منفصل الموسط الثانى فاذا اضيف

اذا مربع منفصل موسط الاول او مربع الذى يصير الكل مع منطق موسطا

الى خط موسط يكون عرصه منفصل موسط الاول او الثانى

|وليكن ايضا خط اب واحدا⁽³⁹⁵⁾ من الخطين الاصمين الباقيين اما

منفصل موسط الثانى واما الذى يصير الكل مع موسط موسطا وليكن خط

ده موسطا⁽³⁹⁶⁾ وموضع هز مساويا لمربع اب وخط فس منطقا وموضع سر

مساويا⁽³⁹⁷⁾ لمربع اب فحط فر اذا المنفصل اما الثالث واما السادس من

قبل ان خط اب اما ان يكون الثالث من الخطوط الصم التى بالتفصل

واما ان يكون السادس وليصير خط تر لفقه وموضع رن مساويا لموضع

تر فلان حط فر اما ان يكون المنفصل الثالث او السادس فكل واحد

من حطى فت تر مباين فى الطول لخط فس المفروض منطقا وهما منطفان

فى القوة مشاركان لخط فس فكل واحد اذا من موضعى ست تر موسط فكل

واحد من موضعى هم نز اذا موسط فلان مربع هد موسط فهو اما مشارك

لموضع هم او لموضع تر او لس هو مشاركا⁽³⁹⁸⁾ ولا لواحد منها لانه ليس

يمكن ان يكون مشاركا لكليها والا صار موضع هم مشاركا لموضع تر اعنى

موضع ست يشارك ثر اى ان خط فت مشارك لخط تر وقد وضع هدان

متباينان⁽³⁹⁹⁾ فى الطول فليكن مربع هد مشاركا لاحد موضعى هم نز فلان

كل واحد من موضعى هم نز موسط وهما متباينان فحط مد ادا فى القوة

مشارك لخط مر ولان مربع هد مشارك لاحد موضعى هم نز يكون خط

17 Junge-Thomson

هد فى الطول مشاركا لاحد خطى مد مز فاحدهما اذا موسط وهما فى
القوة مشتركان فالخط الباقى اذا موسط لان الموضع المشارك للموسط موسط
والقوى على الموسط موسط فخطا مد مز اذا موسطان فى القوة مشتركان
ولان الذى يحيط به هد مد موسط وكذلك ايضا الذى يحيط به [هد] [400]
مز فالذى يحط به دم مز لا محالة مشارك لاحدهما اذ كان حط هد فى
الطول مشارك لاحد خطى مد مز فالموضع اذا الذى يحيط به دمز موسط
فخط دز [401] اذا منفصل [401] الموسط الثانى وان كان مربع هد غير مشارك
لكل واحد [402] من موصعى هم نر فخط هد ادا نسبته الى كل واحد من

Pag. 66

خطى مد مز كنسبة موضع موسط موسط مباين له فكل واحد من
حطى مد مز فى القوة مشارك لخط هد ولان موضع هم مباين لموضع نر
وحط دم فى الطول مباين لحط مز فخطا مد مز موسطان فى القوة مشتركان
والدى يحيطان به اما ان يكون منطقا او موسطا فخط دز اذا منفصل
الموسط اما الاول واما الثانى فقد وجدنا عند ما نظرنا فى جميع الخطوط
الصم التى بالتفصيل [403] ان مربعاتها [403] اذا اضيفت الى حطوط موسطة
احدثت اما منفصل الموسط الاول او منفصل الموسط الثانى كما احدثت
مربعات الخطوط التى بالتركيب الحطين المقابلين لهما اعى الذى من موسطين
الاول والذى من موسطين الثانى

§ 33 وقد يمكنا ان نضف ان اضافاتها بانواع كثيرة وذلك ان مربع الموسط
ايصا اذا اضفته الى كل واحد من التى بالتركب وجدت عرصه واحدا من
التى بالتفصيل وهو المقابل له كما بينا انفا واذا اصفته الى كل واحد من التى
بالتفصيل وجدت عرصه واحدا من التى بالتركيب المقابل له وذلك ان

الموضع الموسط وهو مربع الموسط اذا احاط به خطان مستقيمان فكان احدهما واحدا من الخطوط الصم التى بالتركب كان الباق المقابل له من التى بالتفصل وبعكس ذلك وهذا شىء قد تبين فيما قبل وقد يمكننا اذا اصفنا مربعات الصم التى بالتركب الى التى بالتفصل [404] ان نطلب العروض وايضا اذا اصفنا المربعات [405] التى بالتفصيل الى التى بالتركب وذلك اما متى جعلنا الاضافات الى الخط الموسط او الى الخطوط التى بالتركب [او الى التى بالتفصيل] [404] اتننا بعده كثيره من المعانى الداخلة فى هذه الاشياء

Pag. 67 ورأينا اصنافا من المقدمات وقد نكتمى ما وصفنا اد كان فيه |تذكرة موجزة [406] فى حملة العلم بالخطوط الصم لانا قد علمنا العلة التى من اجلها احتاج الى الاصافات وهى [407] الاشتراكات

§ 34 وقد علمنا ايضا علما كافيا ان عدد الصم كثيرة بل هو بلا نهاية اعى التى بالتركيب والتى بالتفصل والخط الموسط [408] نسه كما بين اوقليدس لما حكم بانه قد نكون من الخط [409] الموسط خطوط احر صم بلا نهاية لا [410] بحسب نوع الخطوط التى تقدم وصفها وان كان يحدث من الخط الموسط خطوط بلا نهاية ها قولك فيما يحدث من سائر الصم الباقية على الترتيب وعلى عير الترتب من اليين عندكل احد اه قد يمكنك ان تقول اه قد يحدث من ذلك عدة عير متناهية مرارًا [411] متناهيه

§ 35 ولكن قد نكتمى ما قلنا فى الصم وقد يمكنا من هذه الاشياء ان نبحث عما يسئل عنه من هذه المسائل اعى اذاكان خط منطق وخط اصم اى الخطوط هو الموسط يينها فى النسبة واى الخطوط ثالثها فى النسبة على ان المنطق يوصع الاول ثم يجعل ايصا الثانى وكدلك يجرى الامر فى

17*

كل واحد من الصم على حدته مثال ذلك ان نعلم اذا كان لنا خط منطق والذى من اسمين او المنفصل اى الخطوط هو الوسط بينها فى النسبة وايها[412] ثالثها فى النسبة وكذلك الحال فى الخطوط الباقية وايضا اذا كان لنا خط موسط وباقى منطق او واحد من الخطوط الصم فانه قد يمكننا ان نعلم ايها[413] هو الخط الموسط بينها فى النسبة وايها[413] هو ثالثها فى النسبة وذلك انه لما كانت لنا عروض اضافاتها محصلة وعلمنا ان الذى يحيط به الطرفان مساو لمربع المتوسط سهل استخراجنا لذلك ٭

تمت المقالة الثانية وتم تفسير المقالة العاشرة من كتاب اوقليدس Pag. 68 نقل ابى عثمن الدمشقى والحمد لله وصلى الله على محمد واله وسلم

كتبه احمد بن محمد بن عبد الجلبل

بشيراز فى شهر حمادى الاولى

سنة ثمان وخمسين

وثلثمـاية .

NOTES ON THE TEXT.

(1) There is no general title to the whole treatise. The first general title which WOEPCKE gives, تفسير المقالة . . لس, is an adaptation of the title of Book II of the treatise. The second is the title of Book I of the treatise minus the first phrase, المقالة الاولى من.

WOEPCKE's title to Book I is a combination of the first phrase of the title of Book I and his own first general title to the treatise. The phrase, — بسم الله الرحمن الرحيم, adopted by WOEPCKE, is manifestly an addition either of the Arab translator, or more probably of the copyist.

WOEPCKE reads لس instead of سس, deceived evidently by a trick of the copyist who, whenever three such letters as "B", "T", "TH", "N", "Y", follow one-another in succession in an Arabic word, prolongs almost invariably the upward stroke of the second more than usual;

as, for example, in يبتدى (p 4, l 10). بين (p. 5, l 4): اثنها (p 12, l 4); ميبها (p. 32, l 3). يبغى (p. 32, l 6), ميسمى (p. 30, l 34); تبين (p 42, l 13): تبين (p. 42, l 11), تبيه (p 48, last).

Some words in the margin which I cannot decipher, may be a note on ذكر, which has in the M S. a sign over it ذكر evidently means "Exposition (See Lane's Dictionary, III, 969, col. III). WOEPCKE translates "Mention".

(2) الاسطقسات gl in

(3) ووقوعا على استخراج gl m. WOEPCKE read تاس instead of تاّى. وقوعا . كان Syntactically تأّى is in the same relation as the preceding would be an accusative of respect in the same relation as جلة

(4) Conj (WOEPCKE) فى كتات t

(5) فنوا gl. m.

(6) The MS has حر by haplography for احر after كما There is, then, a supralineal gloss to اخر, namely, اقتصّ, and also a marginal gloss,

namely, احد واقتص . The marginal gloss probably serves the purpose of giving clearly the correct reading of the text and also the supralinear gloss.

([7]) Gl. m. اومدمس t

([8]) gl m. اطهر

([9]) The marginal gloss, which it is impossible to decipher, must be some word meaning, Respect, Veneration, or Honour, such as مدح, or مرّة or مزيّة. See J. L. HEIBERG's *Euclidis Elementa*, Vol. V, p 417, ll 19—20, where the Greek equivalent of the Arabic phrase is given.

([10]) ان قد استعاض فيهم gl. m.

([11]) بالحياه gl. m.

([12]) صفته gl supra.

([13]) مرور التكون gl. m. WOEPCKE read مرور مدود التكون is probably the Greek ή ροή. التكون and الكون are synonyms as used here.

([14]) Conj. ما ا هده t The l is more likely to be a dittograph than the ه; and gramatically the feminine is to be preferred

([15]) Gl m. عيانه t.

([16]) العوارض gl. supra.

([17]) I read للعار with SUTER instead of WOEPCKL's and the MS's للعار.

([18]) From وليتأمل to قصدنا is given in the margin

([19]) المشترك و is added in the margin

([20]) والمطق is added in the margin

([21]) تصوّر gl m.

([22]) Gl m. هاد t

([23]) والمساوى m

([24]) A curious case of haplography has occurred here In the first place the copyist omitted the first الوقوف: then his eye slipped from the first to the second الحركة; and finally in supplying the omissions in the margin, he began with the second الوقوف, neglecting the first and also the phrase after the first الحركة. The part given in the margin can be read with the exception of one word, of which two letters can still be deciphered and which can be conjectured from the context. For, as a matter of fact, the same word occurs in another form in the very next line (مؤدّيه, يؤ[دّون]). I have, therefore, reconstructed the text on this basis, enclosing, within square brackets what is not given in the text or in the margin

(25) ‏فاما فى الاعظام فالامر‏ gl. m.

(26) ‏فى [التقسيم]‏ gl. supra

(27) ‏والواحد مقابل للكثرة‏ Gl m.

(28) The MS. has ‏مستوى‏ quite distinctly, which could be taken as the pass. partic. of the eighth stem. WOEPCKE gives the commonly used act partic., and his emendation is probably to be accepted.

(29) Conj (WOEPCKE): lacking in the MS.

(30) ‏الثبت‏ gl. supra

(31) ‏علل تباين‏ t Gl m

(32) ‏فقط‏ m

(33) ‏الطول و‏ m.

(34) ‏والتباين فى السبة‏ to m

(35) ‏منطق‏ t. Conj (WOEPCKE).

(36) ‏يتصوّر‏ gl supra

(37) ‏ما‏ m

(38) ‏التى‏ t. Conj (WOEPCKE).

(39) ‏الطول و‏ m.

(40) ‏مثل‏ gl. supra

(41) ‏مطلقة‏ t Conj (WOEPCKE)

(42) WOEPCKE conjectures ‏يولد‏.

(43) ‏احر‏ m

(44) ‏اصغر من قدر‏ m

(45) ‏اقل‏ gl. supra.

(46) WOEPCKE read ‏يتلمه‏.

(47) ‏غير‏ gl supra

(48) ‏عدمنا ٢‏ gl supra. It reads ‏قبد‏

(49) ‏قد‏ m

(50) ‏الوهم‏ gl supra.

(51) ‏وسميه‏ m

(52) Conj. (WOEPCKE). ‏اواسيا‏ t. The second ‏ا‏ is evidently a dittograph.

(53) ‏القدر‏ gl m. ‏العدد‏ is used as a gloss to ‏القدر‏ p. 7, l. 13, note 8 (para. 6). The two words are synonyms in paras 11, 14, and 15; p. 11, l. 21, p. 12, l 1, p. 14, ll. 13, 15, p 16, ll 3—4

(5 1b) ‏ايضا‏ gl. m.

(54) وايصا فينغى gl m.

(55) على الاطلاق فى الاعظام المتناهية gl. m.

(56) يقال gl. m

(57) انها gl m.

(58) المحصلة gl supra

(59) لانه ايضا قد يوحد فى الاشتراك gl. m

(60) تكون m

(61) العدد gl supra.

(62) The MS gives لانعلم with نا above the line after لا.

(63) معروف m.

(64) Gl. m. يكن t.

(65) Conj (WOEPCKE) اصما t.

(66) لامحالة m

(67) كانت is given in the margin to be inserted after لما

(68) المتناسبة gl. m

(69) محاورة ارمم من طيمة gl m WOEPCKE read

(70) اقل gl. m

(71) ومعلم is added here in the margin

(72) لبعضها m

(73) الثالوث gl supra

(74) للكل m

(75) وتحصل gl. m.

(76) تنفد gl. supra.

(77) يعرق gl. m.

(78) فى gl supra

(79) الانواع gl. m

(80) والاحر التوسط to m

(81) WOEPCKE read تشبه The Greek is ἔοιχεν (J L HEIBERG, *Euclidis Elementa*, Vol. V, p. 485, l 3).

(82) حمل gl. supra.

(83) يقلب gl. m.

(84) Gl. m السبب t.

(85) لكن شى بعد شى منها gl m WOEPCKE read لكنه.

(86) A supralinear gloss adds ٠.

(87) WOEPCKE conjectures لما, reading فيا. But the text is undoubtedly فيهما.

(88) تحصيل gl. m.

(89) Conj. (WOEPCKE). موافقه t.

(90) ناوشة gl. m.

(91) ايضا gl. m

(92) The MS. has واحد at the end of the line, and الا انه at the beginning of the next. Obviously the first ا of the second line belongs to واحد

(93) Gl. supra الواحد t.

(94) تحدان gl. supra.

(95) على مذهب m.

(96) The MS. has معيد ان; but the "Ya" is palpably an addition. An asterisk appears above the word, which may serve to draw attention to the introduction of the "Ya" or to indicate that the introduction is an error. Cf. a similar case in Part II, para. 34.

(97) و[هذا] ما ينتهيا للاسان gl. supra

(98) Conj. (WOEPCKE) مشار[كين] t مشتركين gl. supra.

(99) التي gl. m

(100) كانت gl. in

(101) يحدون للخطوط t, يحدر الخطوط gl. m

(102) ذلك gl. ni

(103) The MS. reads, or seems to read, يصحك منه تحميم; but the "Fa" may be a "Ya" somewhat thickly written. The marginal gloss runs: يصحك منه حميم, not just يصحك as in WOEPCKE حميم would seem to be the better reading after جهل. See Trans., Part 1, note 88.

(104) اعنى m

(105) Conj (WOEPCKE) مطق t

(106) اظهر gl. supra

(107) والاقتران gl. supra.

(108) القدر gl. in

(109) [الو]حدة gl. supra

(110) تقصد gl. m

(111) WOEPCKE suggests تحد as a correction, but it is unnecessary

(112) Gl. m واما t

(113) Conj. (WOEPCKE). احدهما t.

(114) تحصيل m.

(115) على الحقيقة طبيعة gl. m.

(116) والحدود gl. m

(^{117}) نبحث gl. supra.

(^{118}) للخط المفروض gl. m. See Trans , Part 1, note 108.

(^{119}) Conj. (WOEPCKE) واصما t

(^{120}) Conj. (WOEPCKE). اصما t.

(^{121}) معمله gl. m.

(^{122}) العلم gl. m. See Trans , Part 1, note 113.

(^{123}) مشتركة to كانت m

(^{124}) ادا m.

(^{125}) ما t., نما m

(^{126}) WOEPCKE proposes مشاركين as a better reading Gramatically he is justified, but in usuage مشترك is often found in this sense

(^{127}) Conj. (WOEPCKE) المشتركة t.

(^{128}) After احر the MS. has يقدر الخط المفروض ايضا WOEPCKE quite correctly omitted them. See Translation and note.

(^{129}) فى الطول is added in the margin.

(^{130}) بالسطح gl m.   ($^{130\,b}$) مشاركين t.

(^{131}) السطح gl. m

(^{132}) السطح gl m

(^{133}) Conj (WOEPCKE). مساحيه t.

(^{134}) فى الخطوط انفسهما m.

(^{135}) ميقيسها gl m

(^{136}) المطقة انفسها m

(^{137}) سب m

(^{138}) Conj. (WOEPCKE) برى يقدر t

(^{139}) WOEPCKE read· وهولاء تشعر Seo Trans , Part 1, note 138.

(^{140}) ان m.

(^{141}) Conj (WOEPCKE). واحد t.

(^{142}) فلدلك gl m.

(^{143}) WOEPCKE suggests مشتركة as a better reading But it is possible that the same phrase as in the previous clause is to be understood

(^{144}) للخط كل to m

(^{145}) Conj (WOEPCKE). الطول t See Translation and note.

(^{146}) Conj. (WOEPCKE). لذانك t

(^{147}) خطان m.

(^{148}) حطان m.

(^{149}) Conj (WOEPCKE) منطقين فى الطول t See Trans., Part 1, note 154.

(150) Gl. m. مير t

(151) والتباين to وذلك m.

(152) منطق m.

(153) Conj. (WOEPCKE). اصما t.

(154) Conj. (WOEPCKE) من الذى من t.

(155) Conj. (WOEPCKE). The MS does not give الذى هو to اصم m

(156) بل قد gl. m.

(157) Gl supra وهى t.

(158) Gl. m. نعلم t.

(159) Conj. (WOEPCKE). احدهما t.

(160) الذى m.

(161) Conj. (WOEPCKE) كله مركب t.

(162) Sic تتلوا t

(163) Gl. m. فالمربع t.

(164) اذا m.

(165) اصم to يسمى m

(166) المركبة m.

(167) ان فصلها m

(168) Conj. (WOEPCKE) اصم t

(169) انا الجزء to m.

(170) Conj (WOEPCKE) و التركيب t The text of the MS is, however, quite intelligible as it stands

(171) Gl m. ينغى t.

(172) هدا m.

(173) فنصرف gl supra.

(174) The MS has ابها after ذكر. It is probably an interpolation The Greek has nothing corresponding to it See J L HEIBERG, *Euclidis Elementa*, Vol V, p 483, no. 133, ll. 11—15, esp. l 14

(175) Conj (WOEPCKE). مشتركان t

(176) مشتركين to فقط m

(177) Conj. (WOEPCKE). مشتركين و الطول t

(178) Conj (WOEPCKE) الاول t Perhaps we should read يجعل. Cf. ياخذ two lines later

(179) مطقا to به m

(180) به m.

(181) Conj (WOEPCKE). التى t.

(¹⁸²) WOEPCKE omits this sentence. But it is presumably the Arabic equivalent of the Greek clause: ἣν ἔχουσιν αἱ κατὰ σύνθεσιν ἄλογοι πρὸς ἀλλήλας, which is represented, then, in the Arabic not only by the status constructus, but also by this sentence. See J. L. HEIBERG, *Euclidis Elementa*, Vol. V, p 551, l. 23.

(¹⁸³) Conj (WOEPCKE). والمفصل t

(¹⁸⁴) Conj. (WOEPCKE). موسط t.

(¹⁸⁵) Conj (WOEPCKE). وكماين فى التركيب t

(¹⁸⁶) فى m

(¹⁸⁷) Conj. (WOEPCKE). عشر t

(¹⁸⁸) الخطوط to الصم m

(¹⁸⁹) Conj (WOEPCKE). عشر t

(¹⁹⁰) Conj (WOEPCKE). الثانى عشر t

(¹⁹¹) فى gl supra

(¹⁹²) Conj. (WOEPCKE). اصيف t

(¹⁹³) Conj. (WOEPCKE). الثالث t

(¹⁹⁴) Conj. (WOEPCKE). الست t

(¹⁹⁵) التى m. At the bottom of this page of the MS., on the left-hand margin, is written قوبل. "It has been collated"?, i. e., the MS copied with another or others

(¹⁹⁶) Gl. supra. المنتظمة t WOEPCKE read المورة m the preceding line as المورة. See Trans, Part 11, note 2 The phrase, بسم الله الرحمن الرحيم is manifestly an addition of the Muslim translator or copyist.

(¹⁹⁷) عما m.

(¹⁹⁸) باحد t WOEPCKE adopted as his reading باحد, but suggested باحدى in his note.

(¹⁹⁹) اصما m

(²⁰⁰) يتم gl. supra

(²⁰¹) واحد m

(²⁰²) وحد gl. supra (وجد؟)

(²⁰³) WOEPCKE read كلحد.

(²⁰⁴) Gl m. ترك المطق t

(²⁰⁵) معصلة? See Trans., Part 11, note 9b

(²⁰⁶) سطح gl. supra.

(²⁰⁷) فقط to وان m.

(208) الموضع m.

(209) After المثال the MS. has خطان, obviously an error, and probably a partial dittograph of the following word.

(210) Gl. m. المعنى t

(211) Conj. (WOEPCKE). العلم t.

(212) Conj. (WOEPCKE) سصفه t.

(213) سطح gl supra

(214) مطق to يحب m

(215) Conj. (WOEPCKE). يحيط t

(216) ان m.

(217) The MS adds كان in the margin after فان.

(218) Conj. The MS has ا for ا and حب for جـ from line 2 to line 9 Cf line 11ff, where the MS has ا and جـ

(219) Conj. The MS. has again حب

(220) Conj. (WOEPCKE). كلاهما t

(221) به conj WOEPCKE) It is the usual construction, but not absolutely necessary

(222) به m But the MS places it after اقليدس.

(223) WOEPCKE suggests that قليلا would be better But قليل is possible.

(224) حطوط m

(225) لا gl. m. لم لا وصف.

(226) Conj (WOEPCKE) المتباية t وصف might be read as وضع. Cf. l. 2

(227) Conj (WOEPCKE) تسمها t.

(228) Conj. (WOEPCKE) مطقا والذى يحيطان به موسطا t

(229) مربعيهما to موسطا m.

(230) Conj. (WOEPCKE) لالذين t A case of haplography, the ١ of اللذين omitted after the ١ of لا

(231) Conj (WOEPCKE) ومربعيهما t

(232) Conj. (WOEPCKE) ومربعيهما t

(233) Conj (WOEPCKE) متباين t

(234) Conj. (WOEPCKE) منطقين t

(235) Conj. (WOEPCKE) اج t

(236) Conj. (WOEPCKE) مرح t.

(237) Conj (WOEPCKE) The MS lacks مطق

(238) مشتركين m

(²³⁹) Conj (WOEPCKE). ولصف t.

(²⁴⁰) Conj. (WOEPCKE). لمربى t.

(²⁴¹) Conj (WOEPCKE) ما t.

(²⁴²) Conj. (WOEPCKE). كل t.

(²⁴³) Conj. (WOEPCKE). مطبي t.

(²⁴⁴) Conj. (WOEPCKE). منطقان t.

(²⁴⁵) Conj (WOEPCKE) واما الموسطة t

(²⁴⁶) منطقا to ه m.

(²⁴⁷) Gl. m يستخرج t But an "Alif" has been written over the "Ya" of يستخرج in the MS.

(²⁴⁸) Conj. فليلفى t WOEPCKE adopted فلنكتف. The copyist probably wrote فليلفى in error for فليكفى, itself an error for فليكف.

(²⁴⁹) Conj. أحدث t.

(²⁵⁰) Conj. (WOEPCKE) يصير does not occur in the MS

(²⁵¹) Conj. (WOEPCKE) فلتفصيل t

(²⁵²) Conj. (WOEPCKE). بالتركيب t.

(²⁵³) Read معصّلة ? See Trans, Part 11, note 9b.

(²⁵⁴) Conj. (WOEPCKE) لذلك t

(²⁵⁵) Conj. (WOEPCKE) من t   (²⁵⁵ᵇ) متحانسين t.

(²⁵⁶) Conj (WOEPCKE). مرتين is lacking in the MS

(²⁵⁷) Conj. (WOEPCKE). أعظم t.

(²⁵⁸) WOEPCKE suggests that the phrase, والذين يحيطان ه موسطا, should be added here to the text. Although not strictly necessary, the phrase completes the argument

(²⁵⁹) WOEPCKE inserts here, مرى اب ه مساو الدى يحيطان به مرتين والذى من The insertion is not necessary. The sense is quite clear without it, although the clarity of the argument is aided by it See Trans, Part 11, note 82.

(²⁶⁰) Conj. (WOEPCKE). حطين t.

(²⁶¹) Conj. (WOEPCKE). أب t.

(²⁶²) Conj. (WOEPCKE). موسط t

(²⁶³) Conj. (WOEPCKE) أب t

(²⁶⁴) Conj (WOEPCKE). ليس معصل t. The text of the MS. is possible.

(²⁶⁵) Gl m يعضل النط .. منطق t يفضل من النطق gl.

(²⁶⁶) WOEPCKE rejects ننتزع and suggests ينتزع.

(267) Conj (WOEPCKE). المحيطين t.

(268) Conj. (WOEPCKE). موسطه t.

(269) Conj. (WOEPCKE). الخطين اللذين t.

(270) Conj (WOEPCKE) الموسطه t.

(271) Conj. (WOEPCKE). بالموسطه t.

(272) and (273) Conj. (WOEPCKE). Not in the MS. The scribe's eye wandered probably from the first الذى before يقوى (272) to the second before يحعل

(274) Gl. m القينا t.

(275) Conj اثنان not in the MS

(276) So given in the MS; for منفصل الموسط; cf. the following text.

(277) Conj (WOEPCKE) مشتركان t

(278) m الكل

(279) Conj (WOEPCKE). القوة t

(280) Conj. (WOEPCKE). موسط t.

(281) Conj. (WOEPCKE) موسط t

(282) Conj. (WOEPCKE). تحيط به بالاصاغر t

(283) Conj (WOEPCKE). فيقوى t

(284) Gl. supra. بالتفصيل t

(285) Conj. (WOEPCKE) حطا t.

(286) The MS has لان simply without the و. WOEPCKE conjectured وكان.

(287) Conj. (WOEPCKE) فدا t, which is possible.

(288) Conj اما الاولة t. Cf p. 48, last line, where context and construction are similar

(289) Conj. (WOEPCKE). منطق t.

(290) Conj. (WOEPCKE). والرابع t.

(291) Conj. (WOEPCKE). اصما t

(292) Conj. مباينة t. See Trans, Part 11, note 114.

(293) Conj (WOEPCKE). التاليقى t

(294) Conj. (WOEPCKE). خطين مستقيمين t

(295) Conj. (WOEPCKE). واحد t.

(296) Conj. (WOEPCKE). التاليقى t

(297) Conj فان حطا اب بج منطقين فى القوة مشتركين t. WOEPCKE suggestes. — فان حطى اب بح منطقان فى القوة مشتركان. Cf. p. 48, 1. 6, where the next case is stated

(298) Conj. (WOEPCKE) للمربع t

(299) Conj. (WOEPCKE). موسط t.

(300) الخطوط to الصم m.

(301) WOEPCKE read تبين.

(302) WOEPCKE suggests بانه. Better perhaps to read simply كل. Observe that the correlative of اما is the ف before يبقى

(303) Conj (WOEPCKE). وأحد t

(304) WOEPCKE omits the و, considering it an error

(305) Conj. (WOEPCKE) اب t

(306) Conj (WOEPCKE). قربي t

(307) Conj. (WOEPCKE). رحب t

(308) Conj (WOEPCKE) رحب t

(309) Conj (WOEPCKE) نزا t

(310) Conj (WOEPCKE) نزا t

(311) Conj (WOEPCKE). وليكن t

(312) Conj (WOEPCKE التى تحيط t.

(313) Conj (WOEPCKE). ار t

(314) Conj. (WOEPCKE) منطقا t

(315) Conj Not in the MS See Trans , Part II, note 126

(316) So given here and subsequently for المفصل.

(317) As WOEPCKE says, we should here road, من الذى من, since as the text stands, من here fulfills two functions (1) As part of the name, من موسطين الثانى, (2) As indicating, ' The square upon''.

(318) Conj. (WOEPCKE). على t

(319) Conj (WOEPCKE). حطين مستقيمين t

(320) من m

(321) بالتسبيل to واكن m

(322) Conj (WOEPCKE). مشتركين t

(*) The figure is not given in the MS

(323) The clause beginning كان الموصعان, ll 22—23, may be a circumstantial clause It might be better to suppose, however, that an اد or even اذ قد had been omitted before كان.

(324) حطان m.

(325) وهو m It is possible that وهو should be placed before الاخر.

(326) الصم m

(327) Conj. (WOEPCKE) بح t

(³²⁸) Conj جع t WOEPCKE accepted the text of the MS. here.

(³²⁹) WOEPCKE suggests جد.

(³³⁰) Conj (WOEPCKE) مشتركين t

(³³¹) الخطوط التى to الخطوط m.

(³³²) WOEPCKE read نحن.

(³³³) Conj. والمنفصل المقابل له t. Possibly we should read: الخط الذى من اسمين والمعصل المقابل له.

(³³⁴) قوة m.

(³³⁵) Conj. (WOEPCKE) مشارك t

(³³⁶) Conj (WOEPCKE) مشارك t.

(³³⁷) Conj. (WOEPCKE). كليهما t. Cf. p. 56, l. 1.

(³³⁸) Conj. (WOEPCKE) مشارك t.

(³³⁹) يصير m.

(³⁴⁰) Conj. (WOEPCKE). ان is lacking in the MS

(³⁴¹) Conj. (WOEPCKE) اضيف t

(³⁴²) Conj. (WOEPCKE) واحد t

(³⁴³) Conj. (WOEPCKE) اصيف t.

(³⁴⁴) Conj (WOEPCKE), The MS does not give مطلقا.

(³⁴⁵) Conj (WOEPCKE). خط t

(³⁴⁶) Conj (WOEPCKE). يكون من الذى not given in the MS

(³⁴⁷) Conj. (WOEPCKE) او not given in the MS

(³⁴⁸) Conj (WOEPCKE) خط t

(³⁴⁹) Conj (WOEPCKE). هز t.

(³⁵⁰) Conj. (WOEPCKE) هز t

(³⁵¹) Gl m. وسم t

(³⁵²) Conj (WOEPCKE) هز t.

(³⁵³) Conj (WOEPCKE) بر t.

(³⁵⁴) Conj (WOEPCKE) هز t. A supralinear gloss gives د ? for ز.

(³⁵⁵) Conj. (WOEPCKE). هز t. A supralinear gloss gives د for ر.

(³⁵⁶) Conj. (WOEPCKE). يكون هل t. المرسوم يكون هل وموضع is probably a supralinear gloss which has crept into the text, هل (i. e. DC) being the line upon which the square is described.

(³⁵⁷) Conj (WOEPCKE). بز ? t.

(³⁵⁸) Conj. (WOEPCKE) موسطا t.

(³⁵⁹) Conj (WOEPCKE). مطق t

(³⁶⁰) Conj. (WOEPCKE) موسط t.

(³⁶¹) Conj (WOEPCKE). ولنصف t.

(³⁶²) Conj (WOEPCKE). لموضع t

(³⁶³) Conj (WOEPCKE) ب t

(³⁶⁴) Conj. (WOEPCKE). بز t

(³⁶⁵) Conj (WOEPCKE) نر t.

(³⁶⁶) Conj. (WOEPCKE). بز t.

(³⁶⁷) Conj (WOEPCKE) ثن t.

(³⁶⁸) Conj (WOEPCKE) هد مريم من فالذى t.

(³⁶⁹) Conj. (WOEPCKE). هز t

(³⁷⁰) Conj مز وحط t. WOEPCKE suggests مد reading the preceding line as مر.

(³⁷¹) Conj (WOEPCKE). هز t

(³⁷²) واحد (احد ?) should be added here, says WOEPCKE

(³⁷³) Conj (WOEPCKE) هز t.

(³⁷⁴) The MS gives ولان WOEPCKE suggests لان The context demands some such word as "When", or "As soon as" (لما). The Greek text had evidently some such phrase as ἐπειδή δε or ὅτε δε, which the Arab translator took in its causal instead of in its temporal sense.

(³⁷⁵) Conj. (WOEPCKE) بز t

(³⁷⁶) Conj. (WOEPCKE) موسطين من اذا دن لحط موسط ادا در لحط t Clearly a case of haplography

(³⁷⁷) Conj. (WOEPCKE). القوة فى مشارك t.

(³⁷⁸) Conj. (WOEPCKE). دن مد وحط t

(³⁷⁹) Better perhaps بهما والدى. Cf p 46, ll 4 & 22.

(³⁸⁰) WOEPCKE suggests that the words, المنصل اب خط كان ان be added at this point

(³⁸¹) In this part of the MS the letters designating the lines of the figure have been rather carelessly written, but there are no real errors as WOEPCKE seems to claim

(³⁸²) Conj (WOEPCKE). حطا t.

(³⁸³) Conj. (WOEPCKE) خطا t

(³⁸⁴) Conj. (WOEPCKE) الثانى t

(³⁸⁵) Conj. وهدان t.

(³⁸⁶) Conj (WOEPCKE) يحيط t

(³⁸⁷) Conj (WOEPCKE) موسطان not given in the MS.

(³⁸⁸) الموسط m

(³⁸⁹) Conj (WOEPCKE). المنفصل t.

(³⁹⁰) Conj (WOEPCKE). مشتركين او متباينين t

(³⁹¹) Conj. والدى t

(³⁹²) Conj. وهذان t.

(³⁹³) WOEPCKE suggests منطقا. But ب with the genitive is also correct.

(³⁹⁴) Conj (WOEPCKE) يحيط t.

(³⁹⁵) Conj (WOEPCKE) واحد t.

(³⁹⁶) Conj (WOEPCKE). موسط t.

(³⁹⁷) Conj (WOEPCKE) مساو t.

(³⁹⁸) مشارك m

(³⁹⁹) WOEPCKE remarks: — Thus the text, better متباينين.

(⁴⁰⁰) Conj (WOEPCKE) به not given in the MS. It is not necessary.

(⁴⁰¹) Conj (WOEPCKE) ادا موسط مفصل t

(⁴⁰²) Conj لواحد t.

(⁴⁰³) Conj (WOEPCKE) اب من مربعاتها t

(⁴⁰⁴) اب to بالتركيب (3 lines later) m The phrase within square brackets an emendation suggested by SUTER

(⁴⁰⁵) WOEPCKE remarks· — Thus the text, better مربعات

(⁴⁰⁶) WOEPCKE read موحدة.

(⁴⁰⁷) Gl. m وموا t.

(⁴⁰⁸) Conj (WOEPCKE) المنطق t.

(⁴⁰⁹) Conj (WOEPCKE) الخطوط t.

(⁴¹⁰) Conj See Trans., Part II, note 173.

(⁴¹¹) Conj See Trans, Part II, note 174.

(⁴¹²) Conj. (WOEPCKE) ايهما t

(⁴¹³) WOEPCKE read انها in both cases

GLOSSARY
OF TECHNICAL TERMS.

In the following glossary *W.* indicates WOEPCKE's text of the Treatise of Pappus, printed in Paris by the firm Didot*: *BH.* indicates Codex Leidensis 399, 1, Euclidis Elementa ex interpretatione Al-Hadschdschadschii cum commentariis Al-Narizii, BESTHORN and HEIBERG, Part 1, Fascicule 1; *H.* indicates Euclidis Elementa, J. L HEIBERG, Leipzig, 1888, vol. V; *Spr.* indicates A Dictionary of the Technical Terms etc., A. SPRENGER, Calcutta, 1862; *T.* indicates Euclid's Elements, translated from the Greek by Naṣir ad-din aṭ-Ṭūsī, Rome 1594, "*Heath*" indicates The Thirteen Books of Euclid's Elements, T. L. HEATH, 1908

١	اخذ	To take for granted, to assume (W., p 47, l 20) Cf الماخوذة, "Adsumptum" (Lemma) (BH , I, pp. 38—39)
	ماخود	Given (W., p. 49, l. 1, "The given line")
	الاسمين	The two terms of a binomial (or major etc) (W , p 58, l. 16)
	ذو الاسمين	The Binomial (W , p. 2, l 3, p. 20, l 20; p 21, l 6, etc)
	الخطّ الذى من اسمين	The Binomial (W., p. 25, l 15; cf W., p 21, ll 8—9: p. 22, l 4; p. 25, l. 21)
	من اسمين	A Binomial (W., p 25, ll 11, 12; p 33, l 13; p 43, l 10)
	خطّ من اسمين	A Binomial (W , p. 21, l. 18).
	الخطوط التى من اسمين	The Binomials (W., p. 55, l. 3; cf. (W., p. 26, l 2)
	خطوط من اسمين	Binomials (W., p. 55, l. 15).
	الخطّ الذى من اسمين الاول	The First Binomial (W., p. 25, l. 22).

* WOEBCKE's pagination has been indicated in this edition of the Arabic text in the margin.

الحطّ الدى من اسمين | The Second Binomial (W , p 25, l. 23).
الثانى

الدى من ثلثة اسماء | The Trinomial (W., p. 21, ll. 10, 19).

من ثلثة اسماء | Trinomial (W., p. 22, l. 5).

الدى من اربعة اسماء | The Quadrinomial (W , p. 21, l 11)

الاصول | The Elements (i. e , of Euclid) Greek, στοιχεῖα
Gloss, الاسطقسات (W., p. 1, l. 1).

تاليف | Harmony (e. g., Theaetetus assigned the apotome to harmony) (W , p 2, l 3).

ب

مبدأ | Beginning or Principle of a thing (As "One" of the numbers) (W , p 4, l. 5).

تبديل | The Difference between or the Variance from one-another A synonym of اختلاف (W , p. 56, l. 6).

بعد | Extension (W , p 14, l 2) Distance or extension between things; shortest distance between things (Spr , Vol I, p 115) Greek, διάστημα.
Radius (BH., I, p. 20, l 11).

الباق | The Remainder after subtraction (T , Book X, p 226) Greek, τὸ καταλειπόμενον.

الدى بينهما | The rectangle contained by the two of them (i. e., the two lines, A and B) (W , p 46, l 4, cf p 46, l. 22). Synonymous with الذى يحيطان به — .

تباين | Incommensurability (W., p 4, l 17). It is the opposite of اشتراك q. v

متباين | Incommensurable (W , p 31, ll 3, 20). Greek, ἀσύμμετρος It is the opposite of مشترك q v
Prime (of numbers to one-another) (T , Book VIII, p 169) Greek, πρῶτοι πρὸς ἀλλήλους.

ت

متناسبة | A Progression (and Retrogression) of Multitude (W , p. 8, l 17, n 5). Greek, προποδισμός (ἀναποδισμός).

ث

ثلثة | The Triad (W., p 9, l 6, cf Translation, Part 1, note 52) The Greek is given, H , Vol V, p. 484, l. 23, ἡ τρίας.

مثلث | Triangle (W , p 50, l. 20).

ج

جزء | The Part (of a line or a magnitude) (W , p. 4, l. 7; p. 39, l. 11). It is the opposite of جملة q. v

Part (i. e., in the restricted sense of a submultiple or an aliquot part (T , Book V, p 108) Greek, μέρος.

جمل (With Acc and على). To multiply (e g , length by breadth) (W., p. 16, ll 21—22).

مَجموع The Sum (of lines or magnitudes) (W , p. 34, l. 5; p. 40, l. 20) Greek, τὸ ὅλον.

مجتمع The Sum (of squares upon two lines) (W., p. 32, l. 19).

اجتماع Union or Combination (W , p. 13, l 9). Greek, ἡ σύγκρισις?

جملة The "Whole" (of a magnitude) (W., p 3, l. 8, p. 4, l 7) It is the opposite of جزء (Part) q. v

The Sum (of two lines; i. e., the whole line composed of the two lines (W , p 32, l 14) Cf. the phrase, جملة الخطّ (The whole line), l. 12 of the same page Chapter or Part of a Book (W., p. 23, l. 10. p. 26, l 7) The Greek is given, H , Vol V , p. 485, l 11; p 548, ll. 2—5, κεφάλαιον

متجانسة Homogeneity (W., p 23, l 19) The Greek is given, H , Vol V , p 484, l 14, συγγένεια

متجانس Homogeneous (W , p 7, l 2) The Greek is given, H , Vol. V , p 418, l 16, ὁμογενῶν.

حجم Bulk or Magnitude (W , p 14, ll 2, 5) Greek, ὄγκος.

حدّد To Define (W , p 11, ll 14, 15)

حدّ The Limit or Bound (W , p 9, l 8, p 13, l 13ff.; p 14, ll 3, 8). It is the Platonic πέρας of the *Timaeus* and *Parmenides*
Standard (i e , a unit of measurement accepted for practical purposes) (W , p 6, l 21. p 7, l 17).
The point of bisection in a line, the line of bisection in a plane, the plane of bisection in a body (Spr Vol 1, p 285)

تحديد Definition (W., p 10, l. 6)

حدود Definite or Determinate (W , p 4, l. 1). The Greek is given, H , Vol V , p. 426, l. 6, ὡρισμένος.

حدث To arise or be produced (W., p. 39, ll 15, 16, 17; p 40, l 8, cf. p 34, ll 10 & 11).

احدث To produce (W, p. 39, ll 13, 14, 15)

حركة Movement (W., p.3, l 19). It is the opposite of وقوف, Rest q v

حصّل فى To be comprised or comprehended in (of a thing in its genus) (W., p. 3, l. 4)

حصّل . تحصيل To determine (a thing), i e, make known its form or character (W, p. 10, ll. 17 & 21: p 11, l 4)

مُحصّل Determinate or Distinct (W., p 4, l. 1)

احاط ب To contain (as the sides of a square the square) (W, p. 10, l 13). Greek, Med, περιέχω

خ احرج To draw (a line) (W., p 50, l 3) (Cf. BH. I, p. 16). To produce (i e, extend a line) (W., p 50, l 8) (Cf. BH I, p 10)

استخراج The finding or discovery of (W, p 23, l. 19) The Greek is give H., Vol. V, p 485, l 15, εὕρεσις
To prove or demonstrate (W., p. 26, l. 8) The Greek is given, H, V, p 551, l 23, ἐπιδεικνύον

خارج Beyond (i e, of a line meeting another, AB, for example, beyond the point B, i. e, not within AB, which is داخل) (W, p. 50, l 10)

خطّ Line

اختلاط Distinction or Difference (W, p 20, l 12) The Greek is given, H, Vol. V, 486, l 4, διαφορά

خالف To be the contrary of (i e, of two homogeneous things to one another (W, p 40, l 19, p 44, ll. 13, 20, 21)

اختلاف Difference (W, p 26, l 8) The Greek is given, H, Vol. V, p 551, l 25, διαφορά
To take the place of one-another (i. e, of areas, e. g., in the forming of the irrational lines sometimes a rational area is subtracted from a medial and sometimes a medial from a rational Cf Translation, Part II, para 16 (W., p. 44, l 17)

اختلاف الوقوف Case (Casus, πτῶσις) (BH, I, p 40, l. 3. see Heath, Vol. I, Introd., p 134)

مختلف Unequal (of magnitudes) (W., p. 33, l. 15). Greek,
ἄνισος.

ذ

ذراع Cubit (as an unit of measurement) (W., p. 6, l. 14).
The Greek is given, H., Vol. V, p. 418, l. 13, πῆχυς.

ذكّر To discuss (teach, explain, show by argument) (W.,
p. 23, ll. 17, 18; p. 26, l. 3). The Greek is given,
H., Vol. V, p. 484, l. 13, and p. 547, l. 24, διδάσκει,
διαλέγεται δεικνύων.

منهب Definition (or Thesis) (W., p. 11, l. 5)

ر

رباطات Bonds (W., p. 9, l. 14). Greek, ὁ δέσμος of *Timaeus*,
31 c.

ربّع To "square" a number, i. e., form it into a square
figure. Cf. Appendix A (W., p. 10, ll. 14, 15; p. 11,
ll. 5, 7, 14, 15). The Greek is the τετραγωνίζω
of *Theaetetus* 148 a.

مربّع Square (of a number) (W., p. 11, ll. 1, 3, 4).
Square (of a figure) (W., p. 10, l. 13; p. 11, l. 1).
The sum of the squares upon (W., p. 24, l. 11). But
this meaning is derived from the context. Cf. مركّب.

مربّع خطّ هز The square upon HZ (W., p. 33, l. 1; cf W., p. 34, l. 3).

المربّع الذى من هز The square upon HZ (W., p. 33, l. 8; cf p. 24, ll. 9,
10; p. 25, ll. 5, 6).

الذى من خطّ اج The square upon AJ. (W., p. 40, l. 21, cf. W., p. 57,
l. 14ff.; NB. l. 18 the phrase (المربّعات انفسها).

مايكون من مشاركه له The square upon a line commensurable (incommens-
مايكون من مباين اه urable) with it (W., p. 55, ll. 7—8 etc.; cf. p. 51, l. 16;
p. 52, l. 3).

رسم To describe (a square upon a line) (W., p. 58, l. 3;
cf. BH., I, p. 24, l. 18).
Line (W., p. 14, l. 5). Greek, γραμμή.

ارتفاع Height (of a rectangle) (W., p. 59, l. 5).

ركّب شىء على To apply (an angle to an angle, a triangle to a triangle etc.

تركيب   Addition (Of magnitudes to one-another) (W., p. 5, l. 2; p 9, l 5; p. 20, l. 18, p. 35, ll 16, 17)

الستة الصم التى   The six irrationals formed by addition (W., p. 26,
بالتركيب   l. 8; p. 40, l. 6). The Greek is given, H., V. p 551, l. 23, αἱ κατὰ σύνθεσιν Cf. W., p. 39, l. 9.

الصم بالتركيب   The irrationals formed by addition (W., p. 24, l. 15; p. 35, l. 16).

الخطوط المركّبة   Compound Lines (i. e., lines formed by addition) (W., p. 20, l 20; p 22, l. 12, cf. p. 30, l. 15)

المركّبات   Compound Lines (W., p 23, l. 8).

الخطّان المركّبان   The two [incommensurable] lines which have been added together [to from a binomial] (W., p. 25, l. 7; cf p 48, l 21)

المركّب منهما   The sum (of two lines, of the extremes) (W., p. 45, ll
(الطرفين)   21, 22).

المربع المركّب من   The sum of the squares upon them (W., p 25, ll 3—4).
مربّعيهما   (Cf W., p. 24, ll 9—10; p 25, ll. 5, 6; p. 46, ll. 3—4; p 41, l 20; p 33, ll. 8, 16; p 36, l. 11)

المركّب من مربّى   The sum of the squares upon HJ., JZ (W., p. 33, ll. 10,
هـج حر   11, 18, 21; p. 34, ll. 2—3, 8—9, 12, 15, 18, p. 41, l. 19) (Cf. W., p 33, l. 12)

المركّب   The sum of the squares upon them (W., p. 37, l 10). The sense is evident, however, from the context.

زاوية — زوايا ز   Angle.

على روايا قائمة   At right angles (W., p. 50, l 4).

القائم الروايا   Rectangle (W., p. 21, l. 22, p. 31, l. 8 etc.).

زيادة   Addition (of lines) (W., p. 23, l. 5)

سطح   س   Area, Plane (W., p 17, l. 17). Here it renders the ἐπίπεδος of *Theaetetus* 148h. On page 30, l. 19, it occurs as a gloss for موضع In T., Book X, p. 268, it gives the Greek, χωρίον). It is used throughout for "Rectangle" (Cf. W., p. 25, ll 4, 5, 6).

المساوى   The Equal (as an abstract idea contrasted with the Greater and the Less, a reference to Plato's *Parmenides*

140b c d.) (W., p. 13, 1 6; cf p. 3, 11. 17, 18, where it is contrasted with the Unequal). Greek, τὸ ἴσον.

غير المساوى The Unequal (W, p. 3, pp 18, 19; see Equal)

متساويا مرارا Numbers such as are the product of equal sides (i. e.,
منساوية factors (W, p. 10, 1 12). The Greek is ἴσον ἰσάκις,
Theaetetus 147 e

ش

شبر Span (W, p 6, 1 14) The Greek is given, H., Vol. V,
p. 418, 1 13, ἡ σπιθαμή

شبّه (With ب & Acc.) To compare one thing to another, i. e.,
to liken or represent them as similar (W, p. 19, 1. 16).
The Greek is given, H, Vol V, p 485, 1 17, ἐξομοιόω

يشبّه ان It seems that (W, p 9, 1 11, p 20, 1 5) The Greek
is given, H, Vol. V, p 485, 11. 3, 23 ἔοικεν.

ما اشبه ذلك And such like (W, p 23, 1 19) The Greek is given,
H, Vol V, p 484, 1 15 ὅσα τοιαῦτα

الشبيه Like (W, p. 3, 1. 17) See المساوى.

غير الشبيه Unlike (W, p 3, 1 18). See المساوى.

تشابه Identity of quality or accident (W, p. 2, 1 15: see
Spr. Vol. I, p 792) The Greek, ὁμοιότης probably.

متشابهان Similar (of triangles with similar angles) (W., p. 50,
1. 21).

الاشتراك Commensurability (W, p 2, 1 5). It is the opposite
of التباين

مشارك ل Commensurable (with something or other) (W., p 18,
11. 7, 8, 9, 10, 11; see especially 1 19) Greek, σύμ-
μετρος.

متشارك Commensurable (with one-another) (T, Book X,
prop 6, p. 230).

مشترك Commensurable (with one-another) (W., p. 18, 1. 16, 19).

مشترك Common, e g., there is no quantity which is common
to all quantities (W., p. 3, 1 10), of a characteristic
common to several things (W., p. 5, 1. 3, N 3); of an
angle made so that it is adjacent to two others and
forms with each a larger angle (BH., 1, p. 24, 1 3)

غير مشترك Incommensurable (with one-another). Cf the use of
ἀκοινώνητος H., Vol V, p 414, 1. 10. Is this the

explanation of the use of the root, شرك, to express this idea ?

شكل Geometrical figure (W, p 14, 1 5).   Proposition (W., p. 50, 1 1)

ص

مصرّف Of various sorts (W , p 25, 1 16)   The Greek is given, H., Vol V, p 534, no. 290, διαποικιλλομένος.

الاصغر The Less (as an abstract idea contrasted with the Greater and the Equal, a reference to Plato's *Parmenides* 140b (d) (W , p 13, 1 6)   Greek, τὸ ἔλλαττον. The minor (the irrational line) (W., p 22, l. 16, p 26, 1 17)

اصم — صم Irrational (of lines or magnitudes), surd (W , p 1, 1 2. p 2, 1 2, and 1 3)   Cf منطق

صورة Form (Idea), as opposed to Matter (W , p. 13, 1 18; p 14, ll 3, 4)   Greek, εἶδος

الصور الهندسيه Geometrical figures (W , p 14, 1 2)

صيّر To form, produce (e. g , the first bimedial by the addition of two given areas) (W , p 41, 1 2)

ض

ضلع — اضلاع Side (of a triangle etc)   Greek, ἡ πλευρά Breadth (of a rational area (Cf T, Book X, p 239, prop 16 — prop 20 of our Euclid)   Greek, τὸ πλάτος Side, i. e , Factor of a number (W., p. 10, l. 14; p. 11, 1 5)   The Greek is the ἡ πλευρά of *Theaetetus* 147d — 148b

اضاف To apply (squares etc to lines) (W., p 26, 1 5, p 30, 1 10, p 38, 1 6)   The Greek is given, H , Vol V, p 548, ll 2- 3, παραβάλλω

اضافة Relation (of quantities to one-another) (W , p 7, 1 5) The Greek is given, H , Vol. V, p 418, 1 18, ἡ σχέσις.

ط

الطرفان The Extremes (i. e , of a series of numbers in continued proportion) (W , p 20, 1. 13)   Cf وسط   Greek, οἱ ἄκροι — (See H., Vol. V, p 486, 1 5)

طمن   Doubt, Suspicion (in the phrase, — طمن لا يلحقها التى, meaning, "Irrefutable", W., p 1, l. 8; p. 2, l. 4). The phrase probably renders the Greek word, ἀνέλεγκτον. Cf. G. FRIEDLEIN, *Procli Diadochi in Primum Euclidis Elementorum Librum Commentarii*, p. 44, l. 14.

على الاطلاق   Simply, Without Qualification (W., p. 24, l. 19; p. 38, l. 22).

مطلق   A "whole" [continuous quantity], i. e., a finite and homogeneous one (W., p. 7, l. 1, N. 2). Cf Translation, Part I, note 36.

مستطيل   Oblong (the figure) (W., p. 10, l. 14).

Oblong (of number, i. e , an oblong number) (W., p. 10, l. 15; p 11, ll. 4—5). The reference is to Plato's *Theaetetus* 148 a. προμήκες. Cf. عدد.

ع

عدد   Unit of measurement, measure (W., p. 6, l. 14, N. 9; p. 11, l. 21; p. 14, l. 15; p. 15, l. 2; p. 16, l 3). See Translation. Part 1, note 34.

عدد مربع   A square number (W , p. 11, l. 4; cf. p. 10, ll. 12—14, for its definition, "A number which is the product of equal factors". The reference is to Plato's *Theaetetus* 147 e.—148 a.)

عدد مستطيل   An oblong number (W., p. 11, ll 4—5; cf p. 10, ll. 12 -14, for its definition, "A number which is the product of a greater and a less factor". See Plato's *Theaetetus* (147 e.—148 a).

عدم   Cf النطق , نهاية , تامى.

عرض — عروس   Breadth (W., p. 26, l 6). Greek, τὸ πλατός (H., Vol. V, p. 548, l 3).

العوارض الهيولانية   Corporeal Accidents (W., p. 14, l. 10).

عظم — اعظام   A Continuous Quantity (W., p. 1, l. 2) At-Ṭūsī says (T., Book X, p. 225, l 1ff.) — , "The continuous quantities are five, the line, the plane, the solid, Space, and Time" الاعظام (W., p. 7, l. 2) = τὰ μεγέθη of H., Vol. V, p. 418, l. 7 Cf. the phrase, الكمية المتصلة of W., p. 3, l. 14

الأعظم The major (the irrational line) (W., p. 21, l. 22; p. 26, l. 17 etc.).

The Greater (as an abstract idea contrasted with the Equal and the Less, a reference to Plato's *Parmenides* 140b. c. d.) (W., p. 13, l. 6). Greek, τὸ μεῖζον

عكس To convert (the two terms of a proposition) (W., p. 15, l. 6).

عكس The converse (of a proposition) (W , p. 25, l. 8 and l. 14). Cf. H., Vol. V, p. 548, l. 3 with W., p 26, l. 6. Greek, ἀντίστροφος.

بعكس ذلك Conversely (W., p. 24, l 10, p. 25, ll. 4— 5).

التعاليم Mathematics (W , p 1, ll. 4 & 9).

معلوم Assigned, Given (of a line) (W., p. 24, l 1) Greek, προτεθεῖσα.

عمود A perpendicular (line) (W., p 50, l. 16).

معنى Definition (W , p. 6, l. 7; p. 56, l. 7). Cf. BH I, p. 40, l 9

مُعَوَّزة Destitute of quality (W., p. 29, l 3). See Translation, Part II, note 2

ف

ورر To cut otf (a rectangle from a rectangle) (W., p 33, l. 1).

مفروص (فرض) Assigned, Given   Greek, προτεθεῖσα (W., p 8, l. 4).

فصل To subtract (one magnitude from another) W., p. 22, ll. 15, 18) Greek, ἀφαιρέω.

فصل Subtraction (W., p 22, l. 18). "Distinctio" (BH., p. 8, l. 5) — distinguit inter enuntiationem ejus, quod fieri potest, et ejus, quod fieri non potest

تفصيل Subtraction (Division) (W., p 26, l 15). Greek, H , Vol V, p 553, l 14, ἀφαίρεσις

Definition or Specification (Greek, διορισμός) (BH. I, p. 36, l 5)   It states separately and makes clear what the particular thing is which is sought in a proposition (Cf. Heath, Vol. I, Introd., p 129).

الخطوط الصم التى بالتفصيل The irrational lines formed by subtraction (W., p. 22, ll. 14, 20; p. 26, ll. 12—13; p. 39, l. 9; p. 40, l. 4.

The Greek to p 26, ll. 12—13 is given, H., Vol. V, p 553, ll. 11, 14; αἱ δι' ἀφαιρέσεως αἱ κατ' αφαίρεσιν.

الخطوط المنفصلة   The irrational lines formed by subtraction (W., p 20, l. 20).

بالتفصيل   The irrational formed by subtraction? (W., p. 40, l. 16).

انفصال   Subtraction (W., p. 22, l. 15; p. 42, l. 15).

مفصول   Subtracted (e. g., the rational and subtracted area; W., p. 42, l. 21)

منفصل   Subtracted from (e. g., the area that is subtracted from a rational area; W., p. 42, l. 16).

Discrete (of quantity) W., p 3, l 13) It is the opposite of متصل (continuous).

The apotome (The irrational line) (W., p 2, l. 3; p. 22, l. 21, p. 26, l. 13) Greek, ἡ ἀποτομή.

المنفصل الاول .   The first, second, third apotomes etc. (W., p. 51,
الثانى . الثالث   ll 12 14; cf. p. 51, l 19)

منفصل الموسط الاول   The first (second) apotome of a medial (W., p 22, l. 16;
(الثانى)   p 26, ll. 15—16; p. 39, ll. 14- 15, p. 43, ll 13, 16).

منفصل موسط الاول   Greek, μέσης ἀποτομή πρώτη (δευτέρα).
(الثانى)

منفصل الموسطات   First and second apotomes of a medial (W., p 57, l. 20).
الاوائل والثوانى

الفصل   The Remainder (after the subtraction of one line from another (W., p 39, l. 11).

ق

مقابل   Opposite, contrary (i. e, of two things within the same genus, e. g, the binomial and the apotome) (W., p., 47, l 14; p 48, l. 23; p. 53, ll. 11, 13) (Cf Spr. Vol. II, p. 1205)

متقابلان   Opposite (of the sides of a parallelogram) (W., p. 50, l. 12).

قدر   Measure or Magnitude (W., p. 3, l. 10; p. 6 (throughout); p. 14, ll 13, 18). See Translation, Part I, note 28.

مقدار   Measure or Magnitude (W., p. 14, ll. 13, 17; p. 6, l 2ff) P 13, l. 7 it gives the τὸ μέτρον of Plato's

Parmenides 140 b. c. d. At-Tūsī defines it as the relation or proportion of one homogeneous quantity to another, or the measure of one to the other. Greek, τὸ μέγεθος.

مقدار النصف(الثلث) The ratio of 1 to 2, 1 to 3 (W., p 7, l. 15).

مقدّمة Enunciation (of a proposition) (W., p. 46, l. 14)

قسم To divide (a line) Greek, διαιρέω.

قسمة Division, Subtraction (W , p 3, l 8; p 9, l. 5. p. 20, l. 18, p 25, l 9) Greek, διαίρεσις.

Term (i e , one of the two terms of a binomial etc.) (W., p. 55, l. 6) Greek, τὸ ὄνομα.

القسم الاعظم والاصغر The greater and less terms (W., p. 55, l, 6).

تقسيم Division (into parts) (W , p 3, l 8; p 4, l. 3)

قطر Diameter or diagonal (W., p 21, l 5) (Cf. BH. 1, p 20, l 6)

قاعدة Base (of a rectangle or square) (W., p 59, l 15)

الشيء الذى هو اقل قليل The (A) Minimum (W , p 3, ll 7, 9). Greek, ἐλα-χιστον μέτρον (See H., Vol V, p 429, l. 27)

شيء هو اقل قليل

قال To enunciate, or to say or state in the enunciation, or to give the enunciation (W , p 36, ll 1, 3, 6)

قول The enunciation (of a proposition (W , p. 35, l 15). Proposition or theorem (W , p 3, l 1; p 5, l 3, p. 10, l 20; p 11, l 19) (Cf BH I, p 36 l. 16)

مقالة Theorem ' (W , p 10, l 17) Part or section (of a book) (W , p 35, l 18)

قائمة Right (of an angle) (W , p. 50, l. 7) See راوية

معوم Established, known, proved, belonging as a property or quality to (W., p 3, l 3; p. 4, l 14) See Translation, Part I, note 12.

مستقيم Straight (of a line) (W , p. 31, l 17).

على استقامة In a straight line (i. e , of the production of a line) (BH , I, p. 18, l 8) (of the placing of two lines, W , p 59, l 9)

قوى على To have the power to form such and such a square,

i. e., the square upon which is equal to such and such an area etc. (W., p 11, l. 17; p. 12, l. 1; p. 19, ll. 6, 21, 22; p. 25, l. 21). The phrase, — فان المربع الذى من الخط etc. —. p. 19, ll. 6—7, reproduces الوسط مساو للموضع and means the same as the phrase, ما صار يقوى على الموضع, before it in l 6. Greek, δύναμαι.

الخط الذى يقوى على منطق وموسط — The (A) side of a square equal to a rational plus a medial area (W., p. 22, l. 1; p. 26, l. 18; p. 35, l. 11; p. 44, l. 1). Greek, ῥητὸν καὶ μέσον δυναμένη.

اسم يقوى على منطق وموسط

الخط الذى يقوى على موسطين — The (A) side of a square equal to two medial areas (W, p 22, l. 2; p 26, l. 18; p. 35, l 14; p 44, l 4). Greek, ἡ δύο μέσα δυναμένη.

اسم يقوى على موسطين

قوّة — Square (W., p 10, ll. 7, 8, 10, 14, 15, 18; p. 11, ll. 2, 9, 11, 12, etc.; p. 12, l. 1). See Appendix A. Greek, δύναμις.

Square root, surd (W., p 11, l. 15). See Appendix A. Here قوة renders the δύναμις of *Theaetetus* 148b. Potentiality or power (W, p. 13, l. 13). Greek, δύναμις.

القوّة المصورة — The representative or imaginative power, the psychological faculty (W., p. 14, l. 5). Greek, δύναμις.

بالقوّة — Potentially (W., p. 13, ll. 17, 18). It is the opposite of بالفعل (actually), p. 13, l. 19. Greek, δυνάμει.

القوى على منطق وموسط — The side of a square equal to a rational plus a medial area (W, p 44, l. 1). See قوى على etc.

القوى على موسطين — The side of a square equal to two medial areas. See قوى على.

الكثرة — Plurality or multiplicity (W, p. 3, l. 20ff.). It is the opposite of الوحدة (Unity). ك

الكثرة — Multitude or many (W., p. 3, l. 20ff). It is the opposite of الواحد (One).

أكثر الكثير Maximum (W., p. 3, l. 13). See اقل قليل.

الكل The sum (of two areas) (W., p 43, l. 10).

كمّيه Quantity (quantum) (W., p 3, l 13)

كون The coming-to-be or the coming-to-be-and-the-passing-away (W., p. 2, l. 16, n. 9). See Translation, Part I, note 7. In the first case it is synonymous with الحدوث and is the opposite of الفساد (corruption). In the second it is synonymous with such terms as الوجود, التحقق, الثبوت. (Cf Spr., Vol. II, p. 1274).

Form (W., p 56, ll 7, 9, 22) See Translation, Part II, note 136.

الاكوان are the forms or ways in which sensible things exist.

التكوّن The coming-to-be (W., p 2, l 16). It is the emergence of the non-existent from non-existence to existence (Cf. Spr., Vol II, p. 1276).

ل

اللفق The "annex" (W., p. 22, l 22, p 26, l 21) P. 22, l 22 it is defined as الخط المفصول المنطق; i. e., the rational line commensurable in square with the whole line, which, when subtracted from the whole line, leaves as remainder an apotome. Greek, ἡ προσαρμόζουσα.

م

المشاء The Peripatetic (W. p. 2, l. 4).

مع 'After' (= Gr μετά?) (W., p 25, l. 15).

من See مركب and مرتع.

ممتنع Impossible (W., p 55, l. 11).

تمييز Distinction (W., p. 26, l. 10). Greek, H., Vol. V, p. 551, l 24, διάκρισις.

ن

انزل To take (e. g., Let us take three rational lines commensurable in square only, W., p. 22, l. 2)

نسبة Proportion, ratio (W., p. 5, l. 1, p. 6, l 6ff.; p 8, l. 14ff). Greek, λόγος.

نسة الضعفين The ratio of 2 to 1 (W., p 7, l 14).

نسة الثلثة الاضعاف The ratio of 3 to 1 (W., p 7, l 14).

على نسة In [continued] proportion (W., p. 21, l 17).

على نسبة ذات وسط وطرفين (In extreme and mean ratio)

حط على نسة فى التناسب الهندسى In proportion. The whole phrase means, "The geometric mean" (W., p. 45, ll 4—5).

حط على نسة فى التناسب التاليفى The harmonic mean (W , p. 45, ll 5—6.

فى النسبة In mean proportion between (W., p 20, l. 6)

النسبة الهندسيه Geometrical proportion (W., p. 19, l. 4) Greek, H, Vol V, p 488, l 23, τὴν γεωμετρικὴν ἀναλογίαν.

تناسب Proportion, ratio (the abstract idea of) (W., p 7, l. 1: p 9, l 4). Continued proportion (W., p. 23, l 7).

التناسب الهندسى Geometrical proportion (W , p. 45, l 5)

التناسب العددى Arithmetical proportion (W., p. 45, l 17)

النناسب التاليى Harmonic proportion (W , p 45, l 6)

خط على التناسب العددى The Arithmetical mean (W., p. 45, ll 15—16).

مناسب Proportional (to something) (W., p 45, l 12, p. 20, l 13)

مناسبة هندسية Geometrical proportion (W., p 45, l 12)

حط مناسب مناسة هندسيه The geometric mean (W , p. 45, l 12)

متناسب Proportional (To one-another) (T , Book X, p 231)

نسف دائرة Semi-circle (W., p. 50, l 3)

عدم النطق Irrationality (W , p. 14, l 9).

منطق Rational (W , p. 1, l. 2 etc.). Greek, ῥητόν See صم . متّصل , موسط . قوى .

منطقة فى الطول وفى القوة Rational lines commensurable in length and square (W , p 5, ll. 6, 8, 9, 10, 11) See Translation, Part I, note 22.

غير منطق Irrational (W , p 63, ll. 13—14).

نظيرة — نظائر Like or contrary (W., p 39, l. 19; p 40, l 2, p. 54, ll. 17, 20). See Translation, Part II, note 71

نطام Standard (of measurement or judgment) (W., p. 2, l 16).

Classification (of the irrationals) (W., p. 29, l. 1)

متظم Ordered (of irrationals) (W., p. 2, l. 7, p 29, l 5)

غير متظم Unordered (of irrationals) (W , p 2, l. 7, p 29, l. 6)

نقص (With Acc & من) To subtract something from (W , p 40, l. 11).

تنقيص Subtraction (of lines in the case of the irrationals formed by subtraction) (W., p 23, l. 6).

تنقّص Reduction, bisection (W., p. 4, l. 15).

منقوص Subtracted from (e. g , the areas subtracted from) (W , p. 40, l. 11)

نقطة A point (W , p 50, l 9).

النهاية The finite (W , p 3, l 15)   Greek, τὸ πέρας.

ما لا نهاية The infinite, infinity (W., p. 3, ll 15, 17, 19, p. 4, ll 1, 3) Greek, τὸ ἄπειρον.

ذوات نهايه Finite (W , p 3, l. 16)

لا نهاية Infinite (W , p. 4, l 2)

الى غير نهاية Ad infinitum or indefinitely (W., p 3, ll. 7, 8).

الى ما لا نهايه Ad infinitum or indefinitely (W. p. 4, l 16)

التناهى Finitude, the finite (W , p 3, ll 18, 21)

متناهى Finite, determined (of magnitudes) (W., p. 3, l. 8; p 7, l 2ff) Greek, H , Vol V , p 418, l 7, πεπε-ρασμένος

Defined (of plurality or multitude) (W , p 8, l 17, N 5). Greek, ὡρισμένος (πεπερασμένος) See Translation, Part I, note 44

هناك ' There", the ideal world (W., p 14, ll 3, 8)   Greek, τὸ ἐκει.

الهيولى المحسوسة Sensible matter (W., p 14, l 1) Greek, ὕλη αἰσθητή. See Translation, Part I, note 104

الهيولى المعقولة Intelligible matter (W , p 14, ll 1, 3)   Greek, ὕλη νοητή. See Translation, Part I, note 104

وتّر To subtend (of a line an angle) (W., p 51, l 4).

وتر Diameter, chord (of a circle) (Spr , Vol. II, p. 1471).

واجب صرورة Necessary, Self-evident (W , p. 55, ll. 6—7, 19)

الوحدة Unity (W., p. 3, l 10)   It is the opposite of الكثرة (Plurality)

الواحد One (as the principle of the numbers) (W., p. 4, l. 4).

متوارى الاضلاع A rectangular parallelogram (W., p. 50, l. 11).

وسيطة — وسائط The means (geometric, arithmetical, harmonic) (W., p. 2, l. 2).

الوسط،الخطّ الوسط The medial line (W., p. 5, ll. 7, 8, 9, 11—12; p. 19, ll. 5, 12, 16). Greek, H., Vol. V, p. 488, l. 21, ἡ μέση.
Pl. الموسطات
الموسطة

موسطة ف الطول والقوة Medial lines commensurable in length and square) (W., p. 5, ll. 8-9, 11). The full phrase, موسطان مشتركان ف الطول (ف القوة) is given, p. 19, ll. 17—18, p. 20, ll. 1, 3.

الذى من موسطين الاول The first bimedial (W., p. 39, l. 14).

التى من موسطين الاوائل First bimedials (W., p. 57, ll 19--20)

من موسطين الاول The first bimedial (W., p. 22, l. 10; p. 36, l. 5)

الذى من موسطين الثانى The second bimedial (W., p 39, l 15)

التى من موسطين الثوانى Second bimedials (W., p. 57, ll. 19—20)

من موسطين الثانى The second bimedial (W., p 36, l 6)

الذى من ثلثة موسطات الاول The first trimedial (W., p. 21, ll. 19—20)

الذى من ثلثة موسطات الثانى The second trimedial (W., p. 21, ll. 19—20)

الذى يجعل الكل موسطا مع منطق The line which produces with a rational area a medial whole (W., p. 22, l 17; p. 26, l. 17; p 44, l. 2).

الذى يجعل الكل موسطا مع موسط (مع الموسط) The line which produces with a medial area a medial whole (W., p. 22, ll 17—18; p 26, l. 18, p. 44, l. 5)

موسط على التناسب العددى The arithmetical mean (W., p. 45, l 15; p. 46, ll. 14--15)

موسط تاليفى The harmonic mean (W., p. 49, l. 5).

الخطّ الاوسط The medial line (W., p 23, l. 19) Greek, H., Vol V, p. 484, L. 14, τῆς μέσης

التوسطات	The means (W., p. 9, l. 9) (geometrical, arithmetical, harmonic).
(.Sing توسط)	
التوسط الهندسى	The geometric mean (W , p. 45, l. 7)
التوسط العددى	The arithmetical mean (W., p 45, l. 8)
التوسط التأليفى	The harmonic mean (W., p. 45, l 9)
متوسط	A mean proportional (W., p. 19, ll. 5, 9; p. 21, l. 15)
متوسط فى النسبة	A mean proportional (W., p. 21, l. 5, p. 24, l. 3).
متوسط على التاسع العددى	The arithmetical mean (W., p. 46, l 16, l. 19)
متصل	Continuous (of quantity) (W., p. 3, l. 14) It is the opposite of منفصل.
المتصل بالنطق يصير الكل موسطا	That which produces with a rational area a medial whole (T , Book X, p 287).
المتصل بموسط يصير الكل موسطا	That which produces with a medial area a medial whole (T., Book X, p. 288).
وضع خطين متصلين على استقامة	To put two lines in a straight line (W., p. 59, L. 9).
وضع	(With Acc. & على) To assign something to something (W., p 19, l 7). Greek, H., Vol. V, p. 485, l. 9, ἔθετο ἐπί
وضع	To posit, i. e., assume for the purposes of proof (W , p 16, l 2).
بالوضع	By convention (W., p. 6, l. 13; p. 14, ll. 14, 15). It is the opposite of بالطبع. Greek, H., Vol. V, p 414, l 4 θέσει
وضع	Hypothesis (W., p 13, l 6) Greek, ὑπόθεσις. The reference is to the first hypothesis of *Parmenides*, 140b. c d. Cf 136 for ὑπόθεσις.
موضع	Area, rectangle (W , p 16, ll 9, 15, 18; p 18, l. 16ff ; p. 19, ll. 6, 7, 9, 10) It is practically synonymous with سطح. See the glosses to p. 16, ll. 9, 15, 18. l 13 سطح is used for موضع. As "rectangle" it represents the phrase, موضع قائم الزوايا. (Cf. p 30, l 19). Greek, H., Vol. V, p. 484, l. 13, χωρίον τὸ.

اوطأ To establish (W., p. 30, l. 19). See Translation, Part II, note 12.

الوقوف Rest (W., p. 3, l. 18). It is the opposite of الحركة (Movement).

تولّد To be produced (of areas, for example, by rational lines, i. e., to be contained by them) (W., p. 39, l. 3).

ى

يقيني Certain, exact (of a method) (W., p 4, l. 12; p. 1, l. 7).

Proclus 40,41,42

CPSIA information can be obtained
at www.ICGtesting.com
Printed in the USA
BVHW081427280319
543977BV00008B/150/P